D0093326

Advance Praise for
Good Products, Bad Products

"This book takes us beyond manufacturing quality to components of overall product quality that are often given too little attention. They are essential, but difficult to quantify. *Good Products, Bad Products* does a remarkable job of clarifying their nature and suggesting specific ways to better employ them. Want to produce products that people really want? Read this book."

—**Dave Beach**, *Professor, Director Product Realization Lab,*
Stanford University, Hasso Platner Institute of Design

"In a world that is constantly creating improved ways to achieve unimproved ends, Jim Adams takes a step back and asks, 'What makes a great product great to begin with?' *Good Products, Bad Products* is a book of practical philosophy, a deep dive into the nuts and bolts of why some things get used and others are cherished. Engineers, designers, and marketers alike will come away from this book wondering how we all went so long without it."

—**Dev Patnaik**, *CEO and cofounder,*
Jump Associates; author of Wired to Care

"Jim Adams delights us once again with a fine product. This book should soon become a foundational read for every student, craftsman, and entrepreneur who truly aspires to make a difference."

—**Nicolas Shea**, *founder of eClass and Start-Up Chile*

"Jim Adams's concepts of what makes for a good product have been an essential part of our product design effort at Forbes Marshall in India for more than ten years. Our products have routinely won national innovation and design awards, and this is due in no small part to having imbibed and practiced Jim's concepts.

"The publication of *Good Products, Bad Products* is an event I have awaited for over a decade. We cannot wait to equip our engineers with their own copy. If you know Jim's work, you will already be in line for this book. If you don't, a great discovery awaits."

—Naushad Forbes, *CEO,*
Steam Engineering Businesses, Forbes Marshall;
Chairman, Innovation Council of Confederation of Indian Industry

GOOD
PRODUCTS
BAD
PRODUCTS

GOOD
PRODUCTS
BAD
PRODUCTS

ESSENTIAL ELEMENTS TO
ACHIEVING SUPERIOR QUALITY

JAMES L. ADAMS

New York Chicago San Francisco Lisbon London Madrid Mexico City
Milan New Delhi San Juan Seoul Singapore Sydney Toronto

The *McGraw·Hill* Companies

1 2 3 4 5 6 7 8 9 10 11 12 13 14 15   DOC/DOC   1 9 8 7 6 5 4 3 2 1

ISBN   978-0-07-178240-1
MHID   0-07-178240-0

e-ISBN   978-0-07-178241-8
e-MHID   0-07-178241-9

Library of Congress Cataloging-in-Publication Data

Adams, James L.
    Good products, bad products : essential elements to achieving superior quality /
James L. Adams.
        p.   cm.
    Includes index.
    ISBN-13: 978-0-07-178240-1 (hardback)
    ISBN-10: 0-07-178240-0 (hardback)
    1. Quality of products.   2. Manufacturing industries—Quality control.   I. Title.

HF5415.157.A33   2012
658.4'013--dc23   2011037909

To Marian, who strives to improve my quality

Contents

Acknowledgments   xiii

Introduction   1

Chapter 1   Products and Quality:
             What Is the Situation?   7
             Future Trends: Population Growth and "Taste"   9
             An Example of Quality Improvement   11
             Beyond Manufacturing Quality   17
             Global Competition   19
             Onward   21

Chapter 2   Problems in Increasing Product Quality:
             Narrow-Mindedness and Attitudes   23
             Thinking, Problem Solving, and Quality   24
             Tradition Runs Deep   29
             Flaws in Economic Theory   35
             The Changing Nature of Design   37
             Increasing Creativity and Innovation   44

Chapter 3   Performance, Cost, and Price:
             Is It a Good Deal?   51
             Quantifying Performance   52
             The Complexity of Cost and Price   56
             The Balancing Act Between Performance
                and Cost   59
             Why Are There Problems?   63

Chapter 4   Human Fit: Does the Product
             Fit People?   67
             Physical Fit   70
             Sensory Fit   75
             Cognitive Fit   81
             Complexity   87
             Safety and Health   91

Chapter 5   Craftsmanship: Joy to the Maker,
             Joy to the User   97
             Why Do We Care About Craftsmanship?   98
             The Pleasure and Pride of Craft   100
             The Industry and Culture Problem   104
             The Nature of Craftsmanship   109
             Some Suggestions   114

Chapter 6   Products, Emotions, and Needs:
             Love, Hate, or Blah?   121
             How Emotions Play a Role   122
             The Complexity of Human Emotions   125
             Diversity in Emotional Responses   131
             The Mechanisms of Emotion   133
             Human Needs   136
             Needs and Emotions   140
             Need Finding   149

Chapter 7   Aesthetics, Elegance, and Sophistication:
             Wisdom Through Experience   153
             Aesthetics and Industrial Products   155
             A Bit of Background on Industrial Design   159
             Elegance and Sophistication   164
             Product Form and Function   170
             Some Concerns on Today's Aesthetics   174

Chapter 8   Symbolism and Cultural Values:
            Who Are We?   181
            Products, Symbolism, and Cultures   183
            Products and National Cultures   186
            Products and Subcultures   190
            Globalism and Cultures   195

Chapter 9   Global Constraints: Does the Product
            Fit a Finite Earth and Its Inhabitants?   203
            Big Problems   204
            The Role of Industrially Produced Products   207
            Why These Problems?   209
            Response to Change   212
            Revolutionary Approaches   216
            The Iceberg   221
            Regulations and Laws   224
            Now What?   229

Chapter 10 Conclusion: What Have We Learned?
            Where Do We Go?   233

Notes   239
Further Reading   245
Index   247

Acknowledgments

First I would like to acknowledge all of the Stanford students who took a series of courses that not only gave me the opportunity to think about the topic of product quality with them, but also provided me with excellent feedback on the course notes that became the basis for this book. This series began in 1984 with a course entitled Technology and Aesthetics, which I taught in the Stanford Values, Technology, Science and Society (VTSS) program, initially ably abetted by Barry Katz, then a lecturer in the program and now a professor of humanities and design at California College of the Arts. Beginning in 1993 this course was listed in the departments of Mechanical Engineering and Industrial Engineering and Engineering Management at Stanford as well as in VTSS as Quality and the Products of Industry. In 1997 it was renamed Good Products, Bad Products, and since 2000 it has been taught by my good friend and colleague Professor David Beach, director of the Product Realization Lab in the Design Group of the Mechanical Engineering Department at Stanford, who has redesigned the course to suit his own style and thinking but has retained some of the previous structure and has continued to use my notes. Should any former students be reading this, thank you—I hope you had as much fun and learned as much in the course as I did.

On the publication side I would like to thank my agent, John Willig of Literary Services, who found the book an appreciative home; Stephanie Frerich, enthusiastic acquisition editor of McGraw-Hill Professional, who shepherded the book through the publication process; Zachary Gajewski, development editor, who did a heroic job of cutting out extraneous material, tightening the text, and generally turning the manuscript into a much more reasonable book; Charles Fisher and the production group, who polished it and put it together; and Julia Baxter and Ann Pryor, who helped make the world aware of it.

I am grateful to several people who read and commented on all or parts of the notes and the manuscript, including not only David Beach but also Naushad Forbes, CEO, Steam Engineering Businesses, Forbes Marshall, Inc., in Pune India, a close friend and former Ph.D. student who repeatedly ordered me to write this book and put the original course notes to work in his company (calling them Jim's rules), giving me invaluable feedback on their usefulness; Professor Sheri Sheppard, my number one writing critic in the Design Group at Stanford; Bob Adams, director of Business Partnerships for Sustainable Conservation (a nonprofit) and a farmer; Dev Patnaik, cofounder and chief executive of Jump Associates, a growth strategy firm in San Mateo, California; and last but certainly not least, my wife, Marian Adams, who reads, comments upon, and edits everything I write because she loves me and because I become grumpy if she does not.

Introduction

This is a book on quality. It focuses on products of technology and industry and argues that in the long term, the best products prevail, positively affecting and advancing the individuals, organizations, and nations that produce and use them as well as the human race as a whole. If we produce things that do not serve us well, they will fail in the marketplace, or in extreme cases, we will actively turn against them—for example, consider the use of poison gas in warfare, or chlorofluorocarbons (CFCs) in refrigeration. Throughout the book, I emphasize hardware products, since that is where my background and interest lie, but the content can easily be extrapolated to less physically tangible products. I also focus on so-called consumer products—items produced for sale to individuals and groups of individuals—although I will from time to time mention aspects of those intended for use by organizations (computer systems, buildings) and commissioned by governments (weapons, space stations, highways).

I believe it is essential that we think harder than we have in the past about the overall quality of industrially produced products. Since I spend much of my time with people in industry, education, and design offices, I can safely say that I am not alone. We are slowly becoming aware that our technology could serve us better and we must worry more about the quality of our lives and our environment; assuming that a reasonable standard of living and satisfaction of basic necessities exist, profitability and consumer happiness depend on quality as well as quantity.

This book is based on notes that I wrote for a graduate class entitled Good Products, Bad Products, which I taught for many years at Stanford University. The class was listed in the Design Division of the Department of Mechanical Engineering, the Department of Management Science and Engineering in the School of Engineering, and the Stanford program in Science, Technology, and Society. But the classes typically included not only students in these programs but also many from the Graduate School of Business and other areas of the university. A large number of remote students working toward their degrees part-time while employed in companies also took part through Stanford's Center for Professional Development. The course still exists, now being taught by a good friend, Professor David Beach, who uses my notes for a text.

Quality is a slippery, complex, and sometimes abstract concept. Dictionary definitions do not help a great deal (e.g., "the standard of something as measured against other things of a similar kind: the degree of excellence of something"[1]). Philosophers have spent a great deal of time dealing with the concept of quality. This is not a book on semantics or philosophy, so for our purposes, we will simply assume that quality means "good." But of course, that leaves us with "good for whom?" "good for what?" "good when?" "good where?" and if you really like to pick nits, "what do you mean by good?" I won't go there, either.

I will examine "good" by considering a number of criteria by which products can be evaluated. These are criteria essential for high quality, and they are perhaps easier to think about than quality as a whole. These factors are vital to product success, but they are often given short shrift by engineers, businesspeople, and others involved in production, partly because there are no easy ways to apply quantitative methods to such factors or use simple rules to achieve them. Why do people seem to be willing to pay so much more for a BMW or a Mercedes automobile than for a Chevrolet? Performance is one reason, but there are many others. The topics covered in this book have much to do with this phenomenon. I will also discuss reasons why these topics are often inadequately considered and tactics to bring them more emphasis.

This book is certainly not a traditional engineering book. There are no formulas or scientific theories that enable us to optimize such things as emotional appeal, symbolism, or cultural fit. Even though I am an engineer, the book pays little attention to topics commonly considered by engineers, such as material selection, stress analysis, electrical and mechanical performance, and reliability. My experience leads me to believe that such considerations receive much more attention and are better responded to than the topics in this book are. I am generally impressed with the ability of most industries to carry out the "technical" part of their work, although I wonder sometimes at their priorities. I am less impressed with their ability with the "softer" aspects of product definition, design, and development.

Neither is this a typical business book. It contains no up-front executive summary and is short of bulleted lists or simple "takeaways." Since I have given a great many talks, seminars, and classes to businesspeople, I know that many have a fondness for simple rules and principles that seem to be the key to better organizational performance and profit. But quality is not a simple thing. The content of this book requires thinking and practice to make it work. I hope it will stimulate such mental vigor, and I encourage you to apply the material by considering various products as you read. I have been told that this book is a taxonomy of aspects of product quality. If you want to learn about the quality of wine, for example, you first learn a related taxonomy (wine-tasting lessons?). Then you drink a lot of wine (critically, of course).

I include a few Thought Problems at the end of the chapters to help you consider and practice applying the concepts. The material in this book is intended to help you strengthen your ability to understand product quality in order to help you produce, promote, or perhaps just appreciate better products. But like most material having to do with thinking (how to be more creative, improve your memory, keep bees, or solve differential equations), it is necessary to integrate what you learn into your mental processes. Over many years of writing books, teaching, and consulting on the topics of creativity and innovation, I have found it is easy to put together entertaining classes, workshops, and books on the material, but difficult to help people do what they say they want to do—become more creative and innovative. The issue comes up because work is necessary to change habits. The thought exercises are provided to give you an opportunity to think more specifically about the material in the chapter—a bit of work, if you would. Or perhaps *practice* would be a better way to put it.

I've found, through teaching and talking about this material, that it seems of interest to consumers of products as well as those who produce them, because it is a framework they can use to analyze their past and future purchases. This aspect pleases me a great deal, because consumers have a huge amount of leverage in improving the quality of products.

The content of the book is based on the many years that I have spent amping up against the question of quality. I have worked as an engineer in companies that strove for the ultimate (the Jet Propulsion Laboratory) and those that should have but did not (General Motors). Including the Good Products, Bad Products class, I have taught courses dealing with design, creativity, aesthetics, organizational behavior, and the nature of engineering and technology. I love machinery (cars, motorcycles, old tractors, what have you), and I am constantly trying to figure out why, as I spend major amounts of time acquiring and fiddling with it and my yard keeps filling with restoration projects. Finally, I have consulted for many companies that produce products and I constantly face questions having to do with quality. Throughout all these activities, I have found that people tend to think about pieces of the quality problem, but not the whole picture.

One of the goals of this book is to help the reader become more aware of some of the aspects of overall quality that are often given inadequate attention. The chapters in the book cover such critical aspects of quality that should be thought about more specifically. Not all of them necessarily apply to all things, but if we, as a society and overall in the world, give them too little attention, we lose. The content of this book reflects my personal values and biases. Feel free to differ and substitute your own. Better yet, write your own book and set me straight—dialogue is the key to better understanding quality. All of us, whether we are involved in producing products, marketing and distributing them, or buying and using them, need to think more clearly about whether or not we are converting our resources into the right stuff.

Products and Quality

What Is the Situation?

The perfect product would be a win for everyone: the makers would become personally fulfilled and wealthy, while the users would be forever grateful because their lives would be so improved. Distributors would be ecstatic because of the demand for the product, and the media would seize on it because of its obvious positive impact. The government would love the perfect product because the balance of payments would be improved, and environmental groups would respect it because it would not use limited resources or pollute the ecosphere.

Of course, there are no perfect products, but there have been some awfully good ones: the spring clothespin, the Volkswagen Beetle, the paper clip, the user interface developed initially by Xerox and further by Apple and Microsoft, the shovel, the DC-3, the Barcelona chair. What distinguishes these from similar products that were apparently not as good: the Pontiac Aztec, the first Apple laptop, the Chernobyl nuclear plant? Why do some products considered outstanding disappear? How do we explain products that are constantly criticized but seem to be eternal favorites, such as the Barbie doll, high-heeled shoes, and toy firearms?

Why do we accept the many day-to-day annoyances we live with? For example, why must we spend so much time playing nursemaid to our computer systems? They're supposed to serve us. Wouldn't it be nice if automobiles all had their gasoline filler caps in the same place and had clocks that did not require reading the owner's manual to reset them? Shouldn't it be possible to more easily open the packages that keep us from our new purchases? Why is it so difficult to find products that are consistent with the needs and desires of those who deviate from the norm, whether in physical dimensions and capability, intellectual interests and background, or sensitivity and taste? There are many people like me who find it difficult to leap agilely from low-slung chairs and who aren't happy campers when confined to a tourist-class seat on a long flight. These problems mostly have to do with the fit between products and the human user, but products also suffer from poor performance and overly high prices, unreliability, difficult maintenance, crude manufacturing, ugliness, ostentatiousness, unnecessary complexity, representation of people or places users don't like, and destruction of natural beauty and future health.

All products could be improved. You have evidence for this in your personal experience—after you have used a product for a while, you become critical of its specific details and can think of ways to make it better. The potential for product improvement can also be seen by watching products evolve—even though some stay constant for long periods (the straight pin) and others become worse ("classic" models of cars), most become better over time. This is not to say that all products are inherently bad—my grandparents would consider many products now on the market astonishing—it is just that they could be better. Since products are designed and produced by bright, educated, and well-meaning people, however, why *aren't* they better?

Looking at our history, it is easy to see why we are somewhat dazzled by the products of industry. We have only had anything approximating what we now call technology and science for about one ten-thousandth of our history. We have been farming, domesticating animals, living in villages, and developing tools for 30 times that period, but as a species, we have spent most of our history with a scarcity of food, shelter, and safety, to say nothing of transportation, medical care, and toys. Much of the world's population continues to live in this way.

In the past few hundred years, the miraculous things that we call industrial products have become available. As areas of the world grew richer and more populated, increasing amounts of resources were devoted to producing and consuming these products. These changes worried some people, such as the Luddites and members of the Arts and Crafts movement, but most considered these products wonderful. It is not surprising that we would develop an extreme fondness for things that fulfill our needs.

Since around 1900, industrial products have proliferated. China is a good present example of this process in action, or look at Orchard Road, the retail and entertainment center of Singapore. Any Walmart store in the United States just before Christmas also displays this phenomenon in maturity. But we do have related problems, including huge gaps in access to products between the rich and poor, weapons that can destroy unacceptable numbers of innocent people, an increasingly contaminated ecosphere, an ominously growing population, soaring expectations, and industrially produced products that should serve us better. Exponential growth, however, never continues forever, despite the hopes of some economists and the theories of Adam Smith, nor do empires, religions, companies, or values. Industrial products and the process that brings them to us will be as different (or more so) 100 years from now as they were 100 years ago.

Future Trends: Population Growth and "Taste"

Future trends in industrially produced products will obviously serve a society with different needs, as populations continue to grow (for a while at least). It can only be hoped that poor individuals will also continue to become wealthier. Will we increase the number of products we produce and consume forever? No—the finite nature of the Earth places limits on us, and it will be a long time before we build cars on the moon. Also, there is a tendency among individuals to become more discriminating about products. As we acquire more money, products, and experience, we are not as tempted to buy things simply because they are cheap or we want new toys. The very wealthy, for example, do not especially buy more products. If Bill Gates were to keep up with me in number of products per dollar of net worth, he would have to fill several thousand houses and yards.

Will "taste" change? Most assuredly. We have all gone to enough museums, read enough books, and studied enough history to know this. I have been fascinated over my 40 years at Stanford University to watch the frequent and radical changes in students' desires for products, starting with the anti-industry hippie days when students were listening to folk LPs, playing acoustic guitars, and wearing bell-bottoms and ending with today's students sporting shorts and athletic shoes while plugging into iPads and laptops, with cell phones in hand. In the interim, there has been continual movement.

Whatever the situation will be in the future, product quality will be essential to business success. Most products are produced by businesses interested in making money for their owners and growing. An essential part of these goals is retaining and motivating high-quality employees. Increasing product quality adds to the pride and satisfaction of employees as well as the reputation of the company. But one way to achieve short-term profits is to decrease expenses by shortening the time to market and lowering the cost of design and production. Another is to decrease expenditures on new product development and product improvement. Both of these will result in lower quality.

Since higher production means lower costs and higher prof-its, products are promoted by advertising and other means of hawking their advantages (whether real or imaginary) in order to increase demand. Such actions boost sales, but they may also result in disappointment if the products do not live up to their billing. Beyond these factors, we in the United States have a culture that venerates "more": bigger, faster, and cheaper. In the process, product quality can be, and often is, compromised. Rapid company growth does not always correlate with product quality.

Improved product quality, however, brings added value, increases competitive ability, does not necessarily add to cost, and leads to higher demand. There also seems to be a stable demand for high-quality products that are not cheap. For example, the Apple iPhone is a high-quality product as far as function and appearance is concerned (until the battery fails). At the time of this writing, the International Data Corporation (IDC) claimed that the iPhone had only 4 percent of the world cell phone market at the end of 2010, but it was apparently making 50 percent of the world's cell phone profit.[1] Apple is fielding many products and services that fulfill the criteria for high quality, and at the time of this writing its gross corporate profit margin was hovering around 40 percent.[2]

An Example of Quality Improvement

The late 1960s and '70s were a rude awakening for the United States in all sorts of ways. For me they were especially rude because I innocently moved from a job as an engineer at Caltech's Jet Propulsion Laboratory (JPL), happily designing lunar and planetary spacecraft, to my life as a professor in a university that was just about to (literally) burst into flames. But certainly, it was a time of questioning and increasing awareness. In the context of this book, it caused many people to become much more critical of technology, and therefore of products.

Before this time, people would often grumble about products that would fail, or that were unusually inconvenient, but seemed to accept product failures in return for their gifts. When I was a child, my grandfather complained about his Fordson tractor, which would overheat and occasionally threaten to kill him by rolling over backward. But he never seriously considered reverting to horses. My mother cursed her Easy Spindrier washing machine because the clothes would never arrange themselves symmetrically enough in the drying drum to prevent the machine from bouncing into things it shouldn't, but she never wanted to go back to a wringer. My first automobile was a 1941 Chevrolet Club Coupe, and although it would not have done very well on a skid pad, I loved it greatly.

Why shouldn't we in the United States have loved our products more unconditionally in the past? After all, they were U.S. products, and therefore, we assumed, the best in the world. Hadn't we in the United States brought the world the Model T, concentrated orange juice, and the atom bomb? Hadn't we built 300,000 airplanes during World War II? In fact, had not our industrially produced products played the major role in defeating unprecedented evil? If there were problems in the world, technology and its products were helping cure them, not add to them. Weren't there to be cars that converted to airplanes and unlimited free atomic energy in the future? Also, the growth of industry and mass production were the engines of capitalism, which brought us all jobs and money. We could all get richer and buy more and more products.

But I was at JPL because of Sputnik, which delivered a cruel message to the United States in 1957. The dreaded Soviet Union had successfully exploded both atomic and hydrogen bombs by then, but we had been first. Now they had done something that we had not. The result was the "Space Race," and since space was fascinating, the technology was exotic, and the country seemed to be uniformly behind beating the Soviet Union in this race, no matter what the cost, how could I not join the Jet Propulsion Laboratory (JPL), which had the leading role in the festivities? As we know, the United States closed the "space gap" and pulled ahead, but to our amazement, people began questioning whether the result was worth the cost. Shouldn't we be spending the money on such things as hunger, health, and equality? Shouldn't we clean up our act on Earth before we colonized the moon? The 1960s were happening, and social conscience was beginning to grow.

In the 1960s, environmentalism hit the front pages (Rachel Carson wrote *Silent Spring* in 1962) and we began to worry about the effects of technology and our capitalistic lifestyle upon the ecosphere. In fact, in the late 1960s we began to worry about all sorts of things that most of us had taken for granted, from ethnic and gender biases to abortion rights and social justice. The products of industry were not ignored, but there was relatively little impact upon industrial or government policy at that time.

In the United States, worry about product quality was to come a few years later, when some of our products and industries were first threatened and then displaced by those from other countries. The impressive success of Japan was a particularly large shock, since we had clearly beaten them in World War II and convinced ourselves that they were only capable of making cheap copies of our products.

In 1997, Charles O'Reilly and Michael Tushman wrote an excellent book entitled *Winning Through Innovation: A Practical Guide to Leading Organizational Change and Renewal.*[3] In the book they listed the following industries in which the leaders (often U.S. companies) rapidly lost their market share through the 1970s, '80s, and '90s:

Watches	Food processors
Automobiles	Microwave ovens
Cameras	Athletic equipment
Stereo equipment	Semiconductors
Medical equipment	Industrial robots
Color televisions	Machine tools
Hand tools	Optical equipment
Radial tires	Consulting services
Electric motors	Computer hardware
Photocopiers	Textiles
Shipbuilding	Airlines
Software	Financial services
Steel production	

They also named the product class leaders they considered to have become victims to their own success (note the United States companies again), which are shown in the following list. All of them lost market share during this period. Some have recovered. Some have not.

ICI (chemicals)	SSIH (watches)
IBM (personal computers)	Oticon (hearing aids)
Kodak (photography)	Bank of America (financial)
Sears (retailing)	Goodyear (tires)
GM (automobiles)	Polaroid (photography)
Ampex (video recorders)	Bausch and Lomb (vision)
Winchester (disk drives)	Smith Corona (typewriters)
U.S. Steel (steel)	Fuji Xerox (copiers)
Syntex (pharmaceuticals)	Zenith (TVs)
Philips (electronics)	EMI (CT scanners)
Volkswagen (automobiles)	Harley-Davidson (motorcycles)

This shake-up occurred initially in such resource-dependent industries as shipbuilding and steel. The initial reaction in the

United States was bafflement, because we considered ourselves rich in resources, production skills, labor, and management and believed that our products were superior. Our rationalization on the success of our competition was that they were cheating through use of low wages, government-industry collusion, and unfair trade practices. However, we then began losing markets in higher value-added products (consumer electronics, automobiles, machine tools) and foreign products began to be seen as "better." Our trade balance suffered as we imported more and exported less. And now that many of these "overseas" companies are manufacturing in the United States, it is difficult to think that countries such as Japan were cheating through low wages and industry-government collusion. We had to accept the fact that they had simply moved ahead of us.

Finally admitting that something was amiss, the United States focused on improving one particular aspect of product quality—*manufacturing quality*, an area neglected after World War II that was particularly approachable by the technical and quantitative thinking of industry. The campaign to improve manufacturing quality has been remarkably successful, both in the United States and in other industrialized countries. The benefits have ranged from increased product reliability (100,000-mile automobile warranties), to cost reduction (remarkably reduced reject rates), to appearance improvement (fits and finishes).

I had the pleasure of watching this process in action in many companies, but particularly at Hewlett-Packard and Ford Motor Company. The CEOs of these two companies, John Young and Donald Petersen, put manufacturing quality improvement at the top of their priorities, and it trickled down to all levels of the companies. The programs resulted in astonishing improvements in the reliability of their products, cost savings, communication between different functions and disciplines, and pride among the employees. U.S. companies in fields such as automotive and electronics learned from companies like Toyota and were able to catch up with the Japanese. A major focus on the improvement of manufacturing quality was to decrease defects and part variability. These factors are key in improving any sort of process quality as focusing on small process details can lead to large improvements.

There were major changes in organizational structure and procedures that were instrumental in improving manufacturing quality, including the strengthening of functional interaction, particularly between designers and manufacturing people. The old approach of "throwing it over the wall," in which designers would complete the design and then ship it to manufacturing, was successfully suppressed, resulting in "design for manufacturing" and increased sensitivity to the manufacturing process. Although designers and manufacturing people lost the pleasure of blaming each other for product problems, the products benefited a great deal. Other benefits came from inaugurating stronger supply-chain management, which included exporting manufacturing quality approaches to vendors, just-in-time inventory, minimizing investment in backlogged parts and assemblies, and standardizing components and parts.

Responsibility for manufacturing quality was pushed down the organization due to the realization that the actual manufacturers not only knew more about the process than managers but also were the people looking after the quality of the work itself. This helped flatten organizations and create high-functioning teams. Total Quality Management (TQM), worker empowerment, motivation of and close work with suppliers, encouragement of creativity in the manufacturing process, and use of more sophisticated quantitative approaches to eliminate waste and improve output all became common. Companies also learned to design more flexible assembly lines and products that could be more easily manufactured.

Unfortunately, not all companies had such campaigns, and it is not clear that the effort has remained as strong in those who

did. W. Edwards Deming and Joseph M. Juran, the original quality gurus who moved to Japan and inspired breakthrough efforts
in increasing manufacturing quality there after their teachings
had little response in the United States, taught that improving
manufacturing quality was to be an ongoing goal. Unfortunately,
I suspect that once the United States learned the new game, many
U.S. manufacturers relaxed again. The effort spent on this "revolution" was immense, as was its success, but it did not broaden
into a revolution in overall product quality. Manufacturing quality, and not necessarily overall quality, was the focus. Improving
manufacturing quality was consistent with the quantitative
approach preferred by managers and engineers in industry, so it
was possible to use measurements and metrics to set specific
goals, while overall quality, less susceptible to such tools, sometimes fell by the wayside.

Beyond Manufacturing Quality

We can learn a great deal from the successful campaigns to
improve manufacturing quality. For instance, we know that it is
possible to dramatically improve product quality, but it may
take major setbacks to cause this to happen. Hopefully setbacks
are not omnipresent, but it certainly was the case with manufacturing quality in the United States. In U.S. industries where
high product reliability was required, such as military missile
and spacecraft manufacturing, attention to manufacturing quality was essential. But many industries simply paid no attention.
U.S. competitor countries had been severely set back during
World War II, and the United States was rightfully impressed
with itself for its manufacturing ability. The post–World War
II demand for products was huge. Profits could be high. And
when things are good, people unfortunately (or fortunately) act
as though they will remain that way—witness the economic

"bubbles" and subsequent "busts" of the 1990s and early part of this century. Think of the companies that have gotten into trouble because they delayed too long in moving to a new technology or those that do not realize performance criteria are changing.

Since U.S. companies had been successful for so many years, they saw no reason to change their practices. Large inventories were comforting, and it was assumed that inspectors could ensure adequate quality. Companies, especially large ones, became complacent with success and underestimated the time and effort it would take to change. And improving quality requires change. Procedures defining allowable deviations in part dimensions were developed during the long period when humans controlled machine tools, so shouldn't they work fine when computers took over? Instead of worrying about production details, top managers saw their jobs as more financial. It took the competition of Japanese companies, using the tools of Juran and the approaches of Deming, among others, to wake the United States up.

It also takes effort to maintain a program to increase quality. Unfortunately, business goals and management theories run in cycles. For instance, the hot topics at the time of this writing seem to be *innovation* and *entrepreneurship*. There is little in the media anymore about manufacturing quality—the little attention that exists is oriented toward potentially radical changes through continued advancement in digital technology, such as products built by three-dimensional printers, input directly by designs created with computer modeling programs. Much of the interest in innovation is focused on breakthroughs in technological processes, applications of the Internet, and discovering the next "big thing" (nanotechnology, for example) rather than toward improving overall product quality.

Could we improve overall quality as radically as we improved manufacturing quality? I think so. And in fact we could use many techniques (goals, benchmarking, rewards, better understanding of the components of quality) utilized in those earlier campaigns to do so.

Global Competition

Fortunately (or worrisomely), the United States has an excellent motivation to increase overall product quality: global competition. Industries in many, if not most, other countries are devoting increasing effort to developing higher-quality products. Airbus is successfully competing with Boeing, and U.S. streets are featuring more German and South Korean cars. The United States is reliving the 1970s and 1980s fears of Japan in the present concern with China, whose name appears on so many products bought in the United States nowadays.

Like many emerging economies, China began its surge on the basis of cost. I bought my first Chinese drill bits about 15 years ago. A full set of fractional, numerical, and letter sizes in a metal box cost just $39.95—unbelievable. My friends laughed at me and said the bits would break. Indeed, they did just that. I just bought another set a year ago—still for about the same price. None of them have broken! China is climbing the quality curve due to practice, education, and the experience of manufacturing components and products for leading industries based in other countries that have higher quality standards. China is also focusing on indigenous products, in which quality is also rapidly rising. China's companies are even broadening their competencies. For example, the country is extremely competitive in international large-scale construction. The new eastern span of the San Francisco–Oakland Bay Bridge contains 24 huge steel modules, each half the size of a football field, manufactured in China and shipped to the United States. Attention gained through local projects such as the Beijing Capital International Airport, and the

Three Gorges Dam has resulted in successful large-scale projects from Saudi Arabia to New York City.

India is coming online as a major player in product exports. It is also following the trend toward higher overall quality, realizing that quality *is* value and there is more profit in higher value-added products. Contrary to old assumptions, the United States does not have a monopoly on good engineers and managers, creative approaches to production, or outstanding marketing and design ability—countries such as India are catching up.

Increased visibility of foreign products in the international marketplace is no surprise to those of us who teach in universities and travel extensively. In the United States, foreign students have been top performers in schools for a long time: the old saw that they are good at theory but bad at application and low in creativity has never been true. Neither is it true at present that U.S. engineers are better because they grew up on farms or spent their youth working on cars and radios. There aren't that many farmers anymore, and cars and radios are no longer easy to repair without proper equipment and a great deal of specific knowledge. It is pretty easy to change ignition points in an older car—you can set them fairly well by eye—but you can't diagnose a modern ignition control system in the same way.

In fact, present U.S.-born engineering students are more typified by their performance in high school math and science courses than their skill at application and their creativity. There is nothing inherently superior about U.S. thinking. A stable economic base and national priorities are all that is needed for engineers worldwide to do outstanding work. If companies are short on required specialties, they can hire them. Nor does U.S. birth automatically guarantee that U.S. businesspeople are better than those overseas. We in the United States have always acknowledged the abilities of managers in European countries, but we are now becoming educated about the abilities of those in other parts of the world as well.

The business ability of Indians, Japanese, Singaporeans, Chinese, and people from other Asian countries is startlingly apparent in businesses ranging from doughnut shops to Silicon Valley start-ups. Consider the people who run the Tata Group in India, which consists of 114 companies that create products ranging from tea to steel and from agrichemicals to Jaguar automobiles. Their 2009 release of the Nano, known as the one-lakh car because it only costs around 100,000 rupees, or one lakh (about $2,500), suggests innovative ability as well.

Onward

Improving product quality must pervade all aspects of an organization. It requires a high-priority effort at all levels and in all functions of a company, which means that the board of directors, CEO, and other top managers must be believers. A goal of universal pride throughout the company from being associated with delivering products that are the best in their class and an appropriate reward and recognition system must be established. Companies producing high-quality products must have a high degree of interaction between all functions, disciplines, and levels of management. In particular, engineering, manufacturing, and marketing need unusually good communication and understanding of each other's capabilities, techniques, and goals. A company seeking higher-quality products should also have a high level of traditional skills in solving engineering and business problems, since sophisticated technology, business ability, and an increasing number of disciplines and approaches are required in producing even simple products.

Pricing and profit receive considerable attention in most companies, as do strategy and the setting of goals, although one can argue about the amount allocated to product development and improvement and the overall attention paid to quality. In the early days of Hewlett-Packard, the founders decided that company growth would be determined by the need to provide enough resources to keep new product development strong and engineers motivated and proud of the product line, and that their products would be the best of their kind. This goal required strong growth, but it is definitely different from a goal simply of beating the profit made in the corresponding quarter of the previous year.

Chapter 1 *Thought Problem*

Choose an industrially produced product that in your opinion exhibits extremely high quality, and one that has extremely low quality. In each case, speculate why this is so. In the case of the low-quality product, what could be done to increase its quality? Could this be done without increasing its cost? If so, why do you think it has not been done?

In the class from which this book grew at Stanford, the students are asked to write a short paragraph justifying their choices. We also encourage them to search widely so they don't all converge on their favorite Apple product and their most hated piece of software. The students' choices and speculations appear on the website of the course so that they can see each other's thinking, which makes for good discussion material. Fortunately for the popularity of the books I write, I am not able to give required assignments to readers. But you might find it interesting to discuss your choices in these exercises with friends, coworkers, your girlfriend or boyfriend, or, if you have a good marriage, your spouse.

Problems in Increasing Product Quality

Narrow-Mindedness and Attitudes

We are creatures of our culture. The United States, for instance, is a relatively young culture, blessed with a large amount of usable space, excellent natural resources, and ambitious immigrant forebears. But young cultures that have prospered on the utilization of natural resources can be a bit raw. As an example, think about the reluctance of many people involved in the production of products to become more comfortable with, and competent at, handling aesthetic and emotional issues in their lives and culture—in a sense, this reflects our history. Our industrial past is characterized by competent, competitive (sometimes ruthless) people and spectacular material gains. We are still fascinated by them in biographies and history books. The stereotypical insensitive male is a major actor in the U.S. story of the past.

We are amused by anecdotes like General Grant's oft-quoted comment on music: "I only know two tunes. One is Yankee Doodle and one is not." He was neither an engineer nor a company president, but he did become president of the United States. Many a "traditional" U.S. male (I once was one until retrained by art school, the university, the women in my life, and time) prefers to gain his pleasures from the outdoors, well-played athletic events, physically attractive women, fast cars and airplanes, good liquor, and perhaps extraordinary business deals. Painting, poetry, dance, and beauty did not fit the U.S. male stereotype of old and were considered, by these men, best left to women.

But such attitudes are not limited to men, or to the United States. I know a large number of men and women in industry who, even though they are highly sensitive people and may have sophisticated knowledge and abilities, are reluctant to apply such thought and skills at work. Many managers in companies, especially those who manufacture hardware, are downright timid in discussing and experimenting with aesthetic factors and educating their engineers and managers about them. The result is that they shortchange aesthetic factors in design compared, say, to people in fashion or architectural design. Professionals who focus on aesthetic considerations have historically been given consulting roles in companies rather than line responsibility, and aesthetic factors seem to take a backseat to those that can be easily quantified.

Thinking, Problem Solving, and Quality

Since I have spent many years working in a university, I can partly blame education for lack of adequate attention to overall product quality. Most engineers and many managers are, after all, products of our universities. We in the university are obsessed with theory, optimization, rigorous and logical thinking, breakthroughs, and the next big thing—not "goodness." We teach critical thinking more than creative thinking, and the three R's over quality. Our faculty members rely upon the written and spoken word, mathematics, and rigorous experiment and quantification when possible. Unfortunately, characteristics of good products, such as elegance, and the emotions involved with outstanding products, namely love, are not easily described by these languages—you can't put a number on elegance or love. It is also difficult to define such things with the degree of clarity necessary to allow for improvement.

Many engineering school faculty members are neither comfortable nor equipped with the proper background to deal with such topics. Even professors whose personal lives actively embrace philosophical, political, and humanistic considerations are hesitant to bring them into the classroom. Courses generally focus on analysis rather than synthesis. Aspects of products that cannot be modeled or described with mathematics are often referred to as "nontechnical." Many of these topics are relegated to programs labeled "industrial design" or "product design," and they are often viewed with suspicion by the majority of engineering school teachers.

This attitude is bound to influence not only admission criteria and course content in engineering schools, but also the attitude of the students themselves. In fact, there is so much emphasis on the logical and the quantitative, and such a heavy diet of left-brain activities in the curricula (mathematical analysis, application of science, relying on precedent, numbers, charts and graphs), that we probably scare off many students who have a real liking for right-brain activities (relating to creativity, emotion, and intuitiveness). Engineering students have too little opportunity to deal with the interaction between people and products or to think about topics outside the traditional engineering curriculum. Business schools are a bit better, exposing students to fields such as organizational behavior, marketing, general management, and strategy. But they also have been increasingly drawn to the quantifiable. Being an engineer, I am certainly a believer in metrics, statistics, and mathematical analysis, but many aspects of quality are difficult to measure.

In the 1980s, there were a large number of publications on the previously mentioned topic of manufacturing quality. Some of the more thoughtful ones were written by David Garvin, then and now a professor in the Harvard Business School. In one widely referenced article, "Competing on the Eight Dimensions of Quality," he discussed eight aspects of quality:[1]

1. Performance
2. Features
3. Reliability
4. Conformance
5. Durability
6. Serviceability
7. Aesthetics
8. Perceived quality

The article's emphasis is mainly on conformance (deviation from standard) with resulting positive effects on performance, reliability, and durability. Garvin's article sets the last two qualities apart with the comment, "The final two dimensions of quality are the most subjective. Aesthetics—how a product looks, feels, sounds, tastes, or smells—is clearly a matter of personal judgment and a reflection of individual preferences." He does not deny that they are important; they are simply less susceptible to universal conclusions. I agree with him, but from my perspective as a designer and consultant, aesthetics and perceived quality, although admittedly difficult to generalize over large populations, often play dominant roles in the success of products. In the context of many people in business with whom I have worked who seem to be allergic to things that cannot be measured and plotted on charts, Garvin deserves a medal for even including the topics—and incidentally an oak leaf cluster for including serviceability, an increasingly neglected component of quality.

The increasing emphasis on marketing in business has been good for the quality of products. When I began my career, many industries seemed alarmingly insensitive to their customers. Products were designed in traditional ways, and since they had no choice, customers were forced to adapt to the products. Now, however, it is standard to attempt to be "closer to the customer." Such techniques as beta testing and focus groups are now commonplace. Sophisticated quantitative techniques including conjoint analysis are aiding in the traditional marketing problem of separating and prioritizing what the customer wants. However, some of the components of quality are not necessarily given high priority by the customer even if they should be—in crasser terms, customers do not always know what they like.

In addition, marketing has always been weak in the case of unprecedented products—it is difficult for people to respond to something with which they have no experience. And marketing is constrained by the strategy of the company. In creating new products, marketing can help, but certain principles must lead. Products should physically fit people, whether they think to specify it in their focus group or not. Elegance is good, even if people have difficulty in describing it. Symbolism is important, even though many customers may deny it.

Marketing, when applied in business, is also biased by the values of the people involved in the business. Apple's first "portable" computer was a failure despite their marketing program. Potential customers said that they wanted full Macintosh function, including eight hours of battery life, in as small a box as possible. This sounded terrific to a company perhaps dominated by engineers. But that box weighed 17 pounds, which was not what the customers had in mind. What they really wanted, it turned out, was something small and light. Apple figured that out for the very successful PowerBook line of computers, in which the design goal became "put all the computer you can in a (small) box." The marketing efforts had missed people's love of small things—the most with the least—but at the time, most computer users would probably not have admitted it.

Finally, the intent of marketing is to define products that will satisfy the customer and fulfill company financial goals. In order to do this, data is typically gathered on past and potential future customer wants and needs. Often the target is individuals or small groups who have purchasing power in companies. But what is good for individuals and companies may not be good for societies. For example, the desire for powerful gasoline engines in large vehicles is not compatible with increasingly expensive fuel, clean air, and crowded city streets.

I am an optimist about engineers and businesspeople, industry, and product quality and am confident that industry is becoming better at designing and producing products. There are many fine designers in the world. However, many products are being designed by people who are not fine designers. Companies have improved greatly at manufacturing quality (whether locally or outsourced), but many are still wanting. The cross-functional interdisciplinary team approach to product design has brought a much-needed degree of integration to the product development process, but it is still not used in many businesses. Some managers appreciate and are sophisticated about good design. Many, although they would deny it vehemently, are not. There are also engineers who value aesthetics and the emotional response of the users of their devices. But there are certainly those who would prefer not to be involved in such considerations.

This situation is improving in the United States, but the changes began relatively recently, stimulated by foreign competition. Asia and Europe, for example, have more established aesthetic traditions than the United States. Over a longer length of time, societies seem to become more sophisticated and less awkward with things aesthetic and intellectual. Michelangelo carved the Pietà and the Chinese were making Ming vases during the 15th century. The Pilgrims did not arrive in America until the 17th century and spent much of their early effort securing food, shelter, and safety. We have also been preoccupied with fighting wars, making money, and becoming a world power. Our relatively recent changes in aesthetic sensitivity reflect not only maturation but also the increasing criticism and social expectations that stem from the late 1960s and the Vietnam War and our increasing awareness of environmental problems ranging from potential global warming to ugliness—and perhaps the increasing participation of women in product design, development, and manufacturing and in positions of influence in industry.

We are still perhaps better at building large farming and construction equipment, tanks, and airplanes than we are at making furniture that is both comfortable and visually sophisticated. At one time of great frustration, I had both a classical Eames chair and an old La-Z-boy rocker in my living room. The Eames chair was exquisitely elegant and beautiful to look at, but it did not fit me at all. The La-Z-Boy rocker was extraordinarily comfortable, but my wife finally convinced me it should move to my shop. Why couldn't I have both beauty and comfort? As a possible hint, I once encountered a letter in a well-known business magazine that has an annual feature in which it names the best-designed products of the year. The letter castigated the editor for using professional designers as judges instead of businessmen. The implication was obvious—good, hardheaded businesspeople are the best judges of design. I wrote a letter suggesting that a panel of professional designers be used to pick the 20 most outstanding businesses. I got no reply.

Tradition Runs Deep

When I worked briefly in the U.S. automobile business 50 years ago, it was stuck in the traditions of its past success. The company I worked for was making a lot of money selling OK machinery in the light of limited overseas and local competition. The diversity of its product line was in name only, because it was seeking to standardize parts across different divisions. There was also little diversity between U.S. car companies. U.S. cars were large, heavy, softly suspended, and sluggish in steering. The top managers of the company were U.S. males with dominantly financial interests. Good designers (whose own automobiles were often foreign in make) tended to leave the company because they simply could not get management interested in a wider variety of products that better fit their customers. The philosophy was "Change its look a little, make it go faster, and advertise the hell out of it." When I pointed out the market penetration of the Volkswagen Beetle, the response often was that it was not good in deep snow. When GM finally responded to the Beetle with the Corvair, it was a Detroit copy that could not compete.

But 50 years later, can we say that the automobile industry has gotten the message? At the time of this writing, due to overseas competition, increasing sensitivity to the finite supply of oil and the environment, and a bit of bankruptcy, there is a long overdue burst of innovation in the design of automobiles. But will it last? Look up an old automobile ad and compare it with the new ones. Mileage figures are increasing, but there have been few radical changes that respond to traffic problems and the decreasing oil stocks in the world. There is more attention to pollution, but the U.S. automobile industry has not been the leader here—in fact, it has fought it. Automotive ads also still promise to make us more desirable, attractive, and effective if we buy this year's model (my automobile does not seem to help my image much, but fortunately I do not expect it to).

U.S. automobile companies are trapped by tradition in their design. Where is the efficient commuter machine? Why do I have to either take a ton and a half of metal to the grocery store or risk a bicycle or motorcycle accident because of an overload of shopping bags? Why was it necessary to wait so long for cleaner, more efficient engines, air bags, and hybrid power? Why does the glove compartment in my pickup hold almost nothing, and why can't the spare tire holder be designed so that my wife can change the tire? The reasons are not simply technical, and they have contributed to the bankruptcy of General Motors and the near-death state of Ford and Chrysler (acquired by Fiat) in the recent recession. After major surgery, these companies are now doing much better, but it remains to be seen how they will respond in the long term—with more advertising or more attention to filling society's needs.

Another tradition the United States has that can reduce quality is our desire to produce extremely large numbers of a given product. There are good reasons for this obsession with huge production volumes due to economies of scale—per-item savings in everything from design and development costs to tooling, and sufficient cash flow to allow large advertising campaigns and sales networks. But there is a potential loss in product quality in massive production.

As an example of quality problems occurring through trying to satisfy a large number of people, consider the full-sized "half-ton" pickup truck. The sales volume of these products is large, but the variation in products, except perhaps for optional features, is small. At the same time, the usage of these vehicles varies widely from boulevard cruisers to trucks. But the design emphasis over time seems to be swinging from carrying cargo to carrying people. With mine, I haul around large, dirty, ungainly loads and I seldom stray from paved or dirt roads. I only need a standard cab because I don't take my family or work crews riding, and I need an eight-foot bed because of the loads I carry. I want one that will last a long time (20 or 30 years), be easily maintainable, and be well equipped with tie-down points and other means of securing loads. I want it to have a comfortable bench seat with indestructible upholstery and simple functional features and controls that do not distract me from driving. I do not want it to use a ridiculous amount of fuel and show off the bruises and scratches that it will acquire over time. There are many users like me, and the pickups presently being produced do not fit our needs—they are just not good trucks.

My last pickup had a small V-8 engine, which was larger than I needed, only four weak attach points located at inconvenient points inside the bed, and a body design that both prevented using the outside surface for securing the loads and flaunted all dings and scratches. The mechanical portion of the truck was satisfyingly reliable, but such things as replacing the randomly failing core packs in the ignition system and checking and replacing spark plugs called for a highly intelligent and extremely patient monkey. Unfortunately, the truck, although far from the "luxury" model, included a large number of electric and electronic bells and whistles that could and often did fail, the reasons for and treatment of the failures being often confusing to even "factory certified" mechanics. As a minor example, for some time I had a problem with one of the switches that sensed whether the doors were ajar. It was buried inside the door behind the latch and collected dirt until it no longer functioned properly, causing a few interior and exterior lights to remain constantly on, the dashboard to give erroneous warning signals, and other annoying malfunctions. I tried removing the pertinent fuses but found I would then disable necessary functions.

The first time this malfunction happened, I gave up diagnosing the problem and took it to a dealer. The serviceperson, after telling me how stupidly the switch had been positioned, told me that in such cases they generally changed the switches on both sides, which was difficult because the doors had to be disassembled, but that they would be glad to do so for $500. He also was honest enough to tell me that my problem would probably happen again. My reaction was to take it to another dealer. Serviceman number two agreed with the diagnosis, told me further negative things about the truck's designers, and then told me it was not necessary to change the switches and squirted a large amount of brake cleaner into the switch area. The problem seemed to be solved, but only temporarily, as it began again in a few days.

The serviceman at dealer number three, having been told of the treatment of serviceman number two, added to my lore of stupidity on the part of the designers and coldly informed me that serviceman number two had been completely off base. He then squirted an even larger amount of penetrating oil into the latch. Under such treatment, the switch seemed to work for a while but once again failed in a few days. At that point I learned how to take the door apart and became an expert replacer of switches and solenoids. One might think that pickups should be designed to survive dirt—apparently not these ones.

Some of my farmer friends had an interesting problem with the same model pickups that were fitted with supercharged diesel engines. The air intakes were so positioned that the engines would suck large quantities of dust into the air filter, causing the truck to require new, rather expensive filter cartridges at an alarming rate, the sticky surface on the cartridge making it impossible to blow the dust buildup off with compressed air. Upon interaction with dealers and designers, my friends got the impression that the designers had not thought much about driving the pickups through dusty fields—this is a truck?

I recently bought a new pickup, and by buying the so-called "working" (stripped) model, managed to escape many bells and whistles, but certainly not all. For instance, this one makes highly obnoxious noises in an attempt to force me to put my seat belt on to move it from my driveway to the garage. But even worse, it is so tall that it requires running boards. I cannot reach loads in the center of the bed while standing on the ground, even though I am significantly taller than most people are. I guess my truck was designed to look cool on Saturday night. Another farmer friend of mine who bought a new 2011 pickup solved the problem by disposing of the standard cargo box and custom-building a flat bed so he could better reach his tools and cargo. I am seriously considering lowering my pickup. If I could more easily reach the objects in the bed, I would love it more.

The majority of pickups sold these days, however, are used more often as cars than as trucks. Unfortunately, they are not good cars, either. Their overall weight, weight distribution, and high center of gravity oppose good handling qualities. The horsepower required to achieve carlike acceleration and top speed ensures the burning of large amounts of fuel. They are cumbersome to park and difficult to maneuver in traffic. If not secured, loads in the bed slide around while accelerating, braking, and turning. Finally, they are decidedly unsafe if driven as a car. Their poorer handling makes evasive action more difficult and braking slower.

Granted that options are available, these trucks are *compromise products*, like most products being manufactured these days in huge numbers, because of the tradition of attempting to sell one design to a large number of customers. With modern automated manufacturing techniques, however, it should be economically feasible to provide a more diverse offering of products, thereby doing a better job of satisfying customer needs.

In the 1990s, more attention was paid to this matter while manufacturers experimented with extremely flexible factories that could offer highly individualized products. An example was the Panasonic division of Matsushita, which offered bicycles through the Panasonic Individual Custom System. This system produced more than 11 million variations of a bicycle. The customer chose the desired components, dimensions, and other characteristics, and the customized product reached the customer within two weeks after the order. Another was Levi Strauss's experimentation with individually tailored clothes.

We are proud of the achievements mass production has brought to us, including many products of high quality: VW Bugs, clothespins, and Apple iPods were, or are, mass produced and do their job well, though not loved by everyone. We have equipped large armies with standardized weapons, put our population on the highway with Model Ts and As, and manufactured products so cheaply that we have attained the materialistically highest standard of living in the world.

But people are definitely not all the same, and larger product variability is consistent with this fact. Perhaps there is a portent in the magazine business, which used to be dominated by general-purpose magazines such as *Life*, *Look*, and the *Saturday Evening Post*. These periodicals are now gone, except for thin shadows. Instead the newsstands are filled with specialty magazines like *Cycle World*, *Vanity Fair*, *BusinessWeek*, *Arms and Ammo*, and *U.S. News and World Report*. With the advent of the Internet, specialization is even more pronounced: mass production is general production. As it becomes possible to economically produce products that allow a better "fit" with individual customers, industry will hopefully continue to move in that direction.

Traditions and values, especially in large organizations such as manufacturing companies, are extremely difficult to change. It takes time to develop new sensitivities and values on the part of consumers as well as producers. We finally accepted the fact that motorcycles can both go fast and be quiet. We are demanding the same for leaf blowers. Private plane producers and owners have not gotten the message yet. The 2008 spike in fuel costs finally awakened us to the gas-gorging habits of SUVs, which, someday in the near future, are going to be remembered with disbelief.

Flaws in Economic Theory

Economic theory seems to have several embarrassing flaws when it comes to product quality. In particular, it has problems in dealing with anything that does not have a price determined by supply and demand. Such factors unfortunately include the pleasure and pride the owner receives from an extraordinarily crafted, well-functioning, elegant, and beautiful product. It is possible to quantify the cost of making a movie and the box office receipts, but not the joy, insight, or education the viewer receives. We may easily put dollar figures on the cost of making a Porsche and the cost of buying one, but not on the positive feelings of the person who owns and drives it. The businessperson can therefore know the exact dollar profit on a product, but not the exact dollar value of the brand, the advertising, or, indeed, the quality of the product.

This situation may be another reason for reluctance to spend money on product attributes that improve quality. If one wanted to place a value on these attributes in traditional ways, it would involve selling the original version and the improved one, then determining the difference between what could be charged for each of them. This comparison could be done in the case of optional features on automobiles in which products come with different quantities of them. It is obviously possible to know the costs of an iPhone with and without 4G and the selling prices, and therefore determine the increased profit from adding 4G (it is appreciable). But can you imagine Apple producing an ugly iPhone to run a test in order to put a value on attractiveness?

When looking at a particular economic system, even more traditional measures and actions that may inhibit product quality can be found. An obvious one is the desire for continual and as rapid as possible growth in company sales. Managers are humans, and competitive, and want their enterprise to be the largest one of its kind because large is seen as good by many. Also, we individuals only live a relatively few years and want to see our efforts bear as much fruit as possible before we die. And we need to grow faster than our competitors, don't we? Then there is Wall Street. Stock prices and the perceived performance of management is measured in terms of quarterly performance, usually in terms of sales in the preceding quarter or the equivalent quarter of the previous year—almost never over a five- or ten-year period. This measurement results in the temptation to maximize short-term profit, often by increasing price and decreasing the costs of developing new and better-performing products.

The Changing Nature of Design

Design is the function in the creation of products that reduces specific (or general) goals of the producer to even more specific inputs for manufacturing. In my admittedly biased view, design plays the critical role in determining product quality. Many, if not most, of the aspects of good quality are in the details, and although many people may have input into the design, designers provide the final details.

Industrial products range from women's clothing to spacecraft to medical equipment. The design process varies widely from industry to industry, from consulting designer to staff designer, and from design of civilian consumer products to that of weapon systems. Designers of unmanned spacecraft may not have to worry as much about the emotions of the human users as designers of lipsticks do because the products are heavily determined by knowledge, science, and analysis, and humans are involved only until they are launched. These designers work on extremely complex systems in large groups and must worry constantly about weight, reliability, and subsystem integration. However, spacecraft must be assembled, tested, and launched by people. Also, when designers reach the limits of science and analysis, they must depend on feelings and intuition. The opposite may be true for the designers of lipsticks, first concentrating on the centrality of feelings and emotions of the users and then worrying about more technical aspects (for example, creation of cases that keep their shape and protect the lipstick and of mechanisms that allow the lipstick to emerge from these cases in a satisfying and reliable manner). Although the importance of various aspects of design may vary over classes of products, they to some degree extend across all design activities. An increasing number of people are using the term *design thinking* to address this commonality.

In order to add to product quality, a design group should have the following attributes:

1. **Creativity:** the ability to have good ideas and implement them (which includes selling the ideas)
2. **Comfort with many intellectual disciplines:** either knowledge of them or ability to interact easily with those who do have this knowledge
3. **Cost consciousness:** constant awareness of how much the product will cost to create
4. **Coordination abilities:** close interaction with manufacturing, marketing, general management, and other related functions
5. **Knowledge of the customer:** ability and desire to acquire a deep understanding of the customer or end user
6. **Understanding of overall quality:** a highly developed sense of what creates quality and the ability to distinguish high quality from low
7. **"Whole brain" thinking:** ability to work with inputs based on knowledge, science, and analysis, but also on feelings, intuition, and judgments

These attributes can be summed up by saying good designers must be good engineers and good artists, but also sympathetic to business and able to work well in a team, the latter requiring social skills as well as technical ones.

It would be nice if all people involved in designing products in an organization were extremely powerful in all of these attributes, but as products become more complicated and sophisticated, greater specialization is needed and more people are involved in the design. The result is that functional and disciplinary groups grow, become formalized, and require increasing organizational skill to ensure that necessary interaction between them occurs.

Design has also increased in sophistication. When I was first introduced to design some 50 years ago, design was simpler. I was hired during my summers in college as a junior engineer at Hunter Engineering, where my uncle was the shop supervisor. The products and business were relatively straightforward—designing custom machinery for industrial customers under contract. I sat at a drafting board surrounded by handbooks and my slide rule and made drawings of parts and assemblies that would then go to the shop to be manufactured and assembled. If I didn't know what material to choose or how to calculate loads, stresses, temperatures, and other such things, I would get help from a more senior person. No one in the group had a degree in engineering. It was a traditional machine design operation, but among other things, the group designed a sophisticated continuous casting, rolling, and painting system that became the basis for the Hunter Douglas venetian blind business.

We needed to be creative, but we were creative in the sense of putting fairly conventional pieces together. We worked with a narrow set of disciplines (mechanical with an occasional switch or motor) and were good at prototyping and testing. We also worked to a budget that, aside from our boss, we were not involved in setting. We did not interact with manufacturing, although we did a reasonable job of designing for manufacture because we had all worked in shops at some time. Since these were industrial products, we worked more to the specifications of our customers and what our boss told us to do than to a deep understanding of clients' needs. In fact, we seldom met representatives of our customer company.

We did not think about beauty or cultural fit, but we had a good sense for quality because we were all machinery freaks. We built parts ourselves and knew about surface finishes, tolerances, and other related matters. We owned what machinery we could afford (motorcycles, tools, boats, and so on) and had an appreciation for elegance, efficiency, cleverness, and outstanding performance. I suppose the group could have been considered expert in both the measurable and the nonmeasurable aspects of machine quality. I remember thinking about this fact much later in life, when my uncle, who had dropped out of school after the ninth grade to become a machinist and spent his life working in shops before he became shop supervisor at Hunter Engineering, decided to retire and build custom machinery in his garage. One product was a very large and complicated machine that automatically made fully packaged lemon tarts at high speed—it was simply amazing. With all of my experience and education, I could not have done as well.

I was to encounter different approaches to design working at Shell Oil Company and at General Motors, and studying and teaching at Stanford University, but my next big insight was working at the Jet Propulsion Laboratory. Time had passed and such technologies as computers, solid-state circuitry, and titanium had arrived. Not only were the products unprecedented and technically sophisticated, but the stakes were high (the Space Race) and the constraints were extremely severe (weight, reliability, and launch survival issues). I was employed initially as a senior engineer and later as a group supervisor, once again deeply involved in the design of hardware. There were 2,000 of us at JPL, plus contractors, working on two projects—the Ranger lunar program and the Mariner planetary program. The work was much different from that at Hunter Engineering. For one thing, design was done by a large number of people with different job titles (engineer, scientist, designer, technician, and so on). This process was an effort of highly integrated and coordinated teams. And we engineers now worked at desks (with perhaps a drawing board in our office) and generally had degrees in engineering.

We all overlapped job descriptions, worked together, and were necessary in the process of designing and building hardware. There were many more people in the "design section" (still on drafting boards), and they had more formal education (typically two years of college and some with engineering degrees) than those at Hunter Engineering. Engineers came in all flavors (mechanical, electrical, civil, test), typically gave the designers sketches of what they were proposing, and then spent time with them as the details evolved. Large mainframe computers were available to analyze complicated structures and simulate communication systems.

I think industry pays a large penalty from associating the word *designer* with the type of person I was and the type of work I did when I started my career. The word is often associated with the memory of rooms full of anonymous people carefully "drafting" parts in the aircraft industry in the 1930s. Maybe *draftsman* was a better word to describe this type of work, but drafting is now done by computers. And design is no longer as straightforward. Designers in industry, however, are still somewhat invisible. As an example, if you look at the membership of the National Academy of Engineering, you find many more managers and academics than people who actually are involved in the details of design. At Stanford, we have the good fortune to have Brad Parkinson, the person credited with the Global Positioning System, on the faculty. That label is fair, since he envisioned it, managed the project while in the U.S. Air Force, and now busies himself finding applications for it. He is an excellent engineer/designer.

A few years ago, Brad was receiving many awards for his GPS work. I asked him once how it felt to be famous, and he replied that it was embarrassing because good engineers are invisible.

That is often the case with good designers as well, even though I have met many who are probably more valuable to their employer than some of the executives are. It is time to upgrade our image of designers in industry and make sure that the people doing the design are consistent with our upgraded image.

The work at JPL, unlike that at Hunter Engineering, was technically extremely interdisciplinary, requiring coordination of many parts (subsystems). We had "systems engineers" and "systems managers," and of course "systems design" to ensure that the spacecraft came complete with handling fixtures and test equipment, the proper number of test prototypes were built, the spacecraft would not be harmed during shipment to the launch site and launch site operations (probably a more hazardous environment than space), and the system was subdivided into subsystems that could be built and worked upon in parallel and assembled into a working unit. Above all, the systems people were in charge of making sure that the spacecraft design was balanced technically and between all of the various interests involved.

The term *technical balance* refers to adjudicating the various demands of the people responsible for the various subsystems—including communications, structure, propulsion, guidance and control, and science. As an example, the communications section at JPL usually wanted a safety pad of around 10 decibels to communicate to Earth, which was typically done through a steerable parabolic dish that necessarily was constrained during launch and extended once in space—a tricky operation. One way to obtain this safety pad was to make the antenna 10 times as large, but the structures people would rather see it 10 times smaller. Enter the systems engineers.

Another ongoing debate was between JPL and the various user interests involved, such as scientists and the funding agency (the government through NASA). The designers wanted reliability, which is often obtained through simplicity, but the pressure from scientists to fly their experiments was intense and resulted in complexity. Also, scientists tended to want things like magnetic field and cosmic ray fluxes, and the public (and therefore the government) liked mind-blowing photographs—another systems problem.

But JPL was not building products for individual consumers. The business side of the product development at JPL was in fact relatively weak (it dealt with budget control—there was no profit). Marketing consisted of selling NASA on a project, which was aided by the fact that we were the NASA center in charge of unmanned exploration of the solar system. Once the contract was signed, there was not much need to worry about customer demand, liability suits, social effects, or, assuming they were politically acceptable, costs. The products turned out to be visually striking not due to any conscious goal but because of the weight constraints, necessary articulations, and surface treatments needed to maintain temperatures—the appearance was totally determined by the function.

After I left JPL, I became a professor at Stanford teaching courses in engineering design, systems design, and product design, which at that time was a joint effort between the engineering school and the art department. The design process has changed a great deal since I joined the university through the availability of powerful new tools and approaches and changes in organizational approaches and global competition. New economic factors and social and individual values have also played a role. Thanks to computers and research, it seems to me that we have perhaps gotten stronger at purely technical problem solving but not necessarily at how to make products that increase the quality of people's lives—a situation that has attracted more and more of my interest.

As to other changes in design, when I arrived at Stanford, Silicon Valley was in full bloom. The presence of digital electronics and improving integrated circuits was opening up huge opportunities. Successful companies could be started on a relatively small amount of capital and, if successful, grow rapidly enough to cause the venture capital business to flourish along with the electronics business. More and more designers seemed to be working in small, growing companies and becoming interested in more idealistic problems. Perhaps because of this rather revolutionary era, and the severe overseas competition visible on the U.S. horizon, there was a great increase of interest in creativity, innovation (a word that implies more practical implementation than creativity), and entrepreneurship.

Increasing Creativity and Innovation

I happened to write a well-timed book on creativity, *Conceptual Blockbusting: A Guide to Better Ideas*, which although the first edition was written in 1974 is still in print, and became heavily involved in studying, teaching, and consulting about such things. Creativity is an essential element of design, and also of organizational change. And increasing quality usually implies change and innovation. The organizational characteristics necessary to encourage creativity are now well known. At one point, I used the following check sheet in my consulting, and also to help my students with their final projects, in which they acted as creativity consultants to organizational groups. The list includes important aspects of encouraging creativity and increasing innovation not only among designers but also in organizations in general.

1. **Are they, the clients, clear on what they want?**
2. **Are they willing to pay the price (in increased uncertainty, failures, perceived lack of control, and resources) for what they want?** Organizations often say they want to become more innovative but are not prepared to tolerate the associated increased experimentation and risk.

3. **Do they understand how people act in situations of increased creativity?** Organizations that have been operating in a given way for a long time are often unaware that increasing innovation often requires treating people differently and that these people will in turn respond differently.

4. **Are they working on the "right" problems?** Organizations often devote their effort to alleviating symptoms rather than solving core problems, since the latter involves more uncertainty and perhaps more pain.

5. **Do they understand cognitive styles and the necessity not only of using them properly but also of increasing communication between disciplines and business units?**

6. **Do they know when and how to use "ideation" techniques (e.g., time-and-effort focusers, set breakers, other people's ideas, crossing cultures, changing environments)?**

7. **Do they realize that their traditional decision-making approaches may be wrong to evaluate the products of increased innovation?** Numbers 5 to 7 have to do with increasing the quantity and quality of concepts and making sure that they are not rejected by old standards. The organization should perhaps think harder about problem-solving habits, learn a few creativity techniques, and pick up more thoughtful decision-making approaches.

8. **Are the proper resources (time, people, and money) available?** This question is a tough one. Organizations often become interested in increasing innovation when they are in financially tough times. There is no magic.

9. **Is the reward system appropriate?** Traditional organizations have reward systems based on fairness and seniority, not on recognizing individual contribution.

10. **Are groups being properly used to produce and implement new ideas?** Traditional groups are converging and safe, but not particularly creative. Creative groups must be managed collaboratively, rather than authoritatively, and managers must worry about the psychological environment as well as schedule and reporting procedures. Although individual creativity is basic, groups can be more creative than individuals in a complex organization can—they have a bigger "brain" and more economic and political clout.

11. **Is implementation rigorously planned for?** It is harder to make new ideas happen than old ones. Organizations often underestimate the time and resources necessary to do this, resulting in one of the main reasons for failure to increase innovation. Organizations devise and test brilliant new concepts but fail to back them strongly enough to take effect.

12. **Do they understand power and politics in the organization and their use in accomplishing change?** There is often ambivalence about power and politics in organizations, especially in institutions such as universities.

13. **Are changes in the organizational culture needed?** Often organizations are "tuned" for one state (plentiful resources, a steady market) and must reconstitute themselves for a new environment.

When I first joined the Stanford faculty, designers of products were necessarily becoming familiar with digital control, computers, and communication. Mechanical and electrical engineering came to overlap to such an extent that a new cross-disciplinary field called *mechatronics* evolved. Designers in start-up companies also became familiar with topics such as seed capital, mezzanine funding, IPOs, and equity vesting, not to mention working long hours under intense pressure. Business had clearly become a factor in design. Start-ups sometimes had only one or two designers, sometimes none, opening up a major opportunity for consulting design offices (IDEO, Frog). Personal computers were becoming widespread, and the first computer-aided design (CAD) and computer-aided manufacturing (CAM) programs became available.

In another 10 years (in the mid-1970s) I was chairing the Industrial Engineering and Engineering Management department at Stanford, which was in the midst of dealing with manufacturing problems and the competition U.S. companies were feeling from Japan and the Asian Tigers and from new organizational insights that affected product quality. Designers were now working ever more closely with manufacturing people as well as businesspeople. Such topics as designing for manufacture and manufacturing quality were key in design.

Ten years later, I was chairing the Stanford Science, Technology, and Society program, as well as teaching and writing in mechanical engineering and industrial engineering and consulting. Computers were now ubiquitous in design and manufacturing. Although designers still sketched, drawing boards had disappeared. Computers were used to produce the majority of graphics work and perform an increasing amount of analysis. Robots, computer-controlled machining centers, and outsourcing played ever-larger roles in manufacturing. Computers also allowed an increasing amount of simulation and simplified iteration and prototyping—all three increasingly used design tools. Business had become global, and digital communication devices allowed widely separated people to work as groups. Designers accepted that design overlaps not only business and manufacturing but also many other activities having to do with better understanding customers, economics, policy and politics, and generally the quality of life. Social and environmental issues impacted by design were also receiving increasing attention.

An indication of future directions in design is a program in the Stanford Engineering School called the Hasso Plattner Institute of Design (informally called the d.school). Hasso Plattner, a founder of SAP, made a large gift to Stanford to start this program, which is directed by David Kelley, a founder of IDEO, a large and successful design and innovation consulting company, who is now a professor at Stanford. The program teaches graduate courses and has ongoing laboratories, offers executive programs and short courses, and is overseen by a number of professors from different schools, departments, and disciplines. The courses change continually but are all based on projects, are taught by at least two people from different academic disciplines, and utilize student teams whose members also represent different disciplines.

People in the program believe that design thinking can be used to solve a wide variety of problems that are not usually thought to be under the purview of design; examples include social and policy problems. They define design thinking broadly and are experimenting with a definition of design that includes not only engineering and business but also a wide variety of other fields, including law, business, education, and many branches of the natural sciences, social sciences, and humanities—potentially all disciplines. The program considers both technical and emotional aspects of design discussed throughout this book, emphasizing creativity (generating alternate solutions), need finding, and other ways of better understanding the customer's true problem and making generous use of rapid prototyping during the design process.

Chapter 2 *Thought Problem*

Choose a product that you suspect might be of higher quality if it were not for narrow-mindedness or tradition on the part of the company that produced it. What might you do if you were chief engineer or president of the company to offset this narrow-mindedness or traditional thinking?

Then choose two more products, one that you believe to be extremely well designed and one that is poorly designed. Upon what do you base your choices? What do you think the causes might have been for both the good design and the bad? If you were CEO of the company responsible for the bad design, where might you look in the company to begin to improve its design competence?

CHAPTER

Performance, Cost, and Price

Is It a Good Deal?

Having thought a bit about the quality problem, inhibitions to solving it, and the process by which quality might be improved, let us move to the seven areas that are critical to product quality, and which, in my mind, do not receive the consideration they deserve. These areas play a major role in how companies define and differentiate their products, but they are rarely analyzed and adequately thought through. They are, of course, interconnected, but by discussing them separately, we can perhaps break the problem of product quality into more manageable pieces.

In this chapter, I will say a few things about performance, cost to the producer, and price to the consumer—three factors that immediately come to mind when thinking about quality. I also want to touch on them because even though they are often expressed quantitatively, they cannot be as logically determined as people think or might like. Quantities are simple for producers and consumers to think about and measure. But as behavioral economists are now proving, we do not think about price logically. Nor do we about performance. I once owned an open sports car and a station wagon, and I could not convince myself that both speedometers read the true speed because my sports car seemed to be going so much faster at 65 miles per hour.

Performance, cost, and price are intimately connected. Consumers are more likely to say, "That's a pretty good coffeemaker for $30," rather than simply, "That's a pretty good coffeemaker." They want performance to be high and price to be low. The producer is more likely to want cost low, price high, and adequate performance to beat the competition. Ideally, and perhaps necessarily, both producers and consumers will be pleased. The producer will make a nice profit, and the consumer will feel that the product is a good deal.

Quantifying Performance

We like to quantify performance—miles per hour, degrees Centigrade, mean time between failures, pixels per square inch, amortization curve, gigahertz, tons, and so on. Our interaction with products is extremely complex, and putting numbers on such things as performance seems to simplify describing the product. But how can the smoothness of shifting gears in a high-quality manual transmission be measured? Or the sound of a live string quartet? Or, conversely, the response to a disposable diaper with low absorbing ability? A saw that will not cut well? Can we really quantitatively compare the performance of an automobile and a motorcycle?

It also simplifies the lives of both producers and consumers to focus on the performance of products when they are brand-new, but high-quality products should have a long lifetime, and performance should be considered over their lifetime. Performance should include reliability, durability, serviceability, and maintainability as factors, since failures, even if for reasons not directly the fault of the producer, reflect poorly on the performance of the product.

As an example, my wife's car has a good reputation for performance and reliability, and it has lived up to this reputation since we bought it. Unfortunately, rodents recently chewed up the wiring harness, which cost some $3,000 to replace. Now my wife does not consider the car as high quality a product as she did, even though the producer obviously was not responsible for the rodents. I, too, view the car as of lesser quality than previously because not only is the wiring harness attractive to rats and mice, but the entire harness is a single assembly that is extremely difficult to repair or replace—it has bad serviceability. In addition, the situation has caused the carport where the car is parked to become an overwhelming collection of rat and mouse traps, poison bait, and sound-producing devices that annoy rats (and me). Checking with friends and neighbors, I've found that this problem is not an uncommon one, and in each case, although the automobiles were of different brands, the owners thought the producer of the car should have installed wiring harnesses that were easier to repair and less tasty to rodents—a perceived loss of quality.

Serviceability and maintainability are among my pet peeves these days. If a high-quality product is at all likely to have a failure in a part or subsystem, that part or subsystem should be easily repairable or replaceable. The cable harness in my wife's car should at least have been modular so it would not have been necessary to remove the entire assembly. I had an iMac computer fail on me recently because of a widespread problem with bad capacitors manufactured by a company in Taiwan. These are old-fashioned discrete capacitors soldered into a sophisticated multilayer printed circuit board with lead-free solder, which melts at a higher temperature than the traditional lead-tin solder. The computer was no longer under warranty, and to have it repaired by a commercial service would have cost nearly as much as buying a new one.

I looked the problem up online and found many entries reporting identical failures, several of which included instructions on how to repair the computer, but each with a warning that the repair would take many hours. I took the computer apart to see if I could repair it (even though there were warnings in the literature and on the computer implying that I should not do so), and my office partner and I worked on the computer for many hours because I thought it was too good a computer and too beautifully made to throw away. Despite our education and experience, however, we failed, and my love affair with Apple slipped another notch. (The first notch, incidentally, was due to the difficulty of replacing the battery in an iPhone, a necessary activity every so often. It is a challenge to the user to do it and costs about $100 to have it done at an iStore.) Of course, when I replaced the computer, Apple made more money and I ended up with better performance and new features and programs, though I neither needed nor wanted them.

As another example of the difficulty of quantifying performance, "more performance" is not necessarily better. My mother was fascinated by multiuse tools and insisted on buying them for me as birthday and Christmas gifts. Of course, I graciously thanked her for them, but in general they could not compete with my more traditional tools. Although they may be convenient for people who have neither the space nor the interest to acquire traditional tools, combination tools do not work for me, except for perhaps the classic Swiss Army knife.

Think about the proliferation of features on the products consumers buy—the so-called feature creep (additional capabilities added to products) being discussed as people realize the downside of dealing with too many bells and whistles. For most of history, the mechanizing of product function required a considerable investment. Additional features required additional mechanical articulations, which in turn required additional costly parts. The availability of low-cost integrated circuits containing the equivalent of millions of electronic components has changed that process. Product features no longer require expensive custom-manufactured mechanical subassemblies. Integrated circuits in automobiles can easily control ignition timing, fuel injection, and emission control systems. They can tune your radio and remember your favorite stations. With the proper sensors, they can tell you not only whether your seat belt is fastened or your door open but also how many times you applied your brakes that month, or maybe someday, whether you are wearing too much perfume, or if your kid has been making love in the backseat. How many of these functions should integrated circuits perform?

Have you been wondering lately whether you need all of the options in your cell phone? I personally could do without the one that seems to keep taking photographs of the inside of my pocket. Do you have trouble remembering how to use all of the features in your home entertainment system and your computer software? Do you really want your dryer to give you a choice as to how dry your clothes become? Do you still ask for wake-up calls because you don't want to figure out how your hotel alarm clock works? (One of my colleagues claims it isn't that she doesn't want to figure out how the clocks work, she just doesn't trust them.)

People seem to be caught in an endless loop of upgrading computers, operating systems, and application software. Users have applications so dated they can no longer open their e-mail attachments. If they decide to upgrade, they may find the new version does not like their old operating system. After installing the current operating system and the new application, the computer is slower. The next step is to buy a new computer and upgrade everything, only to find that they don't know how to use all of the new features. By the time the users begin to become comfortable with all of these changes, the cycle starts again. I, like many of my friends, would love to avoid constantly upgrading in order to focus on using my computer rather than learning to deal with more "powerful" software, but I am trapped by the need to interact with the world. (Strangely enough, my friends and I would all probably qualify as fairly computer savvy.)

In 1996, Clifford Stoll wrote a book entitled *Silicon Snake Oil*. Despite its title, this was not an anticomputer rant. Stoll is a longtime computer user and expert. In fact, his experience dates from assembling an Altair kit in the early 1970s—and if you have been around computers for a long time, you will realize that this gives him impeccable credentials. However, in his book Stoll did have certain criticisms of computers, one of which was that he claimed he had always spent roughly half of his time working on his computer system rather than using it.[1] This may have been an exaggeration, but I certainly sympathized with the gist of it. Although hardware has become more reliable and software more stable, increased complexity keeps the whole game akin to juggling.

We have reached a stage of technological sophistication where we must (or should) think not only of what we want products to do for us but also of what we do *not* want them to do. Many modern products seem as though the designers frantically tried to use more of the capability of the included chips and, in the process, delivered unnecessary and confusing functions. Designers making the best of the "information revolution" utilize increased technical capability to create devices that are easier to use. When it comes to options, "the more the better" no longer holds true, since the capability of computers is increasing more rapidly than the capability of human brains. Thirty years ago, the designers of products did not have the luxury of facing this problem.

The Complexity of Cost and Price

Cost and price are also extremely complicated topics. Customer perception of price depends on a large number of factors, including the wealth of the customer, the price of competing products, and how much the customer wants the product. Providers of products must consider not only the cost of time and materials and the desired profit margins but also the time value of the money involved and the availability of various sources of funding. Modern times have caused people to think about liability exposure, insurability, foreign exchange rates, and other subtleties as well. Consumers must worry about whether to buy, rent, or lease, pay cash or borrow (and if so from whom), pay for maintenance contracts or not, and buy direct or through the Web, as well as deciding about which model, what options, and whether to wait for a sale.

The increasing complexity concerning cost can be seen in the ongoing debate about "true cost." Traditionally, the price of a product has included the cost of design, materials, and production plus associated profits and business expenses that are passed along to the buyer. True cost might also reflect social costs of environmental pollution, cleaning up after the product, or exploitation of scarce resources. For example, should the cost of an automobile include a quantity for the control of smog as well as the construction of roads? Should lumber's cost include an amount for reforestation? Should the government compensate taxpayers by selling communication frequency bands to industries instead of giving them away? Should the price of air travel be sufficient to provide truly adequate air traffic control systems and airports? These questions, among many others, are now being considered.

Like performance, cost and price are factors that should be considered over the life (and death) of the product. The true cost of a product to a customer includes not only the purchase price and any charges on financing but also repair and service, operating costs, insurance, and other costs incurred while owning the product. These costs should be made clearer by producers, as we are far from the days of caveat emptor, and it might actually benefit them to do so. In the case of a high-quality product, the purchase price might seem less daunting compared to the actual cost of owning and operating the product, and the repair and service costs on a higher-quality product should be less than those on one of lower quality.

Companies also expend tremendous effort attempting to change consumers' perception of price and cost. We seem to be overwhelmed with "deals"—sales, rebates, coupons, discount clubs, frequent flyer miles, and so on. If you want examples, check out your local supermarket, shop for a car, or buy something on the Internet. Somehow, such things seem more appropriate to a carnival midway than the acquisition of a high-quality product. Some manufacturers of high-quality products, however, make non-discounting an aspect of quality—Apple, for instance, likes to control distribution through its own stores and website. The producer of high-quality products should attempt to minimize sales gimmicks, even though rebates make money (many people never apply for them) and sales (whether after Christmas, or in the form of "two for one" or "buy one, get one free" or $5.29 for one, $2.95 each for three or more) must be effective or they would not be so prevalent. Unfortunately, people are extremely susceptible to such deals, so they probably won't go away.

The world is awash in advertising in all media featuring performance and price. An extraordinary amount of talent is directed to influencing what we need and want. I love to watch the annual Clio advertising winners because they provide an opportunity to witness pure human genius. The genius, of course, is focused on influencing consumers to more strongly desire the output of the client. No one is immune to the messages of the advertising profession, and to say that they surround us is an understatement. We accept TV movies that are trashed by commercial breaks. The Internet is being gobbled up by advertisements. We don't even question the placing of products on the shelves of our stores, the billboards in the middle of wildflowers, or the graphics that cover the infield walls of our baseball parks (which themselves are named after companies). We even look forward to the ads in the Super Bowl telecast. We are also influenced by the likes and dislikes of people we admire and celebrities—it is not mere charity that causes fashion and jewelry designers to furnish actors and actresses at the Academy Awards ceremony with their wares. We have become conditioned to an amazing amount of input as to what we should buy, and companies are willing to spend a great deal of money to influence us because it is so effective.

But all this advertising and media attention may result in disappointment, as advertising tends to exaggerate the positive qualities of the product that might not lead the consumer to the desired outcome. If you believe the steamy romantic graphics of lipstick ads, you may be let down when Brad Pitt does not leave Angelina Jolie for you, even though you are wearing the lipstick. If you become overly impressed with the low cost of cubic zirconium, you may be surprised when you buy a fake diamond ring for your wife and find that she is not as impressed. It is easy to find beautifully made automobile advertisements that imply that if I buy a particular car, my life will be spent preventing gorgeous young women from forcing their way into it and all over me. Just think—drastically improved sex appeal for $30,000 (nothing down and a rebate, yet). Most advertisements for pickups show the trucks engaged in heroically rugged tasks (off-road racing, receiving huge loads of construction material, dwarfing other equipment). Somehow, the ads never show the damage that would result if a real pickup were put through such paces. If you pursue the low plane fares or hotel rates being offered, you may find that they are sold out.

For producers of high-quality products, honesty is the best policy.

The Balancing Act Between Performance and Cost

The relative importance of performance and cost vary widely, depending upon product and purchaser. A person buying a Ferrari or the military buying advanced weaponry may care far more about performance than price. The teenager desperately wanting an automobile or the underfunded business start-up needing office space may care more about price than performance. However, to some extent we always balance the two when evaluating products. Should price become too high or performance become too inadequate, widespread unhappiness occurs. An example of the former was the famous toilet seat that the government paid $600 for. An example of the latter was the Three Mile Island nuclear plant failure in 1979, which played a major role in turning the United States away from nuclear power. The explanation for the first was that the toilet seat was a unique item and the cost of its development could not be spread over a large number of products. The explanation for the core meltdown in Pennsylvania had to do with the complexity of the system and the training of the operators. But neither explanation seemed satisfying to many members of the media and the general public.

Traditionally, performance and cost goals and selling price are determined by marketing, competition, technical feasibility, organizational capability, and the intuition of various experienced people. They may be set from on high ("We choose to go to the moon this decade"—John F. Kennedy) or low ("Make a pin puller that doesn't need a telemetry channel"—Bill Schimandle, a former boss at JPL). Eventually these goals assume definite, often quantitative form. At that point, they are typically seen as constraints (freezes) on the design. A better computer can be described in quantitative terms such as desired speed, memory, operating system features, and cost. Goals for a sports car might include performance figures such as acceleration, top speed, skid-pad characteristics, steering ratio, and braking distance as well as cost.

But we should keep in mind the nature of the process that produces the goals that constrain and guide the designer or manufacturer of the product. Like many engineers, I started at the bottom and assumed that some godlike person above me was setting the performance and cost goals I was to work to. When I was higher on the totem pole, however, I realized that setting performance and cost goals was definitely done by mortals. Some of these mortals do seem to have godlike qualities (Bill Hewlett, Steve Jobs), but having been involved in setting performance and cost goals for many products, I can state that most do not. Obviously, setting these quantitative and specific goals is good for meeting schedules and integrating subsystems. For achieving high quality, however, it is helpful if people at all levels have a sense of the amount of uncertainty in the process that sets product goals, as quality may be overlooked. Relatively small interventions in the design of the product may result in relatively high gains in quality.

Performance, cost, and price also look different when examined from different viewpoints. As an example, consider farm equipment. In 1830, some 250 to 300 hours of labor were required to produce 100 bushels of wheat. By 1890, due to improved equipment, this amount of wheat could be produced with 40 to 50 hours of labor. By 1965, the same amount of wheat could be produced with 5 labor hours. The total is now down to 2 to 3 labor hours due to modern equipment.[2] This is an astounding increase in human productivity, as defined simply by the ratio of output to labor.

From the technical performance standpoint, the performance of such equipment is high, in that it is necessarily reliable and does its job extremely well. How about price? In the present farming environment, increasing automation still seems to make economic sense, or farmers probably wouldn't buy it. The operators of the combine certainly would not choose to return to an open-air seat in the direct sunlight in the midst of clouds of dust and chaff. Farmers don't mind at all paying fewer dollars in wages and worrying about fewer pieces of equipment. Neither do they mind being able to farm more acres with fewer people, since large farms seem to be the only ones making money these days, partly because subsidy income is proportional to acreage. From the perspective of the farmer, the performance is high and the cost bearable. From the standpoint of the producer, sales and profit are paramount. Since farmers keep upgrading and since the John Deeres of the world are doing OK, the modern combine looks all right from their viewpoint—reasonable performance and cost. So is there a downside?

By changing perspectives, almost any product can be found to have a downside as performance, cost, and price increase. Increasing performance means faster airplanes, bigger computers, and more powerful medical diagnostic equipment. But faster airplanes may carry fewer people. Would passengers perhaps pay more for a slower but more luxurious ride? Bigger computers and more powerful medical diagnostic equipment might require more highly trained operators, as well as being more expensive to produce. And more access to money is necessary to obtain this more expensive equipment—a barrier to smaller businesses.

Think again about farming equipment. The farmers I know love big, powerful, technically sophisticated machinery. Although I am not an agricultural economist, I suspect that from a pure performance standpoint, some of them buy higher-performance equipment than they need sooner than they need it. Not only is new equipment expensive to purchase and maintain, but it also loses its value rapidly. New harvesters cost more than $500,000 and can no longer be casually maintained and repaired by amateurs. The modern tomato harvester, which is capable of harvesting 50 to 70 tons per hour (a lot of catsup), electronically sorts the fruit by color, those not ripe enough ending up either on the ground or in a cull container. I have yet to meet a farmer capable of repairing the extremely sophisticated sensing and decision-making equipment used to do the automatic sorting. In case of failure, farmers need to call on highly paid experts to come replace the expensive modules.

There are other more subtle drawbacks to modern farm equipment, including that it isolates individuals from the farming process—this is a double-edged sword. Much farming labor is on the odious side. But farmers do like to grow things. One of my sons owns a farm in the Sacramento Valley. Last year he harvested part of his wheat crop with a 1960s harvester that I had restored. Although he did sit in the open air in a cloud of dust, and spent a lot more time harvesting the crop than he would have with a modern harvester, he loved it. He has the farm because he likes the process, and the older harvester definitely involved him more intimately than a modern one would.

Pulling back further, look at what has happened to farming. It provides jobs for fewer and fewer people and no longer allows farmers to compete on a small scale. I often hear people begrudging the loss of the small farm. From the standpoint of the sustainability advocate or the champion of the family farm, the huge, expensive, fuel-gulping machines used now might be thought of as lesser quality than older machinery. Equally negative thoughts might be expected from the farmer whose complicated combine or tomato harvester has failed at a time when the crop must be harvested and rain is imminent. So in the case of major farm equipment, the performance of the machinery is high, but the cost, including purchase, operation, and maintenance, is also high. The benefit to the producers of the products is high, and the benefit to the farmers is positive, but what about the benefit to society? Oddly enough, the same thing is happening in many situations where work is being automated. Tool and die makers? Printing press operators? Vanishing breeds. What is the cost of the jobs lost through automation?

Why Are There Problems?

In a capitalistic system, we like to assume that market forces will take care of problems having to do with performance, cost, and price, and they should. Products are produced for profit, so there is not much motivation to design and manufacture them unless people are going to buy them. The market and competition should pull performance up and prices down. Many factors make this behavior likely, including the advancement of technology. Many readers may have heard of the Moore curve, named after Gordon Moore, one of the founders of Intel Corp. The Moore curve says that the number of components on a single integrated circuit seems to double each 18 months with an accompanying decrease in cost per component. This advancement has been going on since 1958 and has been the major factor in the incredible improvements (per dollar) in the performance of computers over the past 30 years.

The performance/cost ratio of a product increases as producers and users become more familiar with it. People, materials, and processes are not perfect. Initial versions of a product will have weaknesses that will become apparent only after the product is built and used. Subsequent versions of the products give the builders a chance to remedy these weaknesses using not only their own experience but also inputs from users. Economies of scale also occur when a product's success results in increased numbers in production. Initially, a product is quite expensive, since its cost must include the expenses of developing it, the associated tooling, and the initial production. As time goes on, design and tooling are amortized and new approaches developed to produce the product at lower cost. Initial prototypes of automobiles may cost half a million dollars, but three years later you can buy them at the dealer for a small fraction of that price.

As more time passes, newer materials and processes can be incorporated, the design and production can be further refined, and the price continues to drop. These increases in the performance/cost ratio reflect themselves in services as well. Over time people learn to decrease mistakes, develop more efficient routines, and acquire more effective technology. In real dollars, the modern supermarket delivers a tremendous variety of products with impressively low operating costs. Consider airplanes: the real cost of a round-trip airfare across the United States has dropped precipitously in my lifetime. The time required for a cross-country flight has dropped from 20 hours (with four stops) to 5 or 6 hours (with no stops). The price of tickets and the time to travel from San Jose to Nashville oscillate widely, but this is due to the strange jousting in the airline business, not to achievable performances and costs. Why, then, are performance and price not always what they could be?

One possible answer might be the complacency mentioned in Chapter 2. When things are good, people unfortunately (or fortunately) act as though they will remain that way. Witness the economic bubbles and subsequent busts of the 1990s and the early part of this century. Think of the companies that have gotten into trouble because they delay too long in moving to a new technology or those that do not realize performance criteria are changing. Another reason for lack of improvement in price and performance might be that performance goals are set too low. A third might be weaknesses in design and production leading to higher costs and/or poorer performance. Or it could be that the producer is attempting to take an unrealistic profit. But the likely answer is simply that we buy much more than what we usually call performance in our products.

Consider luxury products: Louis Vuitton bags, the Bugatti Veyron sports car, Manolo Blahnik shoes, Patek Philippe watches, Purdey shotguns, and five-carat engagement rings. These are indeed fine items, but most people I know would not consider the performance alone of such things to be worth the high cost. Performance-wise, I am delighted with my discount store luggage, my Toyota pickup, my New Balance shoes, my Seiko watch, and my wife's lack of interest in diamonds, and I don't need a shotgun. But many people buy luxury items and obviously think they are worth the cost. Much of the value of such products lies in the less-tangible characteristics considered in the remainder of this book. The same is true for the much less expensive products that most of us purchase. The seductive power of quantification causes us to be overly attracted to performance and to neglect many aspects of quality that are less measurable but nonetheless highly important. It is to these issues that we will turn in the next chapter.

Chapter 3 *Thought Problem*

Considering performance and cost, choose an industrially produced product that in your opinion ranks very high and one that ranks low—in other words, one that performs beautifully for the money and one that is overpriced and/or low in performance for its cost. Again, in the case of the low-ranking one, what could be done to improve it, and why do you think that improvement has not happened?

Problems and Tactics Table: Performance, Cost, and Price

The following table is a list of possible problems within companies that may inhibit producing products with outstanding performance and satisfying profit due to the difference between producer cost and selling price. It also suggests tactics to overcome these problems. Similar tables at the ends of Chapters 4 through 9 may help you think about the material contained in those chapters.

Problems	Tactics
Lack of competence	Train, hire, learn from competitors, and use consultants wisely
Short-term business focus	Implement long-term product planning and advanced development
Traditional thinking	Emphasize creativity and innovation
Complacency, lack of awareness of changes in customer desires and goals, competition, opportunities	Increase social savvy, mix more with customers, up with advances in technology, competitive products
Lack of vision/guts	Reward visionary championing

Human Fit

Does the Product Fit People?

Since products of industry are to serve people, the fit between people and products is an important issue. The desire for such fit is certainly not a new one. In fact, a tremendous amount of time and effort has been applied to this area. The field of human factors engineering, complete with the Human Factors and Ergonomics Society, focuses upon the relationship between people and machines. The term *ergonomics* applies to this area, along with *biotechnology*, which is still defined in some dictionaries as the study of human-machine compatibility, although it has been co-opted by the field of genetic engineering. More recently, the term *human interface* has been used in describing this relationship. Divisions of technical societies such as the Institute of Electrical and Electronic Engineers (IEEE) focus on this area, while journals including the *Journal of Human Engineering*, the *Journal of Engineering Psychology*, and the *International Journal of Man-Machine Studies* report on new understanding of this relationship. You can easily find large numbers of books that contain concepts and data of value in making products that properly fit people.

Still, we have problems with human fit.

Many people have trouble removing the lids from jars. The majority of airplane crashes are attributed to pilot error. Women's high-heeled shoes permanently deform their toes. We worry about carpal tunnel syndrome. Comedians amuse us parodying people who cannot program their DVRs. We can't read the labels on our electronic equipment controls. What is going on?

Good products *must* fit people, and there is tremendous room for improvement. Take a few minutes and think of products that do not fit you—that do not match your body, sensory system, or mind. You should have no trouble doing this, for the world is full of products that ask us to greatly inconvenience ourselves in order to interact with them. Designers should know better than to do many of the things they do when designing a product. Even worse, they often do know better. I taught a course in human engineering to design majors in the engineering school at Stanford. The class was frustrating to teach because the material we covered seemed obvious to the students. Of course an auditory warning signal was better than a visual one if the operator's task required visual attention. Obviously, chairs should be designed to be kind to the skeletal system. Who would design a control panel without grouping controls for related functions and keying controls to related displays? To my amazement, the students, after reprimanding me for the commonsense nature of the course, would then go straight to their design jobs in industry and proceed to violate the very principles they considered so obvious.

Designers often become so distracted by considerations other than human fit that it does not receive the attention it deserves. Product function, cost, appearance, and reliability may dominate the designer's attention. Tight schedules or budgets do not encourage prototypes and usage tests. Even worse, designers may design for themselves: the petite, young, physically fit, right-handed designer may not think about large, older, left-handed users with physical disabilities. In addition, designers are used to taking advantage of the tremendous adaptability and flexibility of humans. People are capable of accommodating to ridiculously poorly designed products and do so surprisingly quickly with a minimum of complaints. Trouble can occur, however, if users have to accommodate to these products too often, rapidly, accurately, or too long. Furthermore, why should we have to?

My classes were often televised, and individual microphones were provided for students in the classroom to provide clearer audio to the remote students. In the room I often used, the students were supposed to grab a small microphone from a rack on the back of the seat in front of them, bring it to their mouth, and press a button before they spoke. The microphones hung so that the side into which the students were to speak faced them. This setup looked all right until you realized that when you grab something at arm's length and bring it to your mouth it rotates 180 degrees. The normal motion therefore brought the back of the microphone to the mouth of the student. The microphones also stuck in their holders. The students could learn to use the microphones, but why should they have to? Needless to say, most of them found it easier either to ignore the microphones when they spoke or not to engage in discussion.

There are also reasons of tradition and culture that cause people to ignore improving the fit of products. A simple example is the Western bathroom. Many years ago, the architecture department at Cornell University did a study on this topic and produced a wonderful book, *The Bathroom*, criticizing almost every aspect of the bathroom. Tubs are unsafe, difficult to enter and leave, and not efficient in cleaning. Toilets are anatomically incorrect. Lavatories do not allow one to wash one's hair without washing the remainder of the room. Mirrors fog up. The study is supported by a great amount of data, including a statistical analysis of male urine streams, concluding that an appreciable amount of them miss the toilet. There also are pictures of people groping for their shampoo while trying to control a rubber hose with a sprinkler on the end. It is, all in all, a damning indictment.[1]

People don't want to think about bathrooms. Nor do they want to experiment. We cling to the bathroom in which we were reared. One of the traumatic memories in the minds of many "Western" people is their first experience with a squat toilet. A bidet is a useful device, but it has never met much of a market in the United States because we don't want to think about its function. Certainly urinals would be useful in houses with a large male population, but a urinal in a house would cause consternation among our friends and neighbors. More handrails would be useful, but they imply that the household residents are not all Olympic gymnasts. Bathrooms and the products within them seem to be culturally off limits, along with functions such as elimination, shaving of the armpits, and treating zits. So we continue to torture our bodies and flush large amounts of fresh clean water away, often to dispose of just urine, a comparatively benign fluid until mixed with the other components of sewage.

Let's consider four categories of fit between people and products. The first is physical—the interaction of our bones, muscles, hearts, and lungs with built objects. The second is concerned with the senses—vision, touch, smell, and so on. The third is cognitive—the mind-machine interaction. Fourth, we will talk about problems resulting from system complexity. Each category demonstrates different aspects of the problem of fit, and each has its own wisdom necessary for the designer of good products. We will end the chapter by briefly considering some issues of safety and health.

Physical Fit

Historically, the physical aspects of fit were the first to be encountered. As designers of tools, we evolved certain shapes that were compatible with the human body. Probably the first rocks to be used as tools were selected because they fit the hand well and had the proper weight to be moved by the arm. If you intend to use a sword in battle, you do not want it to slip out of the hand. If you pitch hay for a living, the diameter of the fork handle is important. Humans also learned the limits of their physical capability—if you shovel dirt all day, you learn how fast you should shovel.

Life through much of history was technically simple enough that such knowledge could evolve slowly and reside in the minds of the toolmakers and users. Unfortunately, such simplicity was not to last. As the great industrialization movements of the 18th, 19th, and 20th centuries swept the world, all manner of new and less natural human activities evolved: working bent over in dark and dusty coal mines, reacting to the speed of steam-powered machines and transportation devices, dealing with the complexity of mass manufacture. By the beginning of the 20th century, industrialization had outrun the poor human. Industrial accidents and job-related illnesses were taking a large toll. Products were being designed that took little account of the strength or flexibility of the operator and demanded tolerance of extreme temperatures, sound levels, smoke, and increasingly toxic substances.

At the time, the industrial worker attracted increasing attention. Historically, the human had defined the work. Now it was necessary to think harder about the relation *between* the human and the work. The main interest of management at the turn of the century was output and profit—to produce more with a given amount of labor. As a result, a whole field evolved centered upon the productivity of human workers. As factories became more complex, it became evident that the integration of people and machines was important.

A much-maligned pioneer in this field was Frederick W. Taylor, who along with colleagues such as Luther Gulick, Lyndall Urwick, Henri Fayol, and others developed the field of "scientific management." This concept included hierarchical management with unity of command and limited span of control. In the early 1900s, the models for successful organizations were the military, the church, and large governments, so scientific management also assumed top-down authority, standardization of job design, and uniformity of behavior. Scientific management viewed people in factories as components of the overall machine and sought to design their jobs accordingly. The concepts of scientific management were extremely successful in increasing productivity, although now they seem rather inhuman. To the advocates of scientific management, the physical design of the job was critical, and once designed the worker should perform it repetitively, automatically, and incessantly. Be that as it may, scientific management was popular in its day, and much effort went into better understanding the physical relationships between humans and machines. Scientific management's weakness lay in not considering the psychological problems associated with endless repetition of trivial acts. (Psychological consideration was to come later with the increasing influence of industrial psychology experiments beginning in the 1930s that showed the importance of such factors.)

A large boost to the understanding of physical fit came during World War II. During World War I, the number of machines was relatively small and the machines' performance was such that control of them presented no great problem. Airplanes were unstable and often tricky to fly, but speeds were low enough that people could learn to deal with the idiosyncrasies of the machine. Tanks were not designed with the human in mind, but they were few in number, were slow in speed, and did not operate over long ranges. The situation was much different in World War II. Speeds became high enough that hard thinking was required to ensure human operators could adequately control the equipment. Missions of such machines as submarines, bombers, and armored vehicles became longer. In addition, the number of machines was enormous, making it necessary to design them in such a way that a wide variety of people could operate them. They necessarily were made more user-friendly. A P-51 took more physical effort to control than a present-day fighter does. However, the plane was a long way from a World War I fighter as far as stability, dependability, and comfort. By the end of World War II and after, standardization and logical control and display layout also were given a great amount of attention.

A great deal of effort from the military, NASA, and industry (perhaps more than the private sector) continues to be focused on further understanding the attributes, performance, and abilities of humans. When teaching my course, I would simply grab a couple of armloads of books and journals on the topic from the engineering library and take them to class. The students were consistently amazed at what information about humans is known. You want to know the average shoe size of women who are in the fifth percentile of height? No problem. A curve of motion-sickness onset versus oscillation frequency? Easy. The interesting thing to me, since I knew about this mountain of information, was that the students, who had been in the library many times, did not even know it existed.

Data exists on almost any physical aspect of the human. In addition, mockups of a product can and should be made during the design process in order to ensure an even better fit to the user. There really is no excuse for products that are not a good physical fit to the humans who will come in contact with them. However, such products exist in abundance. Think of the size and labeling of the controls on audio systems and miniaturized electronics, bathtubs when used by the elderly, and neckties.

The process of designing products for better physical fit is straightforward. The first step is an increase of awareness and the desire to better match product and user. This step requires constant vigilance in organizations. The companies most successful at this often feature a crusading leader who is dedicated to the fact that products should serve people, not make their lives more difficult. The second step is knowledge of the information and data that is available and how to produce more, if needed. The third is adequate testing with users before producing the product. All three of these steps are often neglected.

Although frequent prototyping is invaluable during the process of designing a product, it is often minimized because designers believe they can solve all potential problems in their heads, while organizations attempt to reduce costs. Testing time can also be a problem. I am always amused by watching people in stores testing mattresses by lying on them, and then immediately getting up, thinking that they have adequately judged the product. Obviously sleeping on them for at least one night is required, but if a mattress feels good on initial contact, the customer is satisfied. Designers often use the same approach. If the tool feels good to hold, they assume it will probably continue to feel good after a day or a week of use. Not necessarily! One does not detect carpal tunnel syndrome after the first 20 minutes of using a keyboard. The problem is that not only do theoretical techniques not solve all problems, but some problems will not even be recognized until an actual trial is conducted. It is naive to believe that we are smart enough to predict everything that may go wrong through thinking, analyzing, testing of components and subsystems, and computer simulation.

There are also new reasons for addressing physical fit: demographics show an aging population. No matter what exercise programs, medication, and diets are followed, people's physical abilities and characteristics change. Just because I still fit in my 1970 sports car does not mean that I am still flexible enough to easily get into and out of it. Our expectations also change as we age. We expect more from our products. My foot does not fit on the accelerator of said sports car unless I take my right shoe off. It is a Jaguar XKE, and I bought it a number of years ago for love, not physical fit. At the time, I thought it only reasonable that it required me to take my shoe off, but I don't want to have to do that anymore.

Another reason for addressing physical fit in design has to do with changes in lifestyle. For example, employment patterns are taking more of us out of active work and sticking us behind computers, displays, and buttons. Simultaneously we hear that we need more exercise. The process of designing workspaces, equipment, and methods of acquiring exercise that are compatible with the restrictions of urban life and the human animal is a challenging one.

And how about people with disabilities? Many such people who were formerly neglected in the design of products now must be considered. There will be more and more emphasis on this group as the population ages. For example, vision and hearing impairment will no longer be considered anomalies. Better methods of getting around will propagate. There are already places such as shopping centers in retirement areas where people traveling by automobile or on foot are at the mercy of those in souped-up golf carts and three-wheeled scooters.

The good news is that in general, people, aging or not, seem to be less forgiving of physical products that do not physically fit them than they used to be, and products are becoming more accommodating. The griping about cramped airplane seats is causing airlines to loosen up seating. The SUV became popular partly because automobiles became less compatible with the stuff people haul around in them. I revel in the easy availability of sizes that fit people of my build (6´2˝, but once 6´4˝, 230 pounds—did you know you are going to shrink?). It used to be most difficult to buy long shirts and coats and wide shoes, but now they are all over the place. But there is still a long way to go.

Sensory Fit

The model of reality built by our brain is based on information from our senses. They are usually grouped in the categories that follow:

Vision sense—sight
Hearing sense—sound
Movement senses—vestibular (orientation), kinesthetic
(body configuration)
Skin senses—pressure, heat and cold, pain
Chemical senses—taste, smell
Organic senses—state of body (hunger, sexual satiation, and
so on)
Time sense—passage of time

The first five categories have specific sensors to detect the pertinent information. Sensing is accomplished by the sensors, the nervous system, and the brain acting as a unit. The process involves memory and is affected by emotional and cultural factors. If we fail to hear the phone ringing at a party, it is difficult to say whether the ear did not detect it or whether the brain merely did not attend to it. Our senses do not give us the true or complete state of the world. They have evolved over many millions of years to relay particular information in a way that is consistent with our survival, much of which has been in a hunter-gatherer outdoor existence. Our senses, however, are not particularly optimal for our present lives. Since we now are awake more at night, we would be better off if our vision extended more strongly into the infrared region. It would be nice if our sense of time were a bit sharper to be consistent with the clock-driven culture we have designed for ourselves. Perhaps we need a sense to tell us if we are being hustled.

One of people's most common errors is to assume that their models of the world are reality, when they are actually only their personal reality. These models do not necessarily correspond to nature; they are merely made from the information processed by the brain to which the sensors are sensitive. Obviously in the case of products where the senses are key (such as food, drink, perfume, and wallpaper), designers must be extremely sophisticated about their role. However, the senses are a bit more subtle than the skeleton and the muscles and perhaps less likely to be paid adequate attention by many product designers. For example, you probably have a pretty good picture of what happens when you bend your elbow: a signal from your brain causes the appropriate muscles to contract, pulling upon tendons fastened to bones. But what happens when you smell something? Do particles from the rose blossom actually enter your nose? Probably not. If the scent is conveyed by chemicals, what chemicals correspond to rose smell? Even more, what sensors in your nose identify them, and how? Then the $64 question: How do the signals from the sensors create the sensation that you interpret as the smell of a rose?

Even those senses whose mechanism we think we understand remain a mystery when the brain is involved. We know that the eye, for example, contains a lens and an array of sensors called the retina. These sensors are specialized to recognize different wavelengths and intensities in the image. They then send the appropriate signal through the optical nerve. So far so good. But then what happens? The signals go directly to a three-pound piece of meat, out of which comes your visual reality. How on earth does it do that? I am always amused by the facetious theory that there is a homunculus (a tiny person) sitting in one's head watching a TV set that is connected to the optical nerve.

The first five senses in the list earlier in this section have some characteristics in common. First, they have sensitivity ranges that cause them to detect certain types of intensities and frequencies of information and not others. A term that is often encountered when studying the senses is *threshold*, referring to the level of signal necessary before the sensor and brain recognize something is happening. Thresholds are low for traditional signals (touch—you can feel the wing of a fly falling on your cheek from a distance of one centimeter; smell—you can detect one drop of perfume diffused into the entire volume of a six-room apartment) and high for nontraditional signals (high-frequency sound—you can't hear it at a frequency above 20,000 hertz). Second, the senses tend to be more sensitive to changing information than to a constant input. In fact, the senses typically become insensitive to constant signals over time. Finally, sensitivity to change varies from sense to sense. A change in sound pitch of 1/133 of the original level can be detected, but salinity of water must be increased by one-fifth before a taste difference can be noticed. In general, there is a correlation between sensitivity and survival value. Salinity is a general measure of environmental interest, and it is of importance to us to detect major shifts. Sight and hearing detect instantaneous events that could immediately spell danger.

Successful products take account of all such characteristics. Effective warnings to equipment operators give indications to the eye, the ear, and maybe even touch (stall warning in aircraft). Fire alarms are cleverly tuned to the frequencies to which we are most sensitive. Designers of radar displays are aware of the negative effects of long periods of scanning an unchanging picture. Humans are often assisted by electromechanical devices (camera light meters, carbon monoxide alarms) if they must detect intensities or changes in stimuli that the senses cannot discriminate. However, many products do not take adequate account of these characteristics of the senses. The signals emitted by electronic devices such as cell phones may be inaudible to many aging males who have lost their sensitivity to certain frequencies. Many visual warnings do not take account of the large percentage of males that are color-blind. There are product opportunities in compensating for these characteristics.

Let us consider hearing in a bit more detail in order to gain an appreciation for the limitations of our senses, the distortions that they place upon our perception of reality, and the challenges facing the designer of good products. Hearing is accomplished through a transducer (the ear) that converts mechanical motion to electrical signals. It has been estimated that for the detection of sound frequencies near 3,000 cycles per second, the vibrations of the eardrum may be as small as one-billionth of a centimeter.

The human ear is able to handle tremendous variations in the power of sound. The loudest sound we can stand is about 100 trillion times as powerful as the weakest that we can detect. However, the ear is quite limited in frequency. The usual rule of thumb is that humans can detect signals between 20 and 20,000 cycles per second. However, most of us are not that good. As we age, we lose our ability to detect the higher frequencies.

Like the eye, the ear has evolved to handle the signals that occurred in nature in a less technological time. It is a wonderful device but does a good bit of interpreting, especially when hooked to the brain. Be impressed the next time you are barely able to understand a conversation at a party or over a bad phone connection. If your brain were not equipped with expectations, you would not be able to understand it at all. Also be impressed at how sensitive the ear is at the frequency of a baby's cry.

The inner ear is essential to our ability to detect orientation and movement. The vestibular senses make use of detectors in the inner ear called the utricle and the semicircular canals. The utricle is basically a bowl with pebbles inside and sensors extending through the walls of the bowl that measure movements of the pebbles due to gravity and other accelerations. The semicircular canals are filled with fluid and detectors to measure the motion of the fluid under rotational accelerations. These sensors together give us a combination of orientation and acceleration. However, they cannot measure velocity and displacement directly. The only way the brain can get a sense of velocity and displacement is to integrate the outputs of these sensors, and they are not the most accurate sensors imaginable. The may also fail to deliver accurate data in nonstandard environments, such as space, where gravity does not give its customary signal.

The outputs of the sensors related to hearing are often augmented by information from the other senses, such as vision, touch, and the kinesthetic senses that tell us about the configuration of our bodies. Our senses are integrated. Our appreciation of food depends upon sight, smell, taste, and perhaps touch and sound. Head position is inherent in locating the source of a sound, and a number of our senses may be needed to ascertain whether it is our train that is moving or the one on the next track. Vision helps the inner ear determine our orientation while flying an airplane, and if the world is not visible due to weather, we add an instrument to look at.

It is poor understanding of the senses associated with the ear that causes product problems such as the cell phone the elderly cannot hear, the potential long-term damage from audio amplifiers, and the unmuffled leaf blower. It is the mind's input of expectations based on previous contact with humans that make computer-generated voices so much more annoying than the programmers might expect. One wonders also how much the designers of automotive suspension systems and seats understand about the vestibular senses. Certain "luxury" cars are extremely efficient at inducing motion sickness, as are the rear seats in many buses.

As in the case of physical fit, sensitivity to problems having to do with the senses is necessary in order to produce high-quality products. As an example, smell is one of the most evocative senses and is particularly interesting because of its ability to result in strong feelings and evoke powerful memories. For example, Plasticine clay, the type used in kindergarten, often evokes memories of graham crackers and milk in the elderly, who were served these delicacies in kindergarten. On the other hand, the smell of decomposing animals is offensive to all of us.

It is not uncommon for real estate agents to bake a batch of cookies in a house before showing it. Architects have to worry about the combination of material used in a house producing long-lasting and unwelcome smells. Used cars are often dosed with a bit of "new car" smell. You probably have your own weak spots. One reason I keep the Jaguar that I no longer fit in is that I am a sucker for the mixed leather-and-leaking-oil smell of vintage English cars. As an extreme example, I once had a student who admitted to the problem of loving the smell of new pocket calculators. He claimed he had to hold his breath while passing the calculator counter in the university bookstore or he was likely to buy yet another one. Manufacturers of perfume and food are certainly sensitive to attractive and repellant smells and use their knowledge and skill to entice consumers to use their products. Many other manufacturers, however, are not so sensitive, even though smell could be a major attractor or detractor. I bought a rather nice-looking small rug a couple of years ago that I thought had a slight, but not bothersome, odor at the time of purchase that I was sure would disappear. The smell not only remained but became bothersome indeed, and I eventually gave the rug away.

Cognitive Fit

Though we are rapidly gaining knowledge about the brain through experiments with such research approaches as functional magnetic resonance imaging (fMRI), we are still surprisingly ignorant of how it works. Twenty or thirty years ago, people liked to refer to the "cognitive revolution." They were talking about our increasing understanding of the brain and its function. But people were at the same time talking about the information revolution—our increasing ability to process and transfer information due to developments in technology. The information revolution has been doing much better than the cognitive revolution. Such technological breakthroughs as the microprocessor and the satellite have enabled us to design products that allow access to huge amounts of information. A study at the University of California, Berkeley, by Peter Lyman and Hal Varian concluded that about 5.4 billion gigabytes of new information was stored on paper, film, magnetic discs, or optical discs in 2002.[2] If this information were all converted to print, it would fill half a million libraries the size of the Library of Congress. Forty percent of the information was produced in the United States, which if converted to print would provide eight pickup loads of books for each citizen. And, of course, as the Internet grows, the information stored online will continue to explode.

Unfortunately, there is no indication that shows our brains are becoming more powerful at a rate consistent with our ability to manufacture and store information. Humans therefore have a problem. We are in danger of becoming overwhelmed by information. I could dwell on the point that the majority of this information is of low quality, being collections of data that have been neither sorted nor put in a useful form, but the sheer quantity alone means that we are becoming cognitively more burdened.

It is not surprising that our brain, although inconceivably wonderful and capable of incredibly rich function, is limited, since it is made of a large but finite number of simple cells. If we take into account the slowness of signal movement (the speed of the signal in the neuronal axon—the brain's "information conductor"—ranges between 1 and 250 miles per hour, very slow compared to the speed of an electrical signal in a wire—186,000 miles per second); the redundancy needed to learn new operations and perform parallel processing; and the allocation of neurons to fixed circuits, we realize that the brain is, in fact, severely limited in speed, capacity, the number of things it can do at once, and many other functional ways.

The conscious mind does not like to do two things at once. The only way it can do so is either to alternate tasks or to integrate separate functions into one act. (Does this make you wonder about multitasking? You should. Research being done at the time of this writing indicates that it is vastly overrated.) The conscious mind also does not like to dwell on its own limitations. We don't think about what our products require from the limited mind, or about the reactions of such minds to the products. In fact, we are so used to considering the mind omniscient that we find thought exercises annoying and our response to our difficulty with them surprising. (For example, as quickly as possible, think how many capital letters of the English alphabet have curved lines in them—not that fast, right?) Such exercises are frustrating, and frustration is an emotion that keeps us from apprising ourselves of our limitations. This emotion affects designers, just as the rest of us, and can get them into trouble when they design products. For example, although the human attention span is limited, designers may forget to take this into account when creating displays.

When the mind is involved, people must also consider not only individual products but also the total amount of work they ask their brains to do. I do not believe that any single electronic device is too difficult for the human mind to comprehend. However, some people seem to be baffled by them. It is probable that the rapidly increasing sum of knowledge needed to operate all electronic devices is being resisted by the mind due to its sensitivity limits. Consider present-day organizational systems, complete with voice mail, electronic mail, several types of traditional mail, telephones, smartphones, Facebook and Twitter accounts, intranets, faxes, beepers, cellular phones, satellite links, and a myriad of computer and television networks. Do you worry about increasing demands upon the attention of drivers as automobiles routinely become outfitted with car phones, map displays, and full-function computers that allow the driver to access e-mail, write memos, create spreadsheets, or just chat with friends? You should.

Fortunately, businesses have discovered that money can be made by using technology to help us manage our technology. When I recently redid our home entertainment center, which I have put together from various components over time, we ended up with five separate remote control units (audio, TV, cable box, DVD, VCR). In order to prevent cognitive breakdown, I spent money I didn't want to spend on a Logitech universal remote.

The mind is also not as "logical" as we might think. The human brain is often compared anatomically with the brains of lower animals. Many models use this anatomical similarity to explain similar behaviors between the two groups. In 1960 a psychologist named Paul MacLean proposed the Triune Brain theory, which has had a great deal of influence as a model.[3] This theory divides the brain into three mechanisms—the R (for reptile) complex, the limbic system, and the neocortex, mechanisms for reacting, feeling, and thinking. In general, lower animals engage in ceremony and hierarchy, just as we do. For example, the reptile goes home to lay its eggs, while we humans visit our hometown, even though it may have no logical attraction. Such behavior is sometimes attributed to the hindbrain, common to both reptiles and humans and operating on inherited programming—not logical at all.

The primitive midbrain is concerned with processing and switching signals from the senses and the motivation of the animal. The same is true of our midbrain, which contains the thalamus, which is the relay station for sensory information, and the hypothalamus, which is involved in behavior having to do with basic biological urges (eating, drinking, sex). Many of our basic emotions emanate from the midbrain, which does not always respond in "logical" ways: we fall in love with the wrong person or are unreasonably prejudiced against ethnic groups or homosexuals, even though we are not supposed to be. We are suspicious of strangers, even though we may tend to like people once we get to know them—an emotional response, not a logical one. It is the highly developed human cortex, or forebrain, that we credit with bringing us our logical ability, of which we are rightly proud. But we must remember we do have midbrains and hindbrains.

There are many models that seek to describe brain function. A great deal of research is being done on the topic. Many older but still interesting models are portrayed in a fascinating manner in a book entitled *Maps of the Mind*, by Charles Hampden-Turner.[4] Most of these models speak to a large amount of unconscious function coupled with consciousness. This duality between consciousness and unconsciousness often gets companies into trouble when designing products—they design them consciously. However, when using these products, both designers and consumers employ a mind that is heavily dependent upon past experience and is quite habitual in its actions. Designers therefore necessarily exclude vast amounts of data and options when reaching conclusions, simplifying life in order to cope with complexity. They are not, however, necessarily conscious of doing so while in the process and often fail to produce products that are as compatible as they should be with humans. Designers are at the mercy of their own problem-solving habits, which probably do not match those of the potential user of the product.

As an example, let us think about computer products. Computers do large numbers of extremely simple logical actions at high rates of speed. They are therefore suited well for mathematical calculations and performing other functions where there is a one-to-one correlation between input and output. As their capability has increased, however, computers have been turned to the solving of increasingly complex problems. For some time, there has been an ongoing debate as to how capable computers will eventually become. One pole of the argument (the hard core of the artificial intelligence community) feels that computers will eventually be able to do much, if not most, of the type of problem solving that the human mind now does. In fact, the more visionary extremists feel that a "silicon mind" would be superior to a flesh-and-blood mind, in that it would not be subject to biological death and therefore could keep on learning and developing forever.

The other side of the argument is that barring unpredictable breakthroughs having to do with neural networks, parallel programming, and biological elements, computers are never going to handle the complexity and uncertainties that the human mind does. For instance, if my wife gives me a simple request, such as "Could you pick up some fruit on your way home?" I fill in a tremendous amount of information from my experience. I know that the proper way to respond is to go buy some fruit rather than merely answering "yes." I know that the pick in the sentence is different from a guitar pick or the pick I use to help dig holes in my yard. I know that I have to go to a grocery store and the incredible myriad of details having to do with driving there, finding the fruit, deciding what is the best deal, getting it through the checkout counter, and so on. I can also handle the many unprecedented situations I will encounter driving to and from the store and maneuvering my shopping cart through people of all ages, sexes, and moods. It will be quite a while before a computer can do all of that.

There is a tremendous amount of work going on in the area of computer problem solving, and our society is certainly giving the computer the benefit of the doubt. We are adopting it, learning to use it, and even learning to act more like computers in order to deal with it—but herein lies the problem. Manuals and the Internet contain vast quantities of information often presented in the jargon and framework of computer designers. There are some people who love to decipher this information. However, this is not true of most people, and computer inputs and outputs must become much more sensitive to the way humans think.

The ancient screen saver program After Dark was a good example of a program that was compatible with the human mind. Each routine had similar controls, and each could be viewed and adjusted rapidly before being activated. The Internet and the associated World Wide Web, as I write this book, are not compatible with most human minds. They contain too much redundancy, too much information of little value, and inadequate sorting. Like most of my friends, I find them useful as intellectual entertainment and to find specific things, but otherwise overwhelming. As an example, I just typed "product quality" into Google and received 147,000,000 items—a bit too many to go through. One of the problems may be that it only took the browser program 0.15 seconds to find all of them. Perhaps even computers cannot pay much attention to quality in that amount of time.

Complexity

Humans have arrived at a stage in our history when we have learned to make extremely complex technological systems. Of course, we have been creating complex systems for a long time, as shown by the Roman aqueducts, the British canals, and the American railways. These earlier systems, however, consisted of rather independent components of a reasonably simple nature. It was possible, for instance, for a human operator to understand a locomotive sufficiently to not only control it but also respond to abnormal situations. Now consider present systems such as the space shuttle, modern passenger aircraft, and nuclear reactors: here, we enter into serious complexity. How about nuclear weapons systems and reengineered ecologies? Maybe we are in over our heads. In an excellent, and controversial, book called *Normal Accidents* by Charles Perrow, the author suggests that as long as humans are involved, there will be accidents in systems above a certain complexity. He states that if the result of an accident could be unacceptable to society as a whole, as in the case of a strategic nuclear missile system, perhaps we had better lay off. In a system of great complexity where the costs of an accident seem to be tolerable to the society, such as the U.S. aircraft control system, he says go ahead.[5]

Complexity relates directly with the topics discussed previously in this chapter. Obviously, it is easier for humans to interact with a complicated system that is consistent with their physical, sensory, and cognitive capabilities. However, at some point, complexity itself becomes an issue. As an example of the type of problems we can get ourselves into, let us briefly consider the previously mentioned accident at the Three Mile Island nuclear energy plant in 1979. This accident received a great amount of attention and was thoroughly investigated. In fact, the report of the Nuclear Regulatory Commission's independent special inquiry group directed by Mitchell Rogovin on the Three Mile

Island accident is a fascinating (if long) read.[6] It is a superb portrait of the type of difficulties that can overwhelm an extremely complex man-machine system.

In the case of the Three Mile Island accident, there were no fatalities or detectable radiation-induced illnesses. But the incident so shook up the nation that it caused permanent changes in the way nuclear reactors are designed and operated and to the public's attitude toward nuclear energy. In the view of some, this incident destroyed the nuclear energy business in the United States, although it is showing signs of resurgence at the time of this writing. The accident was due partly to equipment failures and partly to operator errors. For example, when a relief valve failed to properly perform its function (decreasing the pressure in the nuclear portion of the system), the operators didn't know what to do—they had never been in such a situation. In a complicated system such as a power plant, it is almost impossible to train operators by simulating all possible malfunctions—the combinations of possible component failures is simply too great. The information provided to the operators was incomplete and confusing.

As a result of this accident, many changes were made not only in the hardware of nuclear power plants but also in the training of operators. This accident in a complex system was due not only to inadequate instrumentation but also to incorrect decisions made by operators who had not been adequately trained in abnormal reactor operation and who were both overwhelmed by misleading information and deprived of the information they needed. The challenge to designers of complex systems is to prevent such accidents through foresight.

The Three Mile Island operators simply did not understand the system well enough to do the proper things when it was in an abnormal state. This situation is not difficult to understand. We are all taught, for example, to operate automobiles in a normal operating state. Most driver instruction courses do not include skid pads, blowouts, and oncoming cars veering into our lanes—but we might be better off if they did. One of my friends who was a highway patrolman noted that in freeway accidents, few drivers would leave their lane. As a result, as is often the case in crowded conditions and bad weather, dozens of cars would run into each other. My friend claimed that people simply held the wheel steady and slammed on their brakes, ignoring opportunities to steer onto shoulders or into vacant lanes. He argued, convincingly, that drivers should be trained for the unusual. The same argument is made for private plane instruction. It is possible to acquire a private license without ever having been in a spin, but although modern private planes are much less likely to enter spins, not all private planes are modern, and spins continue to be a factor in small plane accidents, so it would seem to make sense that all licensed pilots be prepared to react to them.

Complexity must be taken into account in preparing human operators for emergencies. Designers of such systems as a nuclear reactor plant, air traffic control system, or refinery often understand the systems well enough that they might be able to respond to abnormal or emergency situations, but the systems' operators may not. Either highly sophisticated simulators must be used in training operators, people with more thorough knowledge must be on hand at all times, or systems must be designed to be compatible with the limits of the human operators. Controls, instruments, manuals, and alarms must be more carefully designed as complexity increases. Redundancy must be included, and computer–human control interactions must be considered. It may be acceptable for your computer to simply show you a warning on the screen if something goes wrong, but that is definitely not adequate feedback for the operator of a nuclear reactor.

Individual consumers do not buy nuclear reactors or refineries, but we sometimes forget that we are components of an extraordinary complex system, consisting of ourselves, the infrastructure that we have built upon our planet, and the planet itself, and that we have to operate the components of that system that affect our lives. It isn't that we have difficulty handling a few components of this system; it is the totality that is becoming a significant burden, and a major contribution is the rapidly expanding number and increasingly complex character of products.

Producers and consumers alike should worry about this situation. Customers seem to be eager for innovative products with new and different features and more capability. That's progress, right? I think not if it is carried to the point that individuals and groups of humans spend too much of their time and effort trying to remember how to operate and maintain these products and too much money hiring professional expertise to help. Technology is supposed to help us live a satisfying life, not consume our time and energy in its operation and upkeep. I am in favor of diversification of products, but also standardization of the controls and displays that allow us to operate them. Strangely, the military seems to handle this job better than producers of products for civilians do, perhaps because in battle you don't want to spend time figuring out how to start a vehicle or load a rifle.

At one time, when products were simpler and we were in love more with manufacturing and less with innovation and high technology, there was more standardization among products. As an obvious example, home entertainment systems consisted of radios and record players, the former equipped with a volume dial (on the left) and a tuning dial (on the right), with the on-off switch sometimes integrated into the volume dial (all the way counterclockwise). Sophisticated record players originally had their on-off switch integrated into the arm and later a speed selector and automatic changers, but the change was slow and new features tended to be the same across brands. The television was a separate device. These former systems contained nothing like the number and variation of controls and displays in contemporary systems. The same can be said for kitchen, yard, and laundry appliances, as well as mousetraps, headache remedies, baby strollers, and a myriad of other products of industry. An example of what has occurred can be seen with cars. There was a time when you could climb into any car, roll down the window, and drive it away. No longer.

I rent cars quite often and am tired of starting the windshield wipers instead of the turn signal; experimenting to find out how to turn on the lights; groping to find the hood, parking brake, or trunk release and then experimenting to see if I have the right one (usually not); and trying to figure out the cabin temperature and navigating systems while entering heavy traffic leaving the airport in a strange city. Not only is this frustrating, it is unsafe!

The idea of fighting the complexity of our lives by paying more attention to standardization as well as ease of operation and maintenance of industrial products is perhaps contrary to our ethic of creativity, innovation, and progress through advances in technology. But the burden of interacting with these products is an increasing one, especially for users who don't keep their manuals and handbooks with librarian skill and do not want, for example, to take their laptops out to the driveway to look up information with their greasy hands, while working on the car. There must be a market opportunity here somewhere. We all believe in products being user-friendly, but as individual products become so, our growing panoply of products seems to require increasing numbers of neurons to deal with it.

Safety and Health

Rightly or wrongly, the United States and other developed countries have become increasingly obsessed with safety. This obsession has been explained by a number of arguments, ranging from lack of sensitivity in the past through a desire for immortality to (again) too many lawyers. Our history is somewhat bleak, considering such topics as black lung disease, radiation poisoning, and industrial accidents. We are now spending much more effort protecting ourselves from ourselves.

I recently set out to acquire some climbing equipment, since I had a large dead tree in my yard that had to come down. I finally had to order it over the Internet, because I simply could not find any in rental or retail stores in my area. The reason most often given to me was unwillingness to be involved in any liability for people like me operating well beyond our skill level or physical ability 75 feet above the ground. The conservative stand would be that it is my life, and I should be allowed to risk it if I want. The liberal stand would be that society should protect me against my poor judgment. The intermediate stand is that I should not be allowed to act in a way that would incur the enormous expense to society that would result from my becoming a "vegetable" by falling and not dying (also the argument for motorcycle helmets).

Industrial safety has been an issue for years, beginning in the United States when rapid growth in the textile industry (due to the embargo of the War of 1812) resulted in the establishment of insurance companies that inspected industrial properties and suggested methods of decreasing risk so their policyholders might qualify for low rates. In 1970 the Occupational Safety and Health Act was signed into law, establishing the OSHA administration and the National Institute for Occupational Safety and Health (NIOSH), which set and enforce strict rules for industrial operation.

Consumer safety has a similarly long history. The regulation having to do with food and drugs is a good example. In 1820, eleven physicians met in Washington, D.C., to establish the U.S. Pharmacopeia, the first list of standard drugs for the United States. In 1848, the Drug Importation Act was passed by Congress in an attempt to control the importation of adulterated and unsafe drugs. In 1906 the original Food and Drug Act was signed into law. The emphasis on consumer safety has increased markedly in the past 25 years through the efforts of activists such as Ralph Nader and Bess Myerson, institutions such as the Department of Consumer Safety, and publications such as *Consumer Reports*. Large numbers of products have been taken off the market, ranging from toys that can shed parts children could choke on, to automobiles that ignite in accidents.

Designing products for safety is a most challenging task, since people seem to be at their most brilliant in devising ways to hurt themselves. One of my first engineering jobs was to devise a safety feature for a machine involved in the production of an aluminum part. The difficulty had to do with the cutter speed, which caused it to be almost invisible to the human eye. The noise level in the plant and the repetitiveness and speed of the operation also caused the operator to become careless during the day. The machine cycle required the operator to load the part and then press a button, which caused the part to be fed through the cutter.

My first approach, of course, was to put a guard around the cutter. But the operators would remove the guard, claiming that it inhibited the job. I then redesigned the machine so that the cutter was buried deep within it. However, another accident occurred when an operator was attempting to remove a snarl of chips and accidentally hit the button. The third attempt was to have two buttons, both of which had to be pushed to cycle the machine, thus making sure that both of the operator's hands were on buttons rather than close to the cutter. Operators circumvented this solution by placing their lunch or other objects on one of the buttons. Inverting the button unit to prevent this resulted in one button being pushed by a knee, and so on. I finally made a big step toward helping the situation by simply requiring holes in the cutter so that it made more noise. But this was before OSHA sound regulation limits.

This ability to find danger can be clearly seen among children. My kids would constantly fascinate me by making weapons from the innocuous, tipping over the permanent, and eating the unthinkable. But we grown-ups are certainly not above reproach. Think of your own life. How many things do you do that products should not allow you to? Here are a few of my own:

- I always remove all guards from power tools. I grew up with open blades on circular saws and naked sanding belts and find guards annoying. Guards should be improved to not inhibit usage and then be made an integral part of the machines.
- I am attracted to strong solvents, such as acetone, get them all over my skin, and inhale their vapors. I welcome efforts toward potent but less dangerous chemicals, such as the continuously improving water-based paints, but I wish they would improve more rapidly.
- I ride my bicycle far too fast for its braking ability. Mountain bikes have good brakes—why not put decent brakes on street bicycles?

There are more, but I just include these to encourage you to think a bit. I highlight them with no shame, because I think I am as careful as most people. And like most people, I am not as careful as I think I am. The key to creating safe products is to keep that in mind: it is a difficult task. I find myself insulted by many of the features that are built into products to prevent me from harming myself. But on the other hand, there is great diversity in the population. Probably (hopefully) these features save some people from harm. As in the case of designing products that are consistent with physical, sensory, and cognitive limitations, the key is conscious effort to be sensitive to the human animal. Tremendous creativity and user testing is necessary to predict the possible misuses and subtle negative effects of the products of industry.

Chapter 4 *Thought Problem*

Here we go again. But for a little variety, this time you may choose six products—one that fits you extraordinarily well and one that fits you poorly from first a physical, then a sensory, and finally a cognitive perspective. Why are they good or bad fits to you? If you own them and they do not fit you, why do you put up with them? Again, if they do not fit you well, how could they be improved to fit you better, and why do you think these improvements have not been made?

Problems and Tactics Table: Human Fit

Problems	Tactics
Adaptability of humans—capability of compensating in the short term for products that don't fit people well	Increase testing of product prototypes with human users
Lack of knowledge of human factors in design	Become familiar with existing knowledge and experiment with people
Assumption that users are as knowledgeable as designer	Make sure designers understand what users know about both normal and abnormal behavior of products
Assumption that human fit is less important than other design criteria and constraints (beauty, schedule)	Work on corporate value system—if products don't fit people, what good is engineering (or the products)?

Craftsmanship

Joy to the Maker, Joy to the User

Craftsmanship is the process of making things extraordinarily well. It involves fits and finishes, obsession with details, tender loving care, and pride. The topic was easier to talk about in the age when objects were made by individuals and by hand, though it is still possible to look at sculpture, custom jewelry, fine wood-work, and exquisite "craft" pieces and comment on the crafts-manship. These comments, however, may be off the mark. We amateurs might be terribly impressed by a polyurethane coating, but a professional woodworker would realize that a rubbed mix-ture of alkyd varnish and oil, or simply the bare wood enhanced by the patina of use over the years, would have been a better fit. Still, most people are comfortable in thinking they know what craftsmanship means in the case of individual hand craftsman-ship. How about in the case of airplanes or motorcycles, plastic spoons and pizza boxes, nails, hangers, or any of the other items spewed out of modern industry. Is craftsmanship still an issue? Is it important? And if so, why?

Why Do We Care About Craftsmanship?

To neglect craftsmanship in the production of industrial products is foolish—perhaps in the long run suicidal. Craftsmanship is a state of mind that permeates design and manufacturing and is highly appreciated by consumers. Its importance was obvious in the 1980s in the ascendancy of the Japanese automobile industry. Immediately after World War II, countries such as the United States were convinced that Japanese products were low-quality copies of Western brilliance. In hindsight, this thought was somewhat myopic. In fact, the Japanese have had a long tradition of outstanding craftsmanship and at the time were suffering from the war that had left their economy and industry in a shambles.

In the 1980s, Japanese automobile makers were noticed for their "fits and finishes." Much was made of the extraordinary evenness of the spaces between door, hood, and trunk panels and body panels on Japanese cars, while U.S. automobiles were criticized because their paint jobs were inferior. It was apparent that the care and attention to the manufacturing process in the quality of the exterior was reflected throughout the automobile, accompanied by greater reliability and eventually leading to higher market price and increased sales. The U.S. automobile industry was caught by its complacency and is still scrambling to reacquire its reputation for outstanding quality against not only Japan but also Germany, and soon South Korea.

After World War II, there was a large market for automobiles in the United States because production had been halted during the war effort and now a large number of drivers were returning from military service. U.S. automobile companies were in heaven because many of their former overseas competitors had suffered major economic and physical damage. They were able to operate at the same (or diminished) level of craftsmanship until the recovery in other countries allowed ancient traditions of craftsmanship to become apparent, augmented by new approaches to production such as the Toyota production system. You no longer hear Japanese products referred to as cheap copies.

Good craftsmanship results in aesthetic pleasure and pride both to the manufacturer and to the user. Museums display the ancient implements and artifacts of our ancestors, and even those from the Stone Age have a certain functional beauty. We humans have been making and then using things throughout our history. Therefore it is not surprising that we would derive pleasure from well-made products.

One of Stanford's anthropology professors, John Rick, occasionally entertains people by making tools from flint or obsidian in the quadrangle or in his talks and lectures. The process consists of chipping or flaking the rock until it acquires the shape desired—and the results are quite beautiful. The chipping, if properly done, is fairly regular, but there is always a slight variation to each one that makes the individual finished object somehow more interesting. This phenomenon is well known to anyone who is an artist and associated with handmade objects. The shape of these tools is functional in a simple and satisfying way. A chipped obsidian edge is said to be sharper than a sharpened steel edge and capable of holding its sharpness longer.

Undoubtedly the users of stone tools made and utilized utensils, storage devices, decorations and totems, and other items that have not all survived the years. Those that have and that we respond to most strongly are considered "primitive art" and put in museums to be wondered at. Attendance at so-called crafts fairs shows that we still value handmade objects, which are often imbued with rough and irregular characteristics. Blacksmithing has become a hobby for some, and evening education programs are replete with courses in ceramics, weaving, and other such ancient activities. Many of us build things as a hobby and gain increasing pleasure as our skills become more refined. Craftsmanship encompasses a wide range of human activity, and the pleasure we receive from it has certainly not diminished, even over hundreds of years. As we encounter more recent well-made products—Grecian amphorae, 17th-century suits of armor, Hepplewhite furniture, restored Brass Era automobiles, Barcelona chairs—we respond even more strongly.

The Pleasure and Pride of Craft

There are several reasons for the aesthetic pleasure we gain from well-crafted products. First, we are impressed by surface beauty. Silver is appealing to us because as it wears, the surface acquires a finish (called a patina) that is reflective, but not a mirror. We can see the nature of the material rather than just our reflections. With age, surface patterns are emphasized by oxidation that is missed by the polish rag, and the overall nature of the item takes on a mellow glow. For such reasons, antique silver pieces are often more attractive than newly manufactured ones. Wood is appealing to us because of the variation in color and pattern and because of the glow of a nicely done finish. Perhaps, like me, you wonder at the highly polished, probably urethane-based finish applied to wood used in some automobile interiors. Wood is a difficult material to use in an industrially manufactured product and is undoubtedly there for its appearance. But why cover it with a finish that makes it look like plastic?

Pleasure also comes from the juxtaposition of various materials, shapes, colors, and finishes, one of the attractions of antique mechanisms and instruments and many sculptures. This attraction might make you wonder about the present trend to cover things up. For example, many modern "luxury" cars place shrouds over the engine, so it is not possible to see the details of the engine itself. I suppose they are aiming to please customers with an allergy to things technical, but it is not much fun to lift the hood on such a car. Often the engine is aesthetically much more interesting than the shroud. To me an engine, especially a clean one, or even better one detailed for a roadster show or a concourse, is a beautiful thing. Ferrari has taken advantage of this aesthetic by exposing the engine to view. Similarly, the inside of an electronic device is more interesting and shows more craftsmanship than the outside. For a brief time Apple made a small desktop computer that was available with a transparent cover. Remember that one? I still have one even though I no longer use it because I enjoy looking at its internal workings. If consumers gain pleasure from well-crafted objects, why do producers cover them up?

People also are impressed by things they recognize they could not, or would not, do. I have spent a great deal of time in my life working with wood, metal, and other materials on hobby projects ranging from buildings to steam tractors to model ships. In my professional career I have acquired a fair amount of skill at making things and am, perhaps as a result, filled with immense pleasure (and perhaps a bit of envy) as I encounter things that I do not have the skill or patience to do. A perfect weld bead, a proper and exquisitely crafted wood joint, a flawless paint job, or a machining job that seems to me impossible not only pleases me, but makes me want to get to know the person who brought forth the miracle.

But good craftsmanship brings us more than just aesthetic pleasure. It also implies pride on the part of those who made the product, which is usually an indication that the object not only holds intrinsic beauty but also functions well. If a Lexus, BMW, Mercedes, or Porsche had a crummy paint job and visible rough sheet metal edges, you might suspect it would not be mechanically reliable or sophisticated in its performance—and you would probably be right. Good craftsmanship implies good performance and vice versa. And in the purchaser's eye, craftsmanship implies that a company cares about details and therefore produces outstanding products. Such craftsmanship is highly motivating to the people doing the work, as it is a matter of pride and satisfaction to all concerned. The company loses a great deal of potential if it does not keep this in mind. Craftsmanship is a factor in pride, and pride is a factor in producing high-quality products. Look closely at a Honda motorcycle or talk to the people who make them. The craftsmanship, the pride, and the quality are obvious. And they reinforce each other.

I have worked quite a bit on craftsmanship with a wonderful company in Pune, India, named Forbes Marshall. It is a family company now run by Naushad Forbes, who was a Ph.D. student of mine, and his brother Fahrad, who studied electrical engineering and business and was a Sloan Fellow at Stanford. Naushad is particularly interested in craftsmanship, and the company has done a great deal in that regard. The first time I visited the company some 20 years ago, it, like many Indian firms, was creating products under license to a European company. The reason for my visit was that Naushad was particularly interested in increasing exports and the number of indigenous products the company produced, and he thought I could help.

The first thing I noticed when I stepped into the lobby was one of the impressive products the company manufactured (an electronically controlled valve) on display. But I later found out that it was a unit that had been made in the European plant rather than their own. When I asked the reason, I was told that the European-made one was "better" than the ones they made—a clearly unacceptable attitude. Although the units that Forbes Marshall manufactured were built to the same specifications as the ones made in Europe, the castings were rougher on the outside, the paint was applied by hand with a marginal brush and no use of masking tape, and after completion the units were put in a rough bag made of jute and packed in straw in a somewhat poorly made, though strong, box. The shipping address was then applied to the box with an even more marginal brush. The net result would not have thrilled a customer in Germany.

Because of Naushad's commitment to higher quality and his position in the company, and maybe a little bit because of my ranting and raving, things began changing rapidly. By my next visit, masking tape, sprayed paint, cartons and foam cushioning, and labels had appeared. On a later visit I found that the company had given its foundry suppliers a good going over and the exterior of the cast parts was much improved as well. Now the products in the lobby are made in their own plant.

As the company continues to improve the craftsmanship on its products, the products' reliability and performance also increase, as does the international reputation of the company. And the pride and confidence of the employees has grown to the point where they have a large number of their own internally designed and manufactured products. In a recent visit, I ran across a particular high-precision instrument that measures fluid flow by means of vortices, which at one point worked very well but definitely had rough edges. The item is now beautifully made, and performance and sales have improved along with the craftsmanship—a common story.

There is a tendency to associate good craftsmanship only with surface finish, which is why I stress the fact that craftsmanship requires an attitude that affects anything one works on. But even surface finish can have profound functional effects. Failures are often associated with so-called stress concentrations in structures, which may be due to localized damage during manufacturing or assembly, or to wear associated with heat treatment or finish of parts that move against one another. Thermodynamic efficiency is often dependent on such things as smooth fluid passages and precise burner geometry. Corrosion resistance demands tight control of surface coatings. The list goes on. Quality definitely depends upon the details, and the details depend upon craftsmanship.

Good craftsmanship also implies that the product was designed to be easily manufactured, which in turn implies it was well designed. Good product designers keep manufacturing uppermost in mind. An example of this mind-set is found in the case of plastic model kits. Here the Japanese again took the ball away from U.S. companies because of Japan's attention to the injection molding process and the details of the components. Companies such as Tamiya are able to sell their products at a premium because the parts go together beautifully and the results are unexcelled in realism.

In fact, in smart companies, design and manufacturing engineers work as part of the same team. If you are contemplating acquiring a product assembled by the manufacturer and it shows symptoms of having been difficult to assemble, you should worry. Only dumb companies produce products that have not been designed with assembly in mind. Consumers don't expect high-quality products from dumb companies, and there is little pride in working for an organization that is considered inferior.

The Industry and Culture Problem

Despite its importance, craftsmanship is often inadequately stressed in industry, partly because it is difficult to measure and describe in words and numbers (the usual languages of industry). Engineers and managers are much more comfortable measuring surface finish in micro-inches of deviation from the mean than in beauty. There are few courses, outside of art schools, that deal with craftsmanship and few forums and books on the subject. Many elements of craftsmanship deal with the senses and are fairly right-brained in nature. You probably own something that is beautifully crafted and value it highly. However, can you eloquently explain why? Can you explain why hand-rubbed furniture finishes are more attractive than urethane varnishes? Why hand-thrown pots are more attractive than greenware pots made in molds? Why leather is more satisfying than vinyl? What metrics would you apply to an interior paint job in your house?

The difficulty in addressing problems of craftsmanship in modern industry is due not only to communication difficulties but also to "progress." There was a time, say 150 years ago, when a much larger percentage of the population worked with their hands. After all, the word *manufacture* originally meant "made by hand." Creating something by hand is a good way to build an appreciation for craftsmanship—probably much more effective than reading books or wandering through museums. Even being closely associated with people who work with their hands is useful, an opportunity I had when I was young as a I grew up on an orange orchard in Southern California with my brother, uncle, parents, and grandparents. My grandfather had no previous experience with farming before buying the land, but he picked up the necessary skills and knowledge rapidly and by necessity. He built most of the buildings on the ranch, as well as many of the tools, machines, and pieces of furniture. My grandmother and mother sewed all their own clothes in addition to shirts and jackets for us males. Such people were my mentors.

By the time I became an engineer in the 1950s, U.S. culture had changed a great deal. The industrial surge in the United States after the Depression of the 1930s, and especially during World War II, resulted in a greatly increased supply of affordable products. People began to buy what they had formerly made and replace things they had formerly fixed. The work involved in making products, and therefore much of the appreciation for how they were made and the understanding of their function, was separated from the user. However, at the time, the work was well understood by the engineers and managers, since many of them had "come up through the ranks" and had a good sense of craftsmanship.

When I was in college, the Warner and Swasey Company in Cleveland, Ohio, made extremely high-quality machinery, and I talked with company representatives at length about possible employment. They were somewhat interested in me because of my experience in machine design and my motivation to design fine machinery. They made it plain to me, however, that if I came to work with them I would spend my first two years as a machinist, since my shop abilities were not adequate for a designer. At the time, their president and all other line managers had served their time in the shop. They recognized good work when they saw it and insisted upon it. I did not take the job they offered, but I sometimes look back and think that perhaps I missed a unique opportunity to really learn what the making of machinery was all about.

One reason I did not take the job was that even then craftsmanship occupied a relatively low status in our abstraction-loving society. We value people who talk well, use mathematics, are familiar with scientific theories, and study history and the classics. Many people value others who "work with their minds" more highly than those who can make beautiful things. Think of the difference between the pay of senior shop people and senior managers, or beginning carpenters and beginning lawyers. We tend to invite authors to our parties more than outstanding masons or sheet-metal workers (that's probably one reason why I write books). I am afraid that we are still burdening ourselves with the outmoded social priorities of the ancient Greeks, in which the upper classes did not deal with trade or technology. In the top-ranked engineering school in which I work, most of the faculty members are familiar with advanced mathematics and the theories of science. However, only a handful of them have much of a grasp of craftsmanship. Interacting with the physical world is not their specialty. They do better in life by spending their time transferring their thoughts to publications rather than three-dimensional form.

It is still possible to find companies (usually small ones) in wood and metalworking in which the bosses are themselves extraordinary craftsmen, or at least have worked enough in the trade that they are good judges of craftsmanship. Such companies are highly prized by their customers for the quality of their work. But most customers, most managers, and even many engineers are quite divorced from the actual work of building things. Engineering education has become much more theoretical, with the result that many graduates have little background in making things and little interest in or feel for craftsmanship. More and more managers have gone through business schools and not only obtained their M.B.A. degrees but also happily accepted the belief that management is a transportable skill that can be used almost independently of one's business. It is popularly thought now that you can manage a company that manufactures machinery even though you have spent no time designing, maintaining, or even operating the machinery. After all, management is considered to be about finance, marketing, organizational behavior, and supply chains.

Computer control has also decreased the need for highly skilled workers to the point where more and more people who work in factories are either maintenance technicians or monitor machines to make sure those machines do their job. Others are responsible for moving raw materials to the machines and then the products to the shipping point. Computers are extremely useful in the production of well-crafted objects. But unfortunately, they do only what they are told and don't know a whole lot about craft.

Several years ago, for example, I was visiting a large automobile assembly plant in Detroit that had an interesting problem dealing with the paint line. Automobiles are painted mainly by industrial robots that are programmed by humans. The man in charge of paint quality control at this plant had previously run his own automotive painting business and had years of experience in painting cars. But he was retiring and the company was having a great deal of trouble replacing him. If you have looked for some-one to paint your entire car lately (a "complete"), you may have found that there are few body shops that do so anymore and those that do charge an extremely high price. This situation has occurred partly because the United States is running out of peo-ple who have the background to do such things. We are therefore also running out of individuals who are able to supervise robots involved in such work. Robots neither have a sense of craftsman-ship nor give birth to baby robots that acquire one.

In my lifetime, social values in the United States have changed so that working with one's hands is increasingly thought to be a lesser goal. The United States has for most of the last 50 years been trying to convince itself that we are in a "new economy" that subsists on "knowledge" workers. Many people have pointed out that perhaps "white-collar" work is becoming dumbed down and the world is running short of good auto mechanics, finish carpenters, "fix-it" people, and other such highly skilled folk upon which our society depends. The traditional "vocational" schools continue to be converted to college prep, where calculus, literature, advanced placement science, and other such "upscale" topics are taught. Shop courses lose their funding, and computer programming courses take their place. Most parents want their kids to go to college and get business, law, or medical degrees even if these students might find greater fulfillment as craftspeople.

If you are interested in the role of such training at a deeper level, read a wonderful article entitled "Shop Class as Soul Craft" written by Matthew Crawford and originally included in the Summer 2006 issue of *New Atlantis* magazine.[1] Since that time Crawford has also written a book with the same title. Inciden-tally, as is pointed out in the book *The Millionaire Next Door* by Thomas Stanley and William Danko, many millionaires in the United States these days are self-employed tradespeople.[2]

Modern industry is short, especially at management level, of people who have an appreciation for, and sense of, craftsmanship. You can't place high priority on something that you don't value, are uncomfortable with, or perhaps don't even know exists. I have mentioned previously that the United States has lost leadership, or lost out completely, in many industrial sectors in which it used to lead the world. The excuses have ranged from "cheaper labor over there" to "government collusion" to "U.S. antibusiness policies" to "a lazy workforce." But in some of these cases, isn't craftsmanship perhaps a factor? Comparing Japanese and U.S. cars or machine tools in the 1980s might have given an early indication that U.S. automobile and tool companies were headed for trouble. Looking at the rapid improvement in craftsmanship in Chinese products over the past 10 years and the present rapid improvement in products from India should signal concern for the future.

The Nature of Craftsmanship

If you do not grow up with a trade or craft, craftsmanship is a complex topic. It requires both left-brain and right-brain thinking, involving knowledge, sophistication, and emotion. One of the more provocative discussions of the issue is contained in a book entitled *The Nature and Art of Workmanship* by David Pye.[3] When Pye wrote the book, he was professor of furniture design at the Royal College of Art in London. In the book he points out that there are several types of craftsmanship (or "workmanship," as he prefers—to him craftsmanship is simply good workmanship).

Pye refers to rough, free, and regulated workmanship. Rough workmanship is oriented toward accomplishing the purpose with minimal effort, like the split-rail fence. Such products often have an honest beauty and, as he points out, are often found in rural environments but are rare in cities, despite the efforts of a few architects and interior designers. Rough workmanship is seldom adorned with decoration and usually more focused on form than surface finish. Free workmanship is more refined but is still directly affected by the individual(s) doing the work. Expert carving falls into this category. The strength and message of the piece is of more importance than geometrical perfection. In regulated workmanship, on the other hand, products are expected to be close to the defined dimensions and surfaces, and therefore highly controlled and interchangeable—the grille of an automobile or the fuselage of an airplane would be examples.

Pye also discusses the workmanship of risk as opposed to the workmanship of certainty. The workmanship of risk refers to processes in which the quality of the result is continually at risk. The individual custom furniture maker, for instance, has continuous opportunities to affect the final product. In the workmanship of certainty, the final product is preordained before production begins: it is completely designed, production tooling is manufactured and the plant assembled, then out comes the product. Free craftsmanship may be involved in the making of prototypes and the necessary tooling. Once the button is pushed, however, the effect of humans on the product is minimized. This type of workmanship is what is found in industry.

Pye does not state that one type of workmanship is better than the others. In fact, he feels that industrially made products can have the same extraordinary workmanship as handmade products. However, he is willing to say that rough and free workmanship are important to us and unlikely in products of industry. He also writes that there can be major problems in relying exclusively upon the workmanship of certainty.

Why are rough and free workmanship important to us? Pye bases his argument partly on world history, during most of which workmanship was rough while the human race made tools, implements, and shelters through individual labor for the purpose at hand. Two stone axes, two oxcarts, or even two cathedrals did not have the similarity of two 2011 Chevrolet Malibus. It is probable that attention to "perfection" of human-made objects did not begin until wealth was accumulated. Certainly by the time of the pyramids there was an emphasis toward tremendous control of materials and form. In fact, during the past 5,000 years this attention to control has continued to increase. The engraved armor of the medieval period, the jewelry and glassware of the Renaissance, the furniture of the Victorian age, the skyscrapers of the mid-20th century, and the automobiles and airplanes of today show the trend clearly—everything in its place and fewer and fewer rough edges. Pye hypothesizes that originally this geometrical perfection and regularity must have seemed almost miraculous. It also must have symbolized wealth and power, because only those with both could afford and maintain such objects in the less controlled environments of the time.

The regularity and control in industrial processes together with standardization and economies of scale are basic to our extraordinary material life. Regularity and control are also extremely satisfying to people. As Pye points out, to our forebears, nature was not especially wonderful. It contained uncomfortable levels of cold and heat, scarcities of food and water, and hostile creatures of all sizes. Control must have initially been an extremely satisfying way of defeating the enemy. I have heard other people philosophize upon similar points. In a talk he gave at Stanford, David Billington, a professor at Princeton University who has studied the aesthetic aspects of technology extensively, presented his belief that one reason for the high degree of control in the Netherlands is the hostility of nature. As the North Sea storms, the Dutch behind their dikes produce artists such as Mondrian, power plants that are laid out like Mondrian paintings, legendarily clean homes, and extraordinarily geometrical and neat fields. All of us have a need for predictability and order, even though most of us are not below sea level and the roll of significant hostile creatures has been reduced to viruses and our fellow humans. The products of modern industry satisfy this need.

However, according to Pye, these products must be carefully designed. The designer must be thoughtful in choosing materials, forms, textures, colors, and other characteristics that work together consistently when built. In the long run, wood-grained vinyl on the sides of station wagons was doomed. We interact with products from all distances and with all of our senses. A building designed by an architect may look good from afar, as it is portrayed on the drawing board. However, how about from six feet away? Is the structure boring, or do the features that please the onlooker do so independently of the distance from which we view it? Pye's hypothesis states that the designer working on paper cannot think about the details of design in a complete enough way to provide this diversity. The craftsman, however, is sensitive to small-scale texture, smell, sound, feel, and psychological impressions. The designer who is divorced from the making of the product is limited. This limitation is reflected in many industrial products that are well made and, at first glance, appealing but in the long run turn out to be bland or dull. Controlled products must also be made well. Shiny surfaces, for example, should not end in rough edges. The more refined the design, the better the workmanship must be.

Rough workmanship, alas, is probably disappearing as industrial capability increases and people who live off the land decrease in number. Chain-link fences, barbed wire on prefabricated steel posts, and electrical fences are replacing the split rail. Recently some land not far from where I live was converted to the raising of horses, and I was amazed to see, on driving by it, that it was completely surrounded by brand-new white fencing of the type seen surrounding horse pastures for thoroughbreds. It seemed like a bit of Kentucky in the middle of the Sacramento Valley in California, and opulent beyond belief in an area that raises field crops and fruit. But upon closer inspection, the fence turned out to be plastic, and weatherproof, never to need painting. Interestingly enough, my response turned from awe to disgust. Plastic textured to look like wood, although sometimes impressively done, demeans both plastic and wood. Fake is fake. But such is the direction of our society—check out the interior of a McDonald's.

Free workmanship is also becoming rare as the cost of labor rises and the cost of mass-produced products decreases. It is still widespread in less industrially developed countries, such as India, China, and Mexico, and practiced by makers of high-priced luxury items and industrial prototypes in developed countries. Some practices such as dentistry still employ free workmanship because of varying constraints. However, in many cases free workmanship can no longer compete economically. Even when products are created by hand, they are often copied and produced in large number through a predetermined process.

This trend in decreased free workmanship costs us not only quality but also diversity. Pye contrasts a street of parked cars with a harbor of fishing boats. Somehow the first is depressing (we build parking structures to hide them) and the second is wonderful (we build high-priced restaurants overlooking them). After spending almost all of our two million years with a great amount of diversity, we are now frantically stuffing ourselves into condominium units, which must cause a little internal trauma. We require things that fit our individual values and personalities and that are fun. The present love of funk, kitsch, antiques, and nostalgia products (such as 1960s Detroit cars) is an indication that we need more than beautifully made manufactured, massproduced items.

The United States should offer more recognition and award to outstanding practitioners of free workmanship. Much attention has been paid to Japan's Living National Treasures program. People are selected for this recognition because they do an outstanding job of producing artifacts consistent with Japanese cultural values. But the emphasis is on traditional craft areas such as ceramics, textiles, lacquerware, metalwork, wood and bamboo crafts, and dolls. Similar programs are now underway in countries such as Korea, the Philippines, Thailand, Romania, Australia, and France, but all oriented toward handicrafts and none overlapping industry. I know of no industry honored because of the quality of its craftsmanship. In fact, I know of no cases in which employees within industry are honored for their craftsmanship. This is shortsighted on the part of industry.

Perhaps the United States will rediscover free workmanship, designate outstanding practitioners as living national treasures, and return to teaching such things in our schools. Maybe engineers and managers will be trained to have a better appreciation for and facility in craftsmanship. Also, perhaps the increased flexibility in industry that is coming from more sophisticated computer control and more flexible approaches to manufacturing will allow more diversity in our products. As previously mentioned, craftsmanship is not a topic that is easy to debate and treat in our schools and companies, since it is quite visceral in nature and without a good vocabulary. However, craftsmanship is extremely important to people, and the issue is not likely to go away. Industry is periodically reminded that products that are well crafted simply do better in the marketplace, and they usually result in higher margins of profit.

Some Suggestions

Some motivations for outstanding craftsmanship happen regularly in industrially developed countries. The United States, for instance, does well in aerospace, where the cost of finishing parts is small compared to the overall cost of a project and craftsmanship is directly tied to function. Assembly is necessarily done carefully because of the high cost of a failure, while aerodynamics promotes nicely done finish and external detail. Interiors in upper-class compartments are very carefully detailed because airlines compete for higher-paying passengers.

Great improvement has occurred in areas with intense competition, such as the automobile industry. But there is a great deal of room for continued improvement in all areas. There are a number of steps that can be taken to improve product craftsmanship, but they require investment of time and money. Some of them can be taken at the individual level, many at the corporate level, and some require national or even international attention. Other steps can be done through traditional education or require lifetimes of practice. Some result in lower product cost, some increase the cost. All of them dangle the inducement of higher profit margin. Let's look at seven of these steps to improve craftsmanship that I consider highly worth exploring for the future of industry:

1. Increase awareness in business of the nature and importance of good craftsmanship in general and in the particular product. This must not only be the case with individuals responsible for defining and manufacturing the product, but broadly throughout a company. There is a saying that has been endemic in companies that have drastically improved the quality of their products: "Quality begins at the top." When Hewlett-Packard and Ford Motor Company decided to radically improve the manufacturing quality of their products in the 1980s, John Young and Donald Petersen, who were the CEOs, made it their personal top priority. When CEOs make such a decision, people notice. Manufacturing quality was of such concern in the 1980s that companies consciously made a fetish out of it, with slogans, T-shirts, charts on the wall, and recognition dinners—such is also necessary with craftsmanship. It is possible to increase people's sensitivity to craftsmanship through traditional courses, reverse engineering, and product reviews. Most people can learn to better recognize it. However, to produce something well crafted, there must be a company commitment to develop an acceptable language to discuss it, a system to evaluate it, and the ability to think about the many components of operations that cause it to be.

2. Ensure broad-based acceptance of responsibility for increasing the level of craftsmanship. In a product company, many people have an effect on craftsmanship, from the marketing people and designers through those who manufacture, pack, and ship the product. Everyone must take pride in the craftsmanship of the product and feel the need to perform his or her function in a way that improves it. In many cases craftsmanship can be improved with no additional expense. Sensitivity to good fits and finishes can result in alternate and sometimes less expensive approaches to production. Often, however, time and effort must be spent to improve craftsmanship. More expensive processes must be employed, and more care must be taken in manufacture and assembly. Of course, businesses do not want to spend money on such things unless they can increase the price by at least a corresponding amount.

Once "Made in the USA" signified outstanding strength, dependability, and good craftsmanship. However, as discussed, complacency caused industry to seek profits by producing large numbers of items rather than finely made ones. Only recently has the United States been competing directly with Asians and Europeans, people who make certain products very well. This competition has been good for the country. Cadillac and Lincoln used to be accepted as the U.S. luxury cars, but they have improved rapidly from confronting companies such as Mercedes, Lexus, and BMW (though they have not yet reclaimed their title on the international stage, or even in the United States). U.S. companies have done a good job of ridding the production process of inefficiency and in some cases have improved the design of products markedly. However, would you say that U.S. products are in general beautifully made? This question would not have been asked 50 years ago when the country was happily making things as U.S. companies had always made them, customers were perhaps not as sophisticated, and European and Japanese products were relatively rare.

3. Utilize a concurrent approach to engineering and a cross-functional approach to product design. Craftsmanship can be impaired by poor product integration. The product must be designed from the beginning to maximize the potential for outstanding craftsmanship. For instance, it is difficult to achieve a beautiful paint job if some of the parts are made of materials that reject the primer, or if someone's subassembly causes a geometry that makes it impossible to coat the surface. Anyone who has painted an old car knows it is impossible to avoid drips, runs, and thin spots on them, while contemporary cars can achieve a better finish simply because they do not have strange corners and projections that cause such flaws.

4. Increase the degree of exposure and perhaps hands-on experience that give at least some people in the companies the level of sophistication that traditional craftsmen acquire. The ability to make things beautifully and appreciate fine work is learned through actually making things. People can be sensitized to the nature and importance of craftsmanship through books and lectures, but the ability to produce outstanding work must be acquired by experience—through working with the hands rather than viewing overhead slides or taking a computer course. Like any artist, the craftsman or craftswoman spends a lifetime of practice reaching the level of sophistication needed to produce and recognize the best. But industry, like schools, seems to continually want to decrease this training.

When I began working in machine shops, apprenticeships required four years. They were conducted seriously, with much effort spent to ensure that the apprentice went through the proper steps to learn the necessary skills. I was asked to do such things as file surfaces flat when a milling machine would have accomplished the same job more rapidly simply because, in the judgment of the machinists, I could not file flat enough. This sort of training was obviously not making any money for the company, but they were *investing* in me. When I graduated from Caltech, I joined Shell Oil Company as a production engineer. They put me directly into an oil field, first on a work-over rig, and then on a drilling rig, as the start of their hands-on training program. I rapidly learned a great deal about the craft of drilling a deep hole that was not in the field manuals. It is regrettably rare these days for companies to invest in their employees regarding instilling a sense of craftsmanship and understanding of overall production within an organization.

5. Increase recognition of outstanding work. Craftsmanship must be elevated to higher importance. One way of both encouraging awareness and motivating improvement is through recognition. Companies regularly reward outstanding salespeople, designers, researchers, and clerks. It would be interesting to witness the effects of occasionally selecting people who made outstanding contributions to craftsmanship and raising their salary to $250,000 a year or so.

6. Increase research and development intended to improve craftsmanship. Every time I look at something like a cheap kitchen knife, I realize that it could be made much more nicely with probably little increase in cost. However, the knife company likely spends little effort thinking about how to do so. A bit of investment and the formal expenditure of a few people's time could make a huge difference. Many companies simply produce products the way they always have and have not yet been goaded into thinking how to make them better. Judging from the past 20 years' experience in many product areas, it is better to improve craftsmanship before being goaded instead of after. One exercise I routinely assigned to engineering design students at Stanford was to have them go buy some cheap product (a dollar or two) and figure out how to improve the craftsmanship. They had no trouble succeeding, often by something as simple as removing crummy paint.

7. Increase consumer demand for better craftsmanship and then fill it. Consumers, the United States, the world, and the human race need more craftsmanship. Producers should promote increased appreciation of outstanding craftsmanship among their customers and then produce the products to satisfy the new demand they have created.

Enough about craftsmanship for now. The last chapter was about human fit. The next chapter will be about the interaction between products and human emotions. Craftsmanship has to do with both, so I will visit it again.

Chapter 5 *Thought Problem*

This one is a bit trickier because we have become so used to associating the word *craft* with handwork. But practice using it in the context of industrial production.

Choose an industrially produced product that is beautifully crafted and one that is not. You may be tempted to choose a hand-crafted example, but stay with items that are produced in quantity with much of the work being done by machines. Once again, how do you account for the difference in well-crafted and not well-crafted products? To what extent is money a factor? Sensitivity? Tradition?

Problems and Tactics Table: Craftsmanship

Problems	Tactics
Lack of adequate language to discuss and communicate craftsmanship	More interaction on the topic among designers, manufacturing people, marketers, managers, and customers; promote mixing with people with high standards of craftsmanship in other fields
Designers don't understand craftsmanship	Designers should follow job through manufacturing, and study beautifully crafted and competing products
Inadequate appreciation of and pride in craftsmanship in the company	Recognize and reward outstanding craftsmanship in company
Insufficient time and resources to accomplish high level of craftsmanship	Sensitize marketing people and upper management on the benefits of craftsmanship

Products, Emotions, and Needs

Love, Hate, or Blah?

Despite the fact that we humans pride ourselves on our cognitive abilities, we are heavily, if not dominantly, influenced by emotion when assessing the quality of a product. Although we separate cognition and emotion for convenience in discussing them, they are not independent of each other. At one time people tended to treat cognition and emotion as separate and perhaps conflicting human motivations. In 1956 Benjamin Bloom chaired a group of educators who identified three separate domains of learning: the cognitive (mental skills—evaluation, analysis, comprehension, recollection, synthesis), the affective (growth in feelings or emotional areas—values, motivation, attitudes, stereotypes, feelings), and psychomotor (manual or physical skills).[1] But present-day research shows otherwise, as is not surprising since we only have a single brain to be involved in all of these functions.

Our actions and responses are molded by a combination of thought and emotion. We are creatures of both nature and nurture. In some cases thinking may dominate, and in others emotion. Sometimes our responses are logical, and sometimes they reflect our past and our wiring. Without the emotional element, *Homo sapiens* would not have made it this far because the human thinking process is too slow to handle many of life's difficulties and is not very good with uncertainty and high complexity.

Even in the case of supposedly logical actions and responses, emotions are involved. Emotions can, and do, rapidly summarize situations and provide plans of action. Clinical studies have shown that people who for one reason or another suffer from impaired emotional responses have difficulty in making decisions.[2] Emotions, after all, are responsible for the "feel" that guides the research scientist, the chief executive officer, and the president of the United States. Intuition communicates with us through emotions. Psychologists sometimes use the term *thin slicing* to designate the ability to find patterns and reach decisions based on extremely narrow windows of experience—too narrow to do the sort of thinking we would expect is necessary to complete the task. For example, our rapid sizing up of new people we meet results from this emotional function. Such workings of the mind speak to us through emotion (such as dislike of the person we are meeting for the first time) just as do many, if not most, aspects of product quality.

How Emotions Play a Role

Take something as obvious as the appearance of products. Part of the success of Apple is that people simply "like" (an emotional response) the appearance and feel of the company's products, often independently of function. Logic often takes second place to emotion. Purely functionally speaking, the argument could be made that high-heeled shoes by Jimmy Choo and Manolo Blahnik are not worth the price. But the success of the brands shows that not all people agree. Function is overwhelmed by emotion.

If a user loves a product, everyone involved benefits—if the user hates it, everyone loses. A great deal of effort goes into attempting to measure and predict emotional response by people involved in marketing, design, psychology, and other fields. Such research ranges from simply talking to people through observing them in action, to subjecting them to carefully controlled tests. Unfortunately, or perhaps fortunately, there are no formulas that allow us to optimize emotional responses, nor are there precise metrics that measure them directly. Nor are the mechanisms sufficiently understood to build simulations. Often words, mathematics, and computer simulations fail us when dealing with emotions. For this reason, emotional response is something that many in engineering and business are relatively uncomfortable with, compared to such usually quantified characteristics as performance and cost (although there, too, as discussed in Chapter 3, quantification falls short).

Society demands that all of us to some extent control our emotions. I was fascinated by my grandchildren during their terrible twos. They expressed their emotions beautifully. They alternated between unmitigated outrage, bottomless love, unconstrained laughter, intense dislike, and passionate desire. But for obvious reasons, society (parents?) had already been hard at work attempting to convince them to soften these expressions. Of course, we could not afford to have the seven billion people in the world be as honest about their emotions as two-year-olds, but in a way we have all been trained to conceal, if not lie about, our emotions. This is especially obvious in the case of primitive and vital emotions such as those involved with spreading our gene pool. If we exhibited and acted upon all our true emotions, we would probably be neither as popular nor as effective in life. We have all learned to be nice to people we don't like, modulate our more animal feelings toward attractive strangers, and pretend interest in things that interest our friends.

People not only have been taught to conceal their feelings, and do not have adequate language to communicate them, but also may not always be sure how they actually do feel. This situation certainly handicaps designers and producers of hardware products from matching the needs and desires of the users. Books, magazines, newspapers, movies, and music CDs are products of industries in which great effort is spent on evoking emotional responses in the user. But although industries producing products such as clothing, automobiles, cosmetics, and food necessarily think deeply and continually about emotion, they often still come up short. And how about the makers of crowbars, backhoes, and chain hoists? They perhaps don't even consider emotions that deeply. But they should, because emotions affect both the design of the product and the user's happiness with it.

Companies seeking to produce high-quality products can always benefit from becoming more sensitive to human emotions—their own, those of people involved in selling, manufacturing, using, and servicing the product, and those of their coworkers or employees. And a good way to foster this sensitivity is simply to become more interested in emotions as a central characteristic of humans. Emotions rule us, but we don't know much about them. They involve our senses, our mind, and our bodies, yet they give us simple messages. While going to school for a significant part of our lives, we hear little of them in most of our classes.

Chapters 3 and 4 deal with analytical material, in which specific information is available, parameters can be quantified and measured, and tests can be conducted, but emotions are still involved. Certainly a chair that is comfortable adds more to a user's happiness than one that is not. Many of the problems in human fit result not from lack of information and tools but rather from the relative low priority assigned to fit in the production-consumption process. Why? Maybe the emotions of the people who create products are playing a greater role than the emotions of the end users. Maybe it is more fun for designers to miniaturize devices than to worry about whether they are compatible with human hands. It is possible that designers are more interested in including new features in a product than worrying about whether the user will understand how to use them (conveniently, in many cases people seem to like miniature devices with lots of features more than they do human fit). The term *technically sweet* implies emotion on the part of the maker. As far as craftsmanship is concerned (Chapter 5), standards can be created for making things well and users can be tested for their response. But the aesthetic aspect of craftsmanship is more difficult to deal with analytically. The location of a steering wheel has to do with function, and automobile companies establish rules for such things (though if it is poorly placed, our emotions will come into play). But a beautiful surface finish will please us emotionally even if the surface finish serves no function.

The Complexity of Human Emotions

Even academic psychologists have had trouble dealing with emotion as a topic. They like to research phenomena that can be replicated and quantified, and have traditionally lumped emotions together in the "affective domain," while searching for their research support elsewhere. Most therapists attempt to approach their work rationally and would like their patients to be more "reasonable." Emotions, however, often defy "reasonableness."

There is not even a commonly accepted simple list of emotions. Some years ago Daniel Goleman, who was once editor of *Psychology Today* magazine and later the cognitive science editor of *The New York Times*, wrote a bestselling book entitled *Emotional Intelligence*. In the appendix, he lists the following labels for emotions:

- **Anger:** fury, outrage, resentment, wrath, exasperation, indignation, vexation, acrimony, animosity, annoyance, irritability, hostility, pathological hatred, violence
- **Sadness:** grief, sorrow, cheerlessness, gloom, melancholy, self-pity, loneliness, dejection, despair, severe depression
- **Fear:** anxiety, apprehension, nervousness, concern, consternation, misgiving, wariness, qualm, edginess, dread, fright, terror, phobia, panic
- **Enjoyment:** happiness, joy, relief, contentment, bliss, delight, amusement, pride, sensual pleasure, thrill, rapture, gratification, satisfaction, euphoria, whimsy, ecstasy, mania
- **Love:** acceptance, friendliness, trust, kindness, affinity, devotion, adoration, infatuation
- **Surprise:** shock, astonishment, amazement, wonder
- **Disgust:** contempt, disdain, scorn, abhorrence, aversion, distaste, revulsion
- **Shame:** guilt, embarrassment, chagrin, remorse, humiliation, regret, mortification, contrition[3]

Another influential classification was done by Robert Plutchik in 1980 in which he named eight primary emotions: anger, fear, sadness, joy, disgust, trust, surprise, and anticipation.[4] He considered these emotions essential for survival and believed that they combine in various ways and intensities to provide secondary emotions. For instance, love would be a combination of joy and trust. Fury, rage, hostility, and annoyance would be different shades of anger.

There are many more such classifications, but although they are useful in attempting to achieve a standardized vocabulary and perhaps a model, they fall short of helping us in our quest for product quality. One can also quibble with these classifications. In my opinion Goleman's and Plutchik's categories sorely lack emotions that cause the feelings of desire (wanting, craving, coveting, wishing) and of frustration (thwarting). Such lists do demonstrate that people require a great many words to describe a type of emotion, and even with these words they cannot convey the feelings themselves.

When it comes to products, such lists can mislead through their attempt at simplification. As an example, it might be assumed that enjoyment, love, and perhaps surprise are "positive" emotions that increase quality of life, while fear and anger are negative. I am a firm advocate toward designing projects that stimulate "good" emotions, but is it bad to be angry at products that fail us? If I weren't a bit afraid when I work on the top of tall ladders, I would quit climbing them. Also, there are many situations where people seem to seek these "negative" emotions and the products that stimulate them. Many people love roller coasters, motorcycles, skis, scary movies, and other products that somehow are successful because they induce fear. Do we need periodic adrenaline rushes? Do we gain enjoyment from the relief when the fear recedes? Is it that our harm-avoidance mechanisms need to be exercised once in a while?

University students during finals week have traditionally believed that the anxiety they feel allows them to perform better on their examinations. And there is a stable market for "entertainment" that triggers "negative" feelings. I am fascinated by the difference between my wife and me in this regard. She loves Edward Albee plays—the ones that have a somewhat light and humorous first act, a foreboding second act, and then trash you in the third. She leaves the theater raving about the wonderfulness of the acting and the play. I leave the theater wondering why I do this to myself. The same is true of movies—my wife is a great fan and a major supporter of Netflix. In the evening when I hear violin soundtracks and voices raised in anguish from the TV room, I am certain that she is in there with a box of tissues having a wonderful time.

Sigmund Freud has been pretty much discredited by academic psychologists, but he still lives on in much so-called talk therapy and in our culture. Freud initially believed that we are motivated to maximize our own pleasure (the pleasure principle) and wrote of the instincts for ego (self-preservation) and libido (sex). He soon came to realize, however, that we do not always act in that way. In particular, he could not explain war, in which people sometimes enthusiastically volunteer for an activity that at first glance might seem to be neither pleasurable nor consistent with self-preservation. He therefore added what he called a death drive that opposes the life drive. Freud's life drive moves us toward preservation and happiness, while his death drive moves us in a direction inconsistent with that.

One of the constants in the history of *Homo sapiens* is war, and, especially in the United States, huge amounts of money and effort are spent designing, developing, and producing products for war. (The country seems proud of the ability to produce very "good" ones.) Despite the deaths of many millions, great destruction of property and wealth, and the dangers inherent in war throughout all of history, people continue to follow their leaders off to battle. The country's best minds and a great deal of its capital are put into designing weapons and other war-related equipment. It is quite easy to understand Dr. Freud's need for his death drive to explain the human psyche.

I have known few people who actually desire death, but many are clearly titillated with danger, violence, and evil, and they derive emotional benefits from risk. During a visit to New Zealand a few years ago, my wife and I stopped to watch some people skydiving. To my great amazement, my wife decided she would like to try it. Clearly violence and evil were lacking in this case and the actual risk and danger were low, not only because the sport itself is fairly safe but also because the first times one jumps, one is tied to an experienced jumper. But when you are falling a long distance through the air, you definitely get the impression that you could be in trouble.

When my wife was suited up and ready to go, she began having second thoughts, but there were several excited, much-younger, high-fiving local girls awaiting a ride, and she decided that if they could, she could. Away she went, and securely fastened to her coach, she arrived safely to the ground. When I went out to collect her, she looked fantastic. She was all wide-eyed and open-mouthed and giggly. That evening she announced that she had never been so scared as when she left the airplane, that she felt great, and that everyone should do at least one thing a year that terrified them, especially grandmothers (she is one).

How about you? Do you have a fascination with thrills and spills, with personal and vicarious physical risk? Do you partake in some activity that is perhaps a bit dangerous and slightly foolish? Would you like to go skydiving? Would you like to drive an Indianapolis race car? How about climbing Mount Everest? More than 200 people have died attempting to climb the mountain, and the majority of the bodies remain there.[5] But there seem to be many people still desiring to make the attempt. Is the risk part of the attraction? Equipment used in so-called extreme sports also takes advantage of these emotions. Skis, surfboards, racing catamarans, snowmobiles, accessories for free-climbing, ultimate skiing, and even Rollerblades and skateboards qualify. The colors and graphics usually reinforce the feeling of danger and accompanying exhilaration. Generally the public is accepting of this situation.

Modern societies are ambivalent about products having to do with thrills, spills, and an increased risk of physical harm if the danger is appreciable. Consider the automobile—America's favorite thrill toy. The association of the automobile with danger has been around as long as the automobile itself. All drivers are familiar with the thrill of going too fast or maneuvering too sharply. Car racing is an extremely popular sport, and when attending, fans are quietly excited by the danger to the drivers—quietly because they are not supposed to admit that this danger is part of the appeal.

Automobile manufacturers take advantage of these feelings in their design and advertising, sometimes to a ridiculous extent. Cars and even trucks with average performance at best are often portrayed in advertisements as bouncing over rough terrain, leaping through the air, or drifting around a curve. Automobile manufacturers associate themselves with racing by providing engines and sponsoring stock cars and dragsters with bodies that simulate the styling of production cars. Many innocuous family cars are also named after ferocious animals and racecourses and equipped with numerical designations that hint of experimental fighter planes. A large number of car-accident deaths occur per year in the United States (more than 32,000 in 2010),[6] resulting in a parallel campaign toward safety and the environment, complete with air bags, crashworthiness, and government regulation. Usually the result is a type of honest schizophrenia, with the automobile designers and manufacturers simultaneously attempting to assure customers that the product is safe and that it is akin to a Formula One race car in thrills and performance.

Toys and games often take advantage of this fascination with death and destruction as well. On Halloween night, many more children (and adults) are dressed as Darth Vader than as Obi-Wan Kenobi. Popular computer games place participants in roles of warriors or other adventurers. Toy stores feature a wide variety of weapons, ranging from antique to futuristic. Attempts to do away with such war toys and "violent" games are numerous but only partly successful. I remember the frustration in one of our local nursery schools when the overseers discovered that their boy charges were bringing toy pistols to school. The toys were summarily outlawed, resulting in the children concocting gun replicas from sticks, tape, and pencils. The teachers announced that such action would also be illegal. The children then reverted to using their forefingers—the time-honored way for youngsters to shoot each other. (Fortunately, the school did not try to outlaw forefingers.)

Athletic competition is also successful because of these aspects of our emotions. Certainly football and ice hockey are games whose attraction is based on battle (offense, defense, line). The equipment used emphasizes this idea (for example, decorated hockey masks). There is nothing prouder, nor more incongruous, than a small kid togged out in oversize pads for a Pop Warner football game. The equipment used by motocross racers is reminiscent of both Roman legionnaires and Darth Vader. Professional football players are reasonably normal, although larger persons. But the equipment that makes them look like refugees from a contemporary Roman Colosseum is made by industry.

Most products do not expose the user to the level of fear, anxiety, exhilaration, and excitement that actually accompany danger and derring-do. But many of them try to imply such feelings, sometimes with success. I suspect that the prevalence of black on electronic equipment has something to do with World War II aircraft instruments. Harley-Davidson profits from its slight outlaw image, even though outlaws do not usually have the money to buy its products. Periodically the clothing business blossoms forth in olive drabs, epaulettes, camouflage, lots of pockets, and other such military motifs, and, after all, there are some 200 million guns owned by U.S. citizens, of which one-third are handguns. That's a lot of products.

Diversity in Emotional Responses

A major complexity in dealing with emotion stems from the great diversity in emotional responses among humans. I live on the campus of a top-ranked university located in an attractive and economically well-off region. A hundred miles from here is the agricultural Central Valley of California. For various reasons I go back and forth between the university and a farm owned by a good friend, and I am always amazed by the difference in emotional response to topics such as Barack Obama, the environment, water usage, the Prius, and the *Iliad*. California is an interesting collection of local "red" and "blue." However, I don't have to travel to find this range of feeling. Within a few blocks, I can find the gamut of Mr. Plutchik's or Mr. Goleman's emotions in all degrees of intensity focused on a myriad of issues and objects. I own a pickup in a sea of Volvos, BMWs, and Priuses. My informal clothing is sometimes described by my wife as "homeless wear." I fill my yard with restored and partially restored farm machinery and other equipment. Although my professional credentials are impeccable and, as far as I know, I am well liked, I suspect friends and neighbors have mixed emotional responses to my lifestyle. I am not going to find out.

A good example of the wide variation in emotional response was seen in the 2008 U.S. election. Emotions toward the candidates and the issues, influenced by highly effective advertising and propaganda, were all over the map both in intensity and in direction. Universal health insurance, estate tax, Iraq, Hillary Clinton, Barack Obama, and Sarah Palin caused much of the country to have strong and conflicting emotions. These emotions continue, perhaps egged on by the media. The 2012 election will undoubtedly be worse. The United States seems to be deadlocked, partly because issues are complicated. Although some people claim to simply not care about such issues, they can usually be goaded into taking a stand.

Humans also carry conflicting emotions within themselves. For example, the love-hate relationship is often encountered. In Mr. Plutchik's model, acceptance is related to trust and annoyance to anger. But we often accept annoyances because the cost of doing something about them is greater than the gain. At the time of this writing, when traveling internationally one often finds people who feel both positively and negatively about the

United States. Not too long ago I was undergoing rehabilitation from bilateral knee replacement surgery. When my physical therapist was wrenching upon my new knees seeking more motion, I was overwhelmed by conflicting emotions. I was extremely happy I had had the surgery, but much less happy about the wrenching. I am also happy to be retired but occasionally miss the self-inflicted angst of the university. I love my word-processing software when it points out embarrassing spelling errors, but I hate it when it wants to help me organize my text.

This diversity of emotional response between and within people, whether they are individuals, groups, or nations and religions, makes it difficult to generalize about emotional response—it is a personal thing. Many people share my love of old machinery. Many more think those of us who have it are nuts. Some people spend great amounts of time playing golf. I think they are nuts. That's the glory of the human condition—to each his or her own. But this diversity makes it difficult to build a product that satisfies everyone, which is probably why companies who try to do so eventually run into trouble, and why I hold out for more product diversification.

The Mechanisms of Emotion

Emotion is also extremely complex considering what is known about the mechanisms involved. When I went to school, we were taught that the cortex analyzes signals from the senses and triggers appropriate responses. For instance, you are awakened at night by a strange sound in the house and your cognitive machinery analyzes what it might be. If the conclusion is that it is a prowler, you become frightened. This mode was convenient and cognition-centered. Over the years, however, powerful scanning techniques have been developed to trace the activity in various parts of the brain. It is now thought that signals from the senses go both to the cortex (thinking) and to the amygdala and hip-pocampus. The latter two subsystems of the brain contain some basic memory of sensory signals that connote danger, and if the new signal matches one of these memories, we become frightened *before* the cortex can analyze the data.

The hypothalamus starts the flight-or-fight response, with heart rate and blood pressure increasing, circulation increasing in large muscles and away from the gut, and breathing slowing. The cingulate cortex tones the large muscles, freezes unrelated movements, and causes our face to assume a fearful expression. The locus coeruleus releases norepinephrine, focusing our atten-tion and prioritizing our knowledge and memories. This whole process is automatic. Later, when the cortex reaches its conclu-sion, it may turn all of these functions off if the noise is simply the cat. Alternatively, the cortex's conclusion may reinforce the response. The important point is that emotions lead, rather than follow. This sequence helps explain, for instance, why we often form such a strong first impression of a person, even though sub-sequent experience may slowly teach us that we were wrong. These same emotions play a strong role in dealing with products.

Emotions also vary a great deal in rapidity of response. People may fall in love almost at first sight or over a long acquaintance—this is true of products as well. We may fall in love with products instantly (the iPhone) or slowly (the hybrid car). Of course, people may also fall out of love over time. We may dislike a person or product on first meeting and later become very fond of that per-son or product (for example, a new and complicated software pro-gram). We may become frightened because a loud noise awakens us at night, but we may also become frightened or anxious because the media tells us of weaknesses in the economy week after week. In some cases our emotions are triggered rapidly by a sensed event, and at other times they are triggered slowly by signals received by our senses and processed by our brain over a long time. Some people who study emotions view them as an alarm system—rapid automatic mechanisms that initiate appropriate actions based either on built-in or learned survival needs. When the bear appears in your campsite, for example, your emotions shut off your daydream and start you on appropriate actions. Others are more biased toward cognition and feel that emotions respond more to past experiences, triggered by information gathered over time.

Many theories of emotion classify some emotions as basic, meaning they are necessary for survival and, to some extent, shared among other animals (assuming you are willing to believe that animals other than humans have emotions: dogs, sure, but chickens?). The previously mentioned basic emotions of Plutchik (joy, trust, fear, surprise, sadness, disgust, anger, and anticipation) are typical. Sensory signals announcing danger, hunger, thirst, or worrisome body conditions cause emotions that galvanize the individual into solving the problem. Other basic emotions would be those useful in preparing for the future and living with members of our species in stable packs, tribes, or cultures. Emotions that support increasing the gene pool are obviously essential to the survival of a species.

But not all of our emotions have to do with survival and increasing the gene pool. In an interesting book entitled *How Pleasure Works*, subtitled *The New Science of Why We Like What We Like*, by Paul Bloom, son of the previously mentioned Benjamin Bloom, the author looks at pleasure from an *essentialist* viewpoint.[7] Essentialism is a school of thought in cognitive psychology that says people naturally assume that inanimate and living things and people have deep but invisible essences that define them. In the case of products, this might include such things as association with admired or hated people, history, association with different cultures, and strongly held beliefs about quality. The advertising industry makes good use of such things to influence the attitudes of potential customers about products. Tests discussed in Bloom's book have shown that after you choose a product you like it more and the competitors less, and the longer you have owned it the more you like it.

In his book, Bloom mentions many things of little use that apparently have great value, including a tape measure from the household of John F. Kennedy that sold at auction for $48,875 and the sock from the foot of a photographer that was run over by Britney Spears's car, which was successfully sold on e-Bay. He also discusses the importance of the people or companies that produce the product and the role of imagination, which allows us to build scenarios before acquiring products (which may later turn out to be false) and come to believe that a product we own is superior to identical ones we don't own.

I am not going to attempt to write about the feelings associated with various emotions here. The greatest artists in history have tried to trigger these feelings in others, but probably experiencing the emotions oneself (falling in love, for example) is more vivid to most people than the feelings evoked by poetry, prose, a painting, or a sonata. Since I am not one of the greatest writers in history, I must be satisfied with strongly encouraging producers to become more interested in and sensitive to emotions and feelings in themselves, consumers, and, for that matter, everyone else. It is a fascinating area for thought and observation. For the purpose of this chapter, I will assume that there is commonality between people as far as the feelings resulting from emotions, although, again, there is not nearly as much commonality in what triggers these emotions or how intense they are.

Human Needs

An increasing number of product designers and others associated with producing industrial products are thinking more deeply about people's needs. In a sense, marketing is based on the past experience of people and seeks the improvement of existing products. Studying the people's needs offers the potential of a clearer look at the future, since products are perhaps more fleeting than human needs. Also, it is likely that if products help satisfy human needs, people will be pleased and sales will be good. Products that hinder satisfying these needs tend to be considered bad and do not sell as well. Should a product help us in satisfying a need, we are enthusiastic, perhaps even in love with it. Should it fail to help us satisfy a need or, even worse, hamper our effort to do so, we are frustrated and annoyed. And we may hate it.

There are many ways to classify needs in order to think more clearly about them. One of the most well-known classifications is the venerable one proposed by Abraham Maslow in a paper entitled "A Theory of Human Motivation" in 1943. In this theory, he defines a hierarchy of what he considers basic human needs, in that all humans share them.[8] The theory remains popular so many years later because it is relatively simple and of high practicality, outlining a set of human needs and hypothesizing that if these needs are not satisfied, humans will be motivated to satisfy them. The theory is hierarchical in nature and is often depicted as a pyramid with our physical needs (breathing, water, food, shelter, sex, homeostasis, sleep) at the bottom. If these physical needs are not fulfilled, we first focus upon them.

Once our physical needs are somewhat (not absolutely) taken care of, we consider our safety needs (security of health, employment, resources, family, property), the next layer in the hierarchy. Having satisfied these to some extent we work on our belonging needs (friendship, intimacy, family). Next in line are esteem needs (achievement, respect by others, self-esteem, respect for others). Finally, we reach the self-actualization needs (creativity, morality, acquisition of knowledge, spontaneity, problem solving, lack of prejudice, and acceptance of facts).

But as is the case with many (most?) theories of motivation and behavior, there is disagreement with Maslow in the literature by others who, while not disagreeing with his needs, have found no evidence that they are hierarchical—in other words, if our physiological, safety, love/belonging, and esteem needs are satisfied but our self-actualization needs are not, we still will not be happy campers. We need to satisfy all of them.

Also, times have changed since 1943. Maslow's list of needs now appear to be somewhat naive. Since 1943, the world's population has grown from 2.3 billion to 7 billion, the U.S. population from 136 million to 310 million, and the population of Los Angeles County from 2.8 million to 10 million. People in the United States are much more aware of the rest of the world because of modern communication and have become much more cynical (and more mature?) about the direction our society is taking. I clearly remember 1943, when Maslow wrote his paper, because I was nine years old and World War II was going on, something of great interest to a nine-year-old boy. I listened to the radio news, watched the newsreels in the movie theater, and read the newspaper. But unknown to me, and to most other people, the news was being carefully managed with the cooperation of the media. There was no TV, nuclear weapons had not yet appeared, and as far as we knew everyone was cooperating in a great cause to save the world. Because of such things as the Cold War, Korean War, Vietnam War, vastly improved communication, and increased awareness of issues like genocide and destruction of the ecosphere, life now seems more complicated. Because of the increased population, it probably *is* more complicated. Contrast the presidential campaign of 1944 with that of 2012, which at the time of this writing seems more like a carnival than a campaign.

A somewhat more contemporary look at needs is that by Len Doyal and Ian Gough, first published in 1991 in a book entitled *A Theory of Human Need*.[9] Their approach is often quoted in work having to do with conflict resolution and is somewhat broader than that of Maslow. They feel that the most basic needs are physical health, individual autonomy, and ability to criticize and try to change the culture in which one lives. They discuss a number of what they call *intermediate needs*, or *satisfiers*. These needs are the most basic but can be satisfied in various ways. They include the following:

- Nutritional food and clean water
- Protective housing
- A nonhazardous work environment
- A nonhazardous physical environment
- Safe birth control and childbearing
- Appropriate health care
- A secure childhood
- Significant primary relationships
- Physical security
- Economic security
- Appropriate education

The first six of these needs contribute to physical health, and the last five to autonomy. The authors point out that this list and methods of fulfilling these needs change continually over time. They further maintain that there must be certain prerequisites in a society before it is possible for people to fulfill their needs, including production, reproduction, cultural knowledge, civil/political rights, ability to access the intermediate and satisfier needs, and political participation.

The Doyal/Gough approach gives more attention to societies and cultures than Maslow's does and specifically lists items such as birth control, work environment, and health care. Both lists are a bit high-minded considering the way the human race behaves. Neither of them lists justice (being treated fairly) or power. Maslow lists sex (spreading the gene pool), but Doyal and Gough do not on the grounds that there are people who live happy and successful lives without it. Entertainment may fall under the same rubric, although it seems to be a fairly significant need to many people I know. These theories and many others attempt to define basic human needs, those that not only are universal but also would cause real harm if not fulfilled.

Needs and Emotions

Now let me say a few things about emotional response to products and three classes of needs. I will call them survival needs social needs, and intellectual needs. Although such a simple split is not consistent with the complexity of the brain or modern neurological, anthropological, or biological studies, I will use it because it seems to have strong intuitive appeal. In Chapter 4 I mentioned Benjamin Bloom and his committee dividing learning into the psychomotor, the affective, and the cognitive. I also mentioned Paul MacLean's division of the brain into the R complex, the limbic system, and the neocortex.

An interesting treatment of emotions as they affect the design of products can be seen in Donald Norman's book *Emotional Design*.[10] He proposes considering design at three levels, based on how humans process information. The first, the "visceral level," has to do with brain function that is automatic—programmed and unconscious. The second, the "behavioral level," concerns activities in the brain that control our day-to-day activities. The third he calls the "reflective level," which includes the contemplative activities of the brain. And finally Maslow's needs are sometimes divided into physical, belonging and esteem, and self-actualization needs.

Survival Needs

As humans, we have some strong needs. We are animals that have been around a long time, and like all forms of life on Earth, we are wired to survive. If something threatens this survival—for instance, if we are extremely hungry, thirsty, or starved for oxygen—we will act in extreme ways to remedy the situation. In some functions, such as our need for sleep, our body will remedy the situation even if we cognitively don't want it to. Some of our body's responses are automatic and involve decisions made locally that result in actions to minimize danger before we are aware of emotion (for example, we will automatically drop a hot pan or strive to get our head above water). Other situations that threaten our physical well-being result in negative and longer-term feelings such as those that result from being cold, sleep deprived, or lost.

We are uncomfortable if our sensory signals are impeded. I have spent time in sensory deprivation chambers. It did not take long for me to tire of listening to my heart beat and my blood flow and to want out. If you have ever tried to cover the eyes of a dog or cat, you realize that we mammals have a basic and understandable need for information from our senses. Since we are also uncomfortable with a sensory overload, designers of products should think hard about the proper amount and type of information available to users' senses. This consideration sounds obvious, but it isn't always taken into account. Think of motorcycle helmets, which help minimize brain damage in case of a fall but are often not worn because they impede vision, hearing, and feeling.

From the standpoint of product quality and survival needs, some rules are simple. Good products should never trigger those emotions associated with threats to survival unless there is a good reason to do so. In the case of entertainment, for example, fear, horror, and disgust are sometimes deliberately triggered (think of Steven King novels, computer games, and horror movies). In the case of alarm systems, primitive responses are often triggered (such as loud and disturbing sounds from fire alarms, obnoxious-smelling chemicals such as mercaptan added to naturally odorless cooking gas). But normally, we do not respond positively to feelings of impending doom. Stuffy car interiors (with their perceived lack of oxygen), appliance exteriors that burn users, and diving masks that leak do no one, producers or users, any good.

Conversely, products that make us think that our survival needs are being met make us feel good. "Comfort food" makes us happy because of the salt, sugar, fat, and carbohydrates it contains (once not only essential to humans but also difficult to find). Manufacturers of food understand this fact well, but presently they are caught in a backlash because they have gone so far in pleasing the customer that they seem to be producing food that is deleterious to consumers' health (with hydrogenated oils, fructose sweeteners, chemicals with frightening names, and massive overdoses of calories) and obese customers. Of course, there is a large demand for foods and drinks that are presumably healthier but that satisfy these ancient needs by tricking the senses.

People in the San Francisco Bay area seem to love their household heating and air conditioning even though the climate is extremely benign. But our forebears were killed by heat and cold (as occasionally still happens), and energy is required for homeostasis. At the time of this writing, people in health clubs, riding bicycles, and otherwise getting mild exercise (once more a part of regular life) often drink far more water (once more difficult to find) than they need. In fact, college students often carry water bottles even though they are doing nothing more strenuous than sitting in class. But fresh water is important to survival. And, of course, anything that presumably attracts the opposite sex, or even makes us feel sexy, is a sure hit in the marketplace. And again, there seems to be a strong desire for products that are antidotes to our primitive needs—think of "diet" products and stimulants to keep one awake.

Humans' survival needs have been with us a long time. Evolution being what it is, sensors and information-processing systems have changed, but we retain traces of sensory equipment that serve us just as they served our forebears. Our sense of taste detects saltiness. Our ocean-going forebears needed the proper salinity for their health, as do we. Toxins are often bitter. Sweet and sour things are often nutritious. Things that smell bad to us (excrement, rotting flesh, spoiled food) are not healthy to eat. Things that smell good (pineapples, roast turkey) often are. Successful products take account of these facts.

Since we have minds and memories, we also worry about the future, with the result that we have what Maslow called *safety needs*. It is easy to see this in the success of products that claim to make us safe. Security systems for homes and security software for computers are popular, and approximately half of all households in the United States contain a firearm, even though statistically the inhabitants are more likely to be shot with them than to shoot dangerous intruders.[11] We insure our cars, our houses, and our lives against future uncertainty. But this area is a much trickier one than that of tending to our short-term physical needs, because although our senses reliably tell us when we are hungry, they are less reliable at telling us how secure we are. Our senses are good at telling us that our house is on fire, but not very good at giving us an indication of our risk of having a stroke, being robbed, or having our grandchildren grow up to live in a drastically degraded environment. Here the mind is involved and perhaps not very good at predicting the future.

These safety needs can also be used to influence people, as can be seen in many pharmaceutical advertising campaigns and in the mileage that politicians have gotten from the 9/11 tragedy. Products that can honestly help us to attain future security or allay fears of losing things that are critical to our happiness are popular. But most of us know people who are, in our opinion, suckers for products that promise eternal health and escape from aging and death. Products that prey upon such things as fear of death in potential customers (especially if advertised in a way that enhances the fear) may make money for the producers, but such products can hardly be called "good." We are good enough at being fearful without outside help. We don't need television ads portraying the horrible diseases we may acquire unless we buy the preventative being promoted.

I wish that our longer-term survival needs resulted in stronger signals and responses in certain situations. For example, we as people are facing some major long-term problems (including resource depletion, destruction to the ecosphere, population growth, religious clashes, economic disparities, and nuclear weapons) that could cause great harm to our lives or those of our children. Unless we change our present path, the odds are high that we humans will have our parade severely rained upon by such problems at some point. But we respond slowly, if at all, because we do not "feel" the sort of danger that we feel if we run out of food to eat. We are wired for short-term problems (affecting days, weeks, or a few years) rather than long-term ones (affecting tens to hundreds of years).

Social Needs

Social needs (friendship, intimacy, family, self-esteem, confidence, achievement, respect for and by others) are also basic to humans. Often they are not considered as basic as survival needs because they are thought to be based more on learning and self-awareness and therefore less widespread in the animal kingdom. But humans are pack animals whose groups over time have increased in size from families and tribes to Rotary clubs, religious organizations, cities, states, and international communities. We need such social groups. Consider that one of the more brutal punishments humans have devised is solitary confinement.

If we have a stable, loving family and belong to groups of people that we like and respect, we are happy. If we do not maintain this stability, we are lonely, depressed, and frustrated. These latter emotions may not occur as rapidly or as strongly as the ones that accompany unfulfilled survival needs, but over a longer period they definitely reduce the quality of our lives. Products that help us belong are good, but there is a growing concern about products that seem to be pulling in other directions. For example, TV and computer games compete with activities that once involved the whole family. Fast food and frozen dinners change the character of the kitchen, a traditional crossroads in the home. Computers and digital communication equipment seem to emphasize differences in age and technical sophistication. The media, with its base in modern communication, is thought to contribute to polarization of societies. Knowledge workers in their cubicles are a far cry from construction workers in their gangs, as is the modern mechanized farmer's family (often complete with working spouse, upscale computers, health club membership, and a full load of organized sports, music lessons, homework, and other scheduled activities for the kids) different from the traditional one. The Web is alive with social networking sites, and we have cell phones and instant messaging (both probably used for purposes more social than professional). However, our current situation means there is room for new products that encourage people to build close friendships through personal engagement in more active pursuits.

So-called *esteem needs* are important similarly to social needs. We realize only too well that we are one of 7 billion people and mortal. We need to think of ourselves as unique and valuable in this huge flock. We seek status and need pride. Good products should certainly honor these needs. But as we leave purely physical needs, the task of fulfilling others becomes more complex. As an example, air is necessary to breath, but achievement and respect by others depends on whose opinion is considered and what activities we value. The academic, the construction worker, the businessperson, and the professional criminal are likely to differ a great deal in this regard. The professor is not as likely to define herself by net worth and the professional criminal may not be as motivated to write scholarly articles. The construction worker may place little value in what the professor thinks of him and vice versa, but he may place great value in the opinion of his coworkers. Though some people may think Donald Trump is a jerk based on his performance on television and media appearances, he might not be interested in what they think at all.

Certain products are associated with economic success. In this category we find the "luxury" product—though what we consider luxury, of course, is dependent on how much money we have. For the wealthy, luxury products might include a gray or black top-of-the-line BMW or Mercedes, a marble fireplace in the living room of the executive home, or even the private jet and the yacht. For the economically comfortable, they may be the large-screen hi-def TV or the upscale deer rifle. For those dwelling in a Mumbai slum, any TV may qualify. Status within one's peer group can also come from a product that performs its task extremely well. I usually find myself owning cameras and computers with far more capability than I ever use. I clearly don't need them, but I am a techie and a sucker for highly sophisticated technical products. Is status among my peers part of this? I certainly wouldn't admit it, but I'm sure my wife might suspect such a motivation of me. In most cases, people take pride in products of technology that they consider the best they can afford.

But there are traps in the luxury product. The desire to "keep up with the Joneses" may be a short-term economic boon for producers, but for purchasers it can be self-defeating. There is less pleasure in the marble fireplace, the Lamborghini, and the 8,000-square-foot house if it is based on comparison with neighbors who have as good as, or even more exotic, fireplaces, cars, and houses. Fulfilling esteem needs by considering ourselves better than others is doomed in the long run. Remember the French Revolution: it is safe to say that the reigning aristocrats behaved in a manner that implied they considered themselves superior to the bourgeoisie. The result was the guillotine.

Even in the United States, there are waves of reaction against overly conspicuous consumption and runaway materialism. Such a wave certainly occurred in the late 1960s and early 1970s and reemerged after the Wall Street debacle of 2008. Consider the contemporary electronic or computer business and industry, in which your status is highest if you both are successful and retain the values of the tribe. Respect now comes from other accomplishments rather than from piling up cash through exotic financial instruments. Bill Hewlett and David Packard (known as Bill and Dave) did not have luxurious office suites, and in fact Bill Hewlett was often found in the cafeteria or "managing by walking around." Steve Wozniak and Steve Jobs are still remembered fondly from start-up days, and Jobs was usually seen wearing jeans. Bill Gates, who raised eyebrows by building a huge and luxurious house, is more highly thought of these days because his foundation is doing such good work with his money.

Industrial products can definitely help fulfill confidence and achievement needs. When Howard Head introduced tennis rackets with a larger "sweet spot," he instantly increased the ability of amateur tennis players who acquired them. Certainly Adobe Photoshop and other computer-based graphics programs have increased the ability of people like me to handle visual material. Along with increased ability comes increased confidence. In fact, in this day and age increased understanding of, and ability with, digital devices seems to add to both confidence and achievement. I am not sure the computer has made a better writer out of me, but I can sure move text around more rapidly. Also my confidence is buoyed up when I can solve my wife's system problems, because she is impressed (it is good to be complimented on your abilities by a spouse). But again, as mentioned earlier, traps exist. You can suffer a decrease of both confidence and achievement by being a prisoner of computer systems that constantly leave you frustrated and having to call either the help line or the IT person. The same is true of playing tennis with a crummy racket.

Intellectual Needs

When I talk about intellectual needs—which include creativity, morality, acquisition of knowledge, spontaneity, problem solving, lack of prejudice, acceptance of facts—I focus much more on *Homo sapiens* than other species since these needs stem from the human mind. Thought, enlightenment, and success are all necessary to our existence. You could argue that such needs require transportation, good audio equipment, and fast computers for fulfillment, but when I think of self-actualization needs these days, I think of "software"—of information and education. This thought is perhaps my bias as an academic, but it seems as though there should be much higher-quality material to allow learning and self-knowledge.

It would be nice if the order of magnitude of money and talent that goes into the production and sale of video or computer games could be invested in educational material for all ages. There are good education programs on videos and on TV, and a plentitude of resources available through the media (the Internet, films, painting, sculpture, facts, articles, and books galore), but relatively little has been done in presenting this material in a new and stimulating way to the general public. There are both public and private university programs that utilize TV and the Internet (the British Open University being an outstanding example), but the best ones tend to use a course format and require a good bit of motivation, commitment, and sometimes cash to access them. I sometimes fantasize about high-quality and creative presentations of educational material available to everyone at no cost to help them in fulfilling their needs to learn and to create.

For me, thinking of the needs of humans is an excellent way to think about products and what emotions are likely to result from the use of them. I think the topics in this book are needs—the needs for good deals, human fit, craftsmanship, beauty, cultural identity, and a clean environment—and that satisfying them makes us feel good. Other needs (such as the need for entertainment, control of our lives, making things, using our bodies, novelty, caring for others, free time) can be tucked in a hierarchy or not, but almost any need can catalyze one's thinking and be reframed to think of products that might satisfy it and, in the process, result in positive emotions. It is therefore possible to connect the satisfying of human needs directly to business through design.

Need Finding

The pursuit of greater understanding of the needs of people, in general, and customers, in particular, is attracting more attention in design. The social sciences have developed powerful methods of qualitative understanding of societies. They have been moving toward the natural sciences in rigor and repeatability. Processes of observing and recording data, without influencing those being studied, is increasingly useful in seeking to define human behavior in societies in a way that sheds light on the needs of individuals in those societies that will be useful to the designers of products. Two pioneers in this field, Bob McKim and Rolf Faste, were members of the Stanford Engineering School faculty, and a good bit of this "need finding" mentality can be seen in graduates of the Stanford Design Program.

An interesting and reasonably sophisticated categorization of needs from a designer's viewpoint is contained in an article by Stanford design graduate Dev Patnaik. He is the cofounder of Jump Associates, a product strategy consulting group based in San Mateo, California, and New York City, and presently teaches the course on need finding in the Engineering School at Stanford. His system breaks needs into four categories based on immediacy and universality.[12] The intention of his system is to help the clients of his company not only better understand the needs of their customers but also use this information to help the clients with product planning.

The most immediate and most easily satisfiable category of needs in Patnaik's system includes the needs of people in a particular group that want to do the same things in the same way—perhaps Stanford students who need an easier way to fasten their bicycles to existing racks so they won't be taken by other people. These needs can often be satisfied with an improvement to an existing product (what Patnaik calls a "new feature" solution).

His next category of needs are those of people in a particular group who want to do the same thing, only perhaps in different ways—Stanford students who want to keep their bicycles from being taken by other people. Even though these students may see their need in terms of past tradition—locking their bicycles to racks—their need is actually much broader and encourages a wider variety of solutions—use a beacon, paint the bicycle to look ugly, and so on. In fact, the need as seen by the customer can disappear if other means to the end are taken, such as riding the campus shuttle buses. Obviously, since these students do not especially want to do things the same way, as is the case with the first group, there is more room for creativity and innovation in satisfying their needs. Satisfying these needs may be more difficult, however, not only requiring more creativity and change but also perhaps moving designers and the company into a wider area of competition and new concepts.

The third category consists of needs of people of the same age, profession, religion, or other such affinity group who do not especially want to do the same thing—for example, the need for college students to find the "right" boyfriend or girlfriend, get good grades, or look cool. Whereas the first level of needs can be solved by "features," or improvements on a product, the second and third levels are much more open to what Patnaik calls "new offering" and "new family" solutions.

Finally, there are Patnaik's "common" needs, which are the needs of most people—to be loved, respected, safe (Maslow again). These needs are the most general and the most difficult to satisfy, often needing what Patnaik calls larger "systemic solutions." Common needs also encourage the broadest range of concepts and cause the company to think most deeply about its products.

Patnaik's company combines approaches taken by product designers and social scientists not only to solve problems but also to correlate customer needs with company capability and strategy. The first level of needs can probably be solved soon and relatively cheaply, but competitors can easily follow (or even do better)—for example, by producing a better bicycle lock. The satisfaction of the second level of needs may lead the company to a more and perhaps preferable solution, often one that allows the company to vault over its competitors (for example, an alternate means of transportation). Satisfying the third level is even more difficult because these needs may have little to do with the company's past activities (for example, moving from bicycle locks to alternate transportation to getting good grades). But looking at third-level needs may help the company to think more broadly about its customers and business and lead to something the company might have advantage on because of its experience with college bicycle riders. Finally, common needs might simply be too generic for the organization to want to deal with, but are interesting to think about in the company context for possible future directions.

Satisfying increasingly broadly defined needs may be more difficult, but it can result in a more stable business. Alternate bicycle security systems may appeal to more potential customers. Families of products offer the opportunity of attracting still more customers, building a more powerful brand, building synthesis between products, and surviving individual product failures. Systems solutions promote the sales of products that are compatible with each other and allow even more capability when combined. The product balance of any company is a critical strategic decision, and decisions on defining this balance can be aided by a good map of present and potential future customer needs considered at various levels. A company product strategy and a good knowledge of customer needs are invaluable to designers defining products for the company.

Chapter 6 *Thought Problem*

Choose two products that fulfill your needs and please you emotionally and two that do neither. Do not feel restricted to products you own, although obviously you need to be familiar with them. Why do you consider each successful or not as far as emotions and needs are concerned? See if you can get into an argument with someone who feels differently about them. Why the difference?

Problems and Tactics Table: Emotions

Problems	Tactics
Engineers, businesspeople, managers, not comfortable in dealing with emotions	Do more customer testing; talk about emotions with colleagues, friends, and family
Inadequate language to talk about emotions	Study psychology, read about emotions
Inconsistency between emotional and "logical" responses to products	Experiment; try designing to evoke various illogical emotional responses
Complexity and subtlety of emotions	Become fascinated with emotion—it is one of the most important and motivating characteristics of *Homo sapiens*

Aesthetics, Elegance, and Sophistication

Wisdom Through Experience

This chapter deals with aesthetics—certain sensory signals, or combinations of them, that give humans unusual satisfaction through wonderful images, smells, sounds, feels, and tastes. The source may be a scenic view, a plant, an animal, or an object. We retain the pleasure our primitive ancestors derived from sensing aspects of nature that served them well—the sound of clear, sparkling streams, the feel of soft fur, the smell and color of ripe fruit, the look of verdant landscapes. We love to gaze at the jungle, the tall tree and the game animal, smell the flowers, and experience the first days of spring and the first rainfall of the season. We consider such sensory inputs and experiences beautiful.

We also find beauty, often long lasting, in our own human works: painting, sculpture, printmaking, architecture, dance, music, and theater. Any large museum is a demonstration of that beauty, as is any well-illustrated book about the Italian Renaissance. Much that is written about aesthetics focuses on art, which is not surprising since art focuses upon aesthetics and has always attracted highly intellectual people who are fond of thinking and writing.

We know from cave and rock paintings that art is a human activity at least 40,000 years old. We also know about the art and architecture of the Egyptians, the Greeks, and the Romans, and the exquisite siting of ruins such as Machu Picchu and Casa Grande. But how about human-made objects other than buildings and monuments? Ruins from ancient cultures show that tools, clothing, jewelry, utensils, pottery, and other products have been not only decorated but also surprisingly finely made for many thousand years. Such items were not easy to make in ancient days, so the detail and thought added beyond the purely functional is particularly noteworthy. Interestingly enough, such products are often found in the same museums as art. It is probable that the appreciation of, and need for, beauty has been with us as long as our species has existed—although in the Stone Age it is unlikely people took art history courses and bought knockoffs of Louis Vuitton bags.

But how about the products of industry? Happily, many people also find beauty in them, but there could, and should, be more. Unlike in the arts, however, there are a myriad of factors competing with aesthetic considerations in products, many of them receiving greater attention because of short-term considerations and of the particular sensitivities, or lack of same, of the people involved in designing and producing them. The majority of people involved in defining and producing these articles are not nearly as interested in aesthetics as are artists. I was told once, by a highly placed business executive, that industry was about making money, not beauty. I asked him whether making beauty was perhaps a way to make money. Already he did not like the direction of the conversation and changed the subject.

When I was an engineering major at Caltech, I spent considerable time defending myself, and my fellow students, from the stereotype that we were narrow nerds with few interests outside of science and technology. After all, we took courses in the humanities and social sciences as well. I was interested in art and thought I knew quite a bit about it, and I was a pretty fair musician. If I tried hard, I could usually convince the women I dated to admit I had some grasp of things aesthetic, but I could never escape the "for an engineer" phrase tacked to the end. After working a couple of years as an engineer surrounded by the same stereotype, I enrolled in UCLA as an art student and immediately had my eyes opened. I had never been surrounded by people who were both personally and professionally entirely committed to aesthetic considerations. I had to work hard to reach the lower rungs of the ladder, and it was obvious to me that I would never make the top. After a year, I returned to engineering due to a shortage of money, but it was probably the most valuable year I have ever spent in school. Although I did not get on a path that would lead me to being an artist, I feel that I gained a much better understanding of the world of aesthetics. Even though it took a year of hard work and long hours, the good news was that I realized I was pretty good at it, "for an engineer."

Aesthetics and Industrial Products

Most people involved in the design and production of industrial products do not even spend a year becoming sensitive to, and comfortable with, aesthetic considerations. I remember hearing a talk by a famous industrial designer in which he claimed that one of his greatest problems was that people such as the top executives of a client company, members of the board, and their respective spouses would feel that their expertise in matters such as color and form was as good as, or sometimes better than, that of the highly trained and experienced designers in his firm. I felt his pain. Making good aesthetic decisions in the process of designing and manufacturing products requires training, experience, and sensitivity. The implementation of these decisions requires battling influential people who seem to consider themselves experts in aesthetics. What is the answer to this problem? Managers and engineers in companies must become more sensitive to aesthetic concerns.

There are many factors involved in the aesthetics of an industrial product—line, form, color, texture, weight, as well as those more unique to industry such as use of fasteners, handling of joints, and results of manufacturing (for example, draft and flashing from casting or weld beads). There are various principles of design used in art. Painters are concerned with scale, proportion, balance, unity, emphasis, contrast, rhythm, and variety. Sculptors worry about whether their work appears interesting and three-dimensional from any viewpoint (articulation). Such things may or may not apply to the design of a product, but the designer should certainly keep them in mind as all of them trigger emotional response and are an interesting checklist when thinking about appearance. Of course, aesthetic considerations are not limited to appearance, so feel, smell, sound, and in the case of food products, taste, are equally important considerations with their own elements and principles. Many of these aesthetics can be applied to industrial products.

As far as aesthetic considerations are concerned, however, product designers are more constrained than artists are. Artists, assuming they are able to earn an adequate income, are free to express themselves as they desire. Should they be independently wealthy and of high confidence, they can spend their lives producing works that are unappreciated by others. This is not the case of product designers who are limited to what can be manufactured and what can be sold. While commercial artists, who are necessarily customer oriented, are looked down upon by studio artists, product designers who do not have a good sense of the market are looked down upon by business.

Organizations' product designers work under constraints from marketing, the product sector the firm occupies, the traditions of the organization, and the opinions of everyone from the chairman of the board to the workers on the production line. Rather than sell their final work, they must sell their initial concept, in which it is hard to include aesthetic factors. It is easier to quantify an initial cost saving by ignoring aesthetics than a long-term profit that might result from a more beautiful product. So when companies see a potential profit problem, they tend to cut short-term costs even when that may hurt improvement of the present product or the quality of the next generation of products. Although consulting designers are usually hired to augment the abilities within a company, they too are constrained by those who hire them. While most artists operate as individuals and are constrained mainly by their artistic abilities and their capability to raise sufficient funding, most designers of products are influenced by the culture and constraints of an organization and the society in which they operate.

Constraints on product designers also occur because products tend to lose diversity over time. Before the Industrial Revolution and mass manufacturing, individually made products revealed much more of the maker and offered the purchaser the opportunity to select something that would resonate with his or her own values. This diversity is certainly still the case with contemporary products exhibiting rough craftsmanship and free craftsmanship (as discussed in Chapter 5). If you want a split-rail fence for your maple sugar farm in New Hampshire, you know that if you select a fence maker based on the maker's past production, you will end up with something that pleases you. If you buy a piece of hand-made furniture, you know that no other piece of furniture will be quite the same and that it reflects both the taste of the maker and your own taste. You can have as much choice of products as you do of individual makers, but the number of industries producing a given product tends to decrease over time.

New technologies are often accompanied by an explosion of small companies applying them to products. As time goes on, some companies flourish, absorbing others and growing, and others die. Eventually only a few may exist. In 1908, there were 253 U.S. companies that manufactured automobiles in the United States. By 1929, there were 44.[1] Now there are three big ones and a few small ones. If you go to a show of "brass" cars (cars with brass fittings made in the early 20th century), there is great aesthetic diversity due to the large number of manufacturers and the fact that more components are exposed, rather than being enclosed in a sleek body. If you look at a parking lot these days, automobiles have converged to a few basic models. As the number of companies producing a particular product shrinks, and as the remaining companies grow, there is an obvious incentive on the part of the remaining companies to produce products that please an increasingly large number of people. This aim to please places increasingly severe constraint upon the product designer. A product that is "acceptable to everyone" may be boring for one individual.

Producing industrial products is also complicated by the necessity to be aware of, and react to, changes in technology and in fad and fashion, either of which can obsolete a product, sometimes rapidly. Fad and fashion are a bit more insidious, especially in the area of consumer products, because people in industry tend to forget how fickle people are. We humans like comfortable change. If the change is too abrupt we are uncomfortable with it, but if there is no change, we become bored. Just as our senses are most sensitive to changing inputs, we are excited by the new and different. We also like to be associated with a peer group that we admire and to which we belong. One way that we can comfortably accommodate to change is if our peer group, culture, or society changes with us. Whatever is presently "in" is called fashionable—but fashion changes.

Consumer products are subject to change, whether clothes, cars, food, or whatever. Around Stanford it is now fashionable to drive a Prius, wear black clothes, and shop at the farmer's market—not a very pleasing development to Chrysler, makers of tartan plaids, or Safeway stores. The manufacturers of these "in" items will change, but so will the culture of the area. Producers of products are aware of this fact and place great effort into trying to predict change and, as far as possible, to influence the future through good advertising and market research. But the future will continue to be uncertain with changing fads. I looked through some old photographs that included me at different times and was reminded that I had worn Levi pants with three-inch cuffs, suede shoes, charcoal and pink shirts, mirrored Ray-Bans, and bell-bottomed pants at various times in my life (not all at once). I was also reminded that automobiles used to be lowered in the back rather than in the front. Fads can be seen clearly in diets and physical exercise, too. Carbohydrates and margarine were in a few years ago and are now out, and the convenient availability of tennis courts on the Stanford campus is a remnant of a short-lived tennis fad.

A Bit of Background on Industrial Design

If you come across an old wheel lock rifle or a 19th-century steam engine in a museum, you will probably notice that significant effort was spent on these products for reasons beyond their ability to perform their job. They are often impressively decorated with graphics, inlay, intricate castings, and polished metals. It doesn't take a student of design to realize that something has changed in product design and development since that time, because such objects are now in the province of collectors rather than being available on the market. There is a definite machine aesthetic that has evolved throughout the world. To oversimplify a complicated story, the world fell in love with machinery, industry discovered ways to decrease the cost of machinery by simplifying forms and materials, and, at the same time, a sizeable number of strong and influential people aesthetically rationalized the result.

One of the first major figures in industrial design was Peter Behrens, who was initially hired by a large German electrical company (AEG) as "artistic adviser" and was committed to integrate art with mass production. He designed products that applied the cerebral concepts of German Modernism to AEG products, developed consistent company graphics, designed a modernistic factory featuring concrete and exposed steel, and was a founding member of the German Werkbund (1907–1934, reestablished in 1950), a national designer's organization formed to help Germany's economic competitiveness. The Werkbund became an influential forum for discussing issues such as the role of craftsmanship in industry, the role of beauty in commonplace objects, and to what extent forms could and should be determined by function.

One of the better-known institutions dedicated to this design approach was the Bauhaus, founded by Walter Gropius (another Werkbund founder) and begun in 1919 in Weimar, Germany. The Bauhaus included on its faculty such influential people as Behrens, Ludwig Mies van der Rohe, Marcel Breuer, László Moholy-Nagy, Wassily Kandinsky, Josef Albers, and Paul Klee. At the time of its establishment, German Modernism was strongly influencing German art, and the institution saw its mission as not only supporting this philosophy but also carrying it beyond the arts to fields such as architecture and industrial product design. Eventually the resulting emphasis on simplified, rationally and functionally determined forms unburdened by ornamentation and the reconciliation of art and industry were carried throughout the world and were to greatly affect design. In architecture these ideas gave birth to the severe forms of the so-called international style, and in product design they gave birth to many aesthetic values that were to define industrial design up to and including the present.

Although the concept of allowing form to be dictated by function was not originated by the Bauhaus, it was certainly emphasized in its teachings. The concept was also exported through staff and students of the Bauhaus who either were citizens of other countries or immigrated to them. In the 1920s and 1930s, the profession of industrial design came of age in the United States, led by people such as Henry Dreyfuss, Raymond Loewy, and Walter Dorwin Teague, all of whom had been influenced by this approach. They tended to have backgrounds in fields where visual aesthetics were important (stage design, architecture) and were equipped with personalities that allowed them to mix easily with managers of manufacturing enterprises. They were to set up large consulting offices and acquire the responsibility for the design of many products produced in great numbers by the influential companies of the day. They capitalized on the desire of customers to have "modern" products, the need for more attention to be paid to human fit, and the clumsiness of companies of that era with aesthetic concerns.

We in the Western world (and more and more all of the world) are the inheritors of this design tradition, as can be seen from comparing modern products with those designed in the period before the Bauhaus. Decoration for decoration's sake was to disappear, and forms were to become sleeker, simpler, and more determined by function. However, there is a downside to this extreme emphasis on technical function. Think of computers, automobiles, and kitchen appliances. They are certainly simpler and more consistent with manufacturing than those of the early 20th century, and their forms have a certain sleek beauty, but are they as interesting? When I rent cars, I am always amazed at the similarity of the products of various manufacturers. How about some variety? I know a number of people who collect, restore, and drive antique cars. Modern cars are far better from a performance standpoint. But there was something going on aesthetically in the older cars that is appealing to us moderns, and there is something satisfying now about driving a car that has some uniqueness. I have a 1910 steam tractor in my backyard and a late-19th-century pedal-powered jigsaw in my living room, and they are both wonderful collections of swirling castings, gears, pulleys, belts, and other machine elements, and in the case of the steam engine, pipes and valves. They are the antithesis of Bauhaus design, but visitors always want to play with them rather than with our modern cars.

Product simplification and design standardization even sometimes cause similarities between very different products because of the role of fads and fashions in design. In the 1930s, there was a great love affair with streamlining, at that time a teardrop shape that moved through air or water with little drag. This form showed up not only on airplanes and high-speed cars but also on many consumer goods. Looking at books on the history of design, it is difficult to avoid a pencil sharpener designed in the Loewy office that looks like it could move through the air at a very high speed. Nineteen fifties appliances were well known for their color palette, with avocado green one of the most popular. At the same time, automobiles went first to two-tone and then to three, sometimes explained as a release from wartime olive drab. Now there are a few standard colors on vehicles, and the same on appliances—no three-tone or avocado. The same is true of digital electronic devices. Washers and dryers tend to look the same and refrigerators, stoves, and dishwashers have a family resemblance even though their functions are different. When traveling, the problem of identifying your bag on the carousel is increased by the fact that the vast majority of suitcases are black and similarly shaped. Parties of designers feature people in black clothing, just as the streets of financial sections of cities are filled with black raincoats during wet weather.

An assignment that I often used to give students required them to go buy two of some low-cost product and improve the aesthetics of one according to some criteria. They would then bring both the original and the improved versions to class and we would discuss the results. Engineering students would typically improve their product by eliminating details that had nothing to do with technical function, simplifying the form, removing paints and platings that masked the identity of the materials, and polishing the overall result. Occasionally a student, usually majoring in the visual arts, would modify the product by adding details and surface treatments and changing the form to be more interesting in its own right. Such changes caused consternation on the part of the other students, who were not only unable to easily evaluate the result but also not sure that it was acceptable. This situation was particularly confusing if the students were attracted to the modified product even though the modifications were not consistent with technical function. A more personal example is that my wife loves our sleekly modernist Saarinen table and "egg" chairs. But she also likes her more garish bottle opener that features the Stanford University Band playing "All Right Now" when the opener is used.

It is easy to do a bad job of modernist design, but difficult to do a good one. You must evoke the hoped-for emotional response with a minimalist approach. Simple forms can be clumsy and uninteresting. Surface finish is critical in such designs because of their scarcity of detail. A box with square corners, for example, can be pretty boring. If the corners are drastically rounded, however, the box may turn into a lump. So what is the best radius for a corner? People respond strongly to color, and as you know from selecting colors on your computer, there are a lot of them. By varying hue, value, and chroma, you can produce what seems like an infinite number of colors. So how do you pick the best color? At the least, you must experiment with a large number of them, though it is even better to spend time and effort becoming more "expert" at color. And how about forms that although functional, go beyond what is necessary, such as Philippe Starck's tarantula-like orange juicer? A good solution, of course, is to find an expert to do such things. But how do you know how to pick an expert or whether to believe that expert? The only answer I know is to climb partway up the ladder oneself.

Elegance and Sophistication

When dealing with aesthetics, especially in the world of fine arts, one comes upon words that have a particular meaning in the field being discussed. Some of these words are specific to the nature of the work, such as the Italian term *chiaroscuro* (modeling by use of light and dark) and *painterly* (referring to the way paint is applied). But others are more general, such as *subtle* (don't use paint straight out of the tube), *interesting* (I don't know quite what to think about it, but it may be terrific), *marvelous* (I like it lots), *elegant*, and *sophisticated*. Let us discuss the last two, since they not only apply to products but also imply a high level of quality.

When I was an undergraduate student at Caltech, I noticed the word *elegance* used a great deal. "What an elegant proof." "What an elegant mechanism." "What an elegant experiment." A mathematics professor, in an informal moment, confided to us that he had chosen his career because he was addicted to elegance. What did all this mean? People would try to tell us: "Precision, neatness, and simplicity" (*Webster's Third New International Dictionary*). "The most with the least." "Technical sweetness." We had a vague idea. But, after all, we were undergraduates and had not been admitted to the inner sanctum. Elegance, when used in a scientific or engineering context, seemed to have to do with efficiency, insight, cleanliness; with making the most with the least. An elegant mechanism was one with no extra parts, in which each piece did its job optimally. An elegant solution to a problem was both simple and ingenious. Unfortunately, since undergraduates spend their time swamped with huge quantities of relatively pedestrian problems in textbooks, we had little chance of personally coming to appreciate the beauty of doing original work really well.

At Caltech we also talked about sophistication and came up with two very different meanings. On the technical side, sophistication had to do with things that are highly complex and developed. "Modern accelerators are incredibly sophisticated compared to the first ones." "Spacecraft are extremely sophisticated compared to automobiles." "I enjoy teaching graduate students because they are more sophisticated." Of course, being in college, we also were concerned with increasing our personal sophistication—another flavor of the word that seemed to have to do with reading certain books, becoming conversant with certain issues, becoming less clumsy at interacting with the opposite sex, learning to drink, and generally becoming more worldly and urbane.

Later, when I was an art student at UCLA, I once again heard the word *elegance* used a great deal. At times it implied simplicity, precision, and neatness, as in "What an elegant little dress," referring to the newest, sleekest, simplest frock (an application of the principle of "the most with the least"). "What an elegant portrayal of anger" might refer to a single bold stroke of strong color in a painting. However, in art school, another definition of *elegance* was often used. "What an elegant use of colors" could be applied to a complex painting with a large variety of restrained hues. "What an elegant chair" might refer to one that was richly decorated. "What an elegant passage" could be a segment of music that was evocative of an 18th-century drawing room and certainly not "simple." I also heard the word *sophistication* being used widely and more specifically. "That is an extraordinarily sophisticated sculpture for your level of training" or "I enjoy Rauschenberg because of his sophistication."

The problem in verbally pinning down words having to do with aesthetics is that the language is inadequate when it comes to describing sensory experience. The words *elegance* and *sophistication* mean different things to different people and are subtly interlinked. That becomes clear if you look through dictionaries to find the formal meaning of the words, as you will find multiple meanings. Let us use the *Webster's New World College Dictionary* as an example.[2] (There is a colloquial meaning of *elegance* that we will not consider here, although I like it because *elegance* was one of my father's favorite words. In this usage, *elegant* simply means excellent—as in "This is sure an elegant day," or "This pie is elegant.")

There are three main groups of words in the usual definitions of *elegant*. One seems to refer to people and two to products:

People
E-1 "Characterized by a sense of propriety or refinement;
impressively fastidious in manners and taste."

Products
E-2 "Dignified richness and grace; luxurious or opulent in a
restrained, tasteful manner."
E-3 "Marked by concision, incisiveness, and ingenuity;
cleverly apt and simple."

(Aha. E-2 must refer to Louis XIV chairs and E-3 to mechanisms.)

The word *sophisticated* continues the confusion because here again we find a single word being defined in two ways, one applying more to people and one to products.

People
S-1 "Not simple, artless, or naive. Urbane, worldly-wise,
knowledgeable, perceptive, subtle."

Products

S-2 "Highly complex, refined, or developed, or characterized by advanced form, technique, etc. Designed for or appealing to sophisticated people."

(Aha again. S-2 must apply to spacecraft and Rauschenberg paintings.)

Should these words apply to industrial products and the people who design them? The E-3 type of elegance is to me universal. Not only does the definition point toward economy and reliability, but I believe that everyone admires this type of elegance, whether they know why they do or not. Type E-2 elegance is a must in so-called luxury products—the Bentley, high-end home-theater components, and expensive furniture. E-2 obviously applies less in products such as motocross motorcycles, backhoes, and gopher traps. As far as sophistication is concerned, definition S-2 should apply to any complex high-performance product.

How about the people concerned with designing and producing good products? Should they be both elegant (E-1, "a sense of propriety or refinement; impressively fastidious in manners and taste") and sophisticated (S-1, "urbane, worldly-wise, knowledgeable, perceptive, subtle")? Some of these characteristics are universally necessary ("knowledgeable" and "perceptive"), while others are less so ("impressively fastidious in manners"). It would indeed be impressive to see a product-based organization staffed with people with all of these characteristics. In an organization that produces products intended for customers with these characteristics, the people in the organization must at least be able to understand and value all of these characteristics, even if they do not possess them.

Many areas of design include a high percentage of highly sophisticated people, and it is necessary to be somewhat sophisticated in order to interact with them in a productive manner.

You do not have to be Beethoven to appreciate his quartets, but you probably have to listen to a good bit of music, and perhaps know something about music, to truly enjoy them. The people I know who are not professional musicians and love string quartet music the most are full-time professionals in fields other than music who are members of amateur string quartets. They have no intention of performing on the stage. They play for their own enjoyment and to become better able to extract pleasure from listening to professionals.

Should CEOs of companies design products as a hobby in order to become more familiar with the process and better utilize the professionals at their disposal? Unfortunately, most managers focus on short-term goals and want to please customers today, not challenge and stimulate them. Also, due to the criteria used to select and promote executives in industry, many of the most influential people in manufacturing organizations are both highly opinionated and much less sophisticated than those who actually spend their time with products. I have known of many instances where, in my humble opinion, company executives with product responsibility have given strong and poorly advised input to the design of products. In fact, I have known people with ultimate responsibility for design who, once again in my opinion, had very little in the way of design sophistication.

Products please us by satisfying certain criteria in our mind. Some of these seem innate, such as pleasure from things that are precise, neat, and simple, and therefore probably efficient and dependable. Others are learned, such as our appreciation of a fine piano, automobile, or piece of flatware. Elegance and sophistication are important to us, whether their literal meanings are confusing or not. Designers and producers must be sophisticated in design to produce elegant and sophisticated products, though I am convinced that such products are appreciated by all of us, even if we are not sophisticated about design. Sophistication in doing design requires training, exposure, and sensitivity. We are not likely to design an elegant mechanism if we do not know what we are striving for. When people ask me how one learns to design elegant and sophisticated products, my response is that they must love such products and wallow in them.

As an example of increasing appreciation of elegance and sophistication through exposure, think of music. Typically the music that appeals to younger listeners has repetitive and straightforward rhythms, harmonies, and melodies. Think of childhood standards such as "Twinkle, Twinkle, Little Star" and "Jingle Bells." As listeners age, their tastes change. The music that attracts adolescents usually speaks to their problems and, incidentally, is happily alienating to other age groups. It is fascinating to watch subtle variations in rock music allowing high school students to refer to the "in" rock of two years ago as passé, even though it all sounds identical to older people. At a later age, although some people seem to have a universal love of music, most people somewhat specialize in that they like a particular genre (jazz, classical, rock) more than others. Although they may retain an appreciation for all types of music, they will become more deeply sophisticated in at least one genre. Those who have a special fondness for classical music will initially like Tchaikovsky, discover Dvorak, move to Beethoven and Mozart, at some point begin appreciating quartets and trios, and add Stravinsky, Schoenberg, Mahler, and more contemporary and experimental sounds. However, their tastes will also broaden. Eventually classical music buffs may increasingly turn to jazz, show tunes, folk music, maybe even back to rock. They will also reappreciate Tchaikovsky.

The same can be said for jazz fans, who after beginning with Dixieland and moving through various Latin forms, swing, bebop, and more abstract improvisational sounds may embrace classical, pop, and Dixieland again. The directions that people take as they become increasingly exposed to and knowledgeable of music are surprisingly consistent—this is why music appreciation courses are possible. This consistence is a large boon to the music business. We also have no trouble correlating these directions with increased sophistication. The same is true of the other arts. Painting begins with photographic realism, proceeds through impressionism, expressionism, abstraction, and finally perhaps an appreciation of all forms. Art history courses help the process.

The same situation is, of course, true of designers of products. Designers and users develop increasing sophistication through practice and usage. Think of bicycles. Those who love bicycles learn through exposure, knowledge, and guidance to appreciate the subtleties of construction, mechanism, balance, and handling that make up an outstanding bicycle. Good designers of bicycles, who are usually also users, are hopefully even more sophisticated.

Product Form and Function

Simple forms that have evolved through usage often become extremely elegant because the unnecessary has been stripped away over time—wooden airplane propellers are examples. They are extremely functional and technically quite sophisticated, but their form is beautiful and without distractions and awkward transitions. A well-known sculpture is *Bird in Space* by Constantin Brancusi and is on display at the New York Metropolitan Museum of Art. If you view it, you will hear other viewers remark both about its similarity to an airplane propeller blade and upon its elegance.

The same is often true of products that require close contact with people. An ax handle is one example. A simple cane is another. I have a framed toilet seat in my office, and people who have never been there often ask me why (or at least probably wonder) when first entering the room. The answer is that if we didn't know what it was, we would have to agree that a toilet seat has an extremely elegant form—it is an exquisite collection of subtle curves and variations. Other products are elegant because of the direction design has taken in the company. Apple products are an example. Fashionable high-heeled shoes are another. Some products are elegant because performance requirements cause them to be so, such as the racing bicycle or the high-speed aircraft.

Abstract lines and forms can have this type of minimalist elegance independent of function. Lines with varying curvature tend to be more elegant than lines with constant curvature. Forms with slight curvature tend to be more elegant than forms with none. And then there are mechanisms. Optimally designed mechanisms for aerospace applications in which weight is critical are normally more elegant than those in agricultural applications in which it is not. Mechanisms that have fewer parts, and in which the functions and articulations are clear to the observer, tend to be more elegant than Rube Goldberg devices. Engineers, managers, and others in industry are relatively comfortable with this "most-with-the-least" type of elegance (E-3), although they may not have the sensitivity or the skills to produce it. However, they often overlook it in their eagerness to add physical function, to implement a feature cheaply, or to come up with a unique solution in a product. Devices such as the combination tool—the same ones I mentioned my mother bought me as a child—that combine a screwdriver, saw, pliers, bottle opener, scissors, and whatever else—may be useful, but they are usually not elegant, aside from the venerable Swiss Army knife, which seems to be able to combine everything up to running water in a sleek form. The same is true with most things suffering from the concept of "feature creep," discussed in Chapter 3, in which increased function leads to a type of complexity.

In the case of a complicated system, adding elegant components can decrease the elegance of the whole. I remember one great argument from my past over the use of localized damping to solve a structural dynamic problem. The situation had to do with a spacecraft that was being developed on a tight schedule (planets do not wait for you) and with extremely specific weight constraints. Rocket launches subject the payload to very high vibration levels. When the prototype spacecraft was subjected to simulated launch vibration during developmental testing, a few of the components that were mounted on the basic structure bounced around unacceptably. One solution to this problem would have been to redesign, rebuild, and requalify the structure, but there was not adequate time to do so.

The solution that was proposed was not to change the structure but rather to attach lightweight dampers between the main spacecraft structure and the pertinent components. To the engineers responsible for the bouncing components (I was one), this was an elegant solution because the problem was solved within minimal time and cost. To the structural engineers, it was a most inelegant solution, because the structure alone should have been able to handle the problem without the addition of these extraneous parts. In the engineering world, fixes such as this are sometimes disapprovingly referred to as "Band-Aids" or "kluges," and they are seen by those responsible for getting a product to work as efficient and clever, but by others as a testimony to a lousy design: efficient to some but not to others—elegance to some and ugliness to others.

Elegance of an initially complex product usually improves as it goes through various iterations to increase ease of use and reliability and decrease cost. An obvious demonstration of this progression is in the human interface of software. I have been writing these chapters with the help of Microsoft Word, a widely used word-processing program. I have been using Word through many editions, both for PCs and Macs, and in each release, many features are better designed than in the previous. For instance, this current release has more screen icons for commonly used commands, allowing me to escape iterating back through the menu commands. But unfortunately, this increasing simplicity of use (user-friendliness) is sometimes obscured by the provision of additional capability, and this, as I just mentioned, is a legitimate concern. Most of my friends do not need the additional options contained in word-processing programs and occasionally yearn for a simpler program. In fact, several of them refuse to move from very early releases for this reason. However, even they realize that this software is commonly used throughout many professions and that many users find the increased capability highly valuable.

The trade-off between elegance and complexity in cases such as Microsoft Word is a difficult one, since, as I previously mentioned, we all seem to like features and capability that we do not use, even though it may complicate the product. For example, I have a Canon PowerShot camera and a Nikon single-lens reflex (SLR) camera. Which is the more elegant? For taking snapshots, the PowerShot would get my vote. However, the Nikon has many more capabilities (it lets me take pictures fully automatically or manually control combinations of speed, aperture, and focus, carries a wide variety of lenses, and offers the convenience of through-the-lens viewing). The Nikon is more flexible and capable of taking excellent pictures in situations where the PowerShot would have trouble. Unfortunately, I use the Nikon camera so seldom that I often have to relearn what some of its functions do and therefore tend to lose sight of how well it does its complicated job. Both cameras are elegant for their particular purpose. I also have an old Pentax film camera—an SLR I used years ago. Occasionally I take shots with it for old time's sake and must admit I love it a lot. That feeling is obviously an emotional response stemming from my long acquaintance with the camera and the fact that I used it when I was a much more serious photographer.

I can apply the word *elegance* to the Pentax in its art-school mean-ing—evoking past glories, even though they were mine.

Some Concerns on Today's Aesthetics

Looking at the history of product design, it is clear that the development of the machine aesthetic in this century has simplified life for those who create the products of industry. Most people in industry are more comfortable with function than what is now called decoration, and the rules of "modernism" are now well known. Through most of history, products have included some details purely for aesthetic pleasure. But now the word *decoration* has become an almost pejorative term, referring to modifications of form and surface treatments that are added to a product for aesthetic reasons but that do not improve the function. Are such things bad? Not if they do not impede function and if function is defined broadly, including bringing the user emotional pleasure and cultural satisfaction. For example, a more interesting shape for the vertical fin on an airplane might make the airplane more attractive (or in the case of a fighter more vicious looking) at no cost in performance or expense.

But the machine aesthetic requires attention to detail. Surface treatments are extremely important and must be given close attention. Finishes need to have integrity to them. For example, new items trying to look old do not quite work—consider antique furniture replicas with urethane finishes and new interpretations of 1920s limousines. Old things trying to look new also miss the mark, such as the overly restored gas pumps and crank telephones found in antique shows. I am also concerned that makers of industrial products are so comfortable with what I have called the machine aesthetic that they are not experimenting with future trends. Where are our postmodernist product designs?

Many well-known designers of the past (Frank Lloyd Wright, Battista Pininfarina, Elsa Schiaparelli, Raymond Loewy) became extremely sophisticated at design and were able to influence general trends. Henry Dreyfuss, for instance, had little faith in the design sophistication of consumers or businesspeople. He believed that products should be defined by the designer, who, after all, was primarily involved in attempts to define exceptional products. His offices still depended heavily on customer and client input and relied upon a large amount of user testing during the development of a product, but he believed that products should be as sophisticated as the customer would accept in order that customers might grow to appreciate them. Often, Dreyfuss's client companies (such as AT&T) had large market share, and the customers often did not have a lot of choice, and since Dreyfuss would typically acquire high prestige in the client company, his office had a great amount of influence.

Presently, many well-known designers (Philippe Starck, Frank Gehry, Bob Lutz, Stella McCartney, Burt Rutan, Ralph Lauren) are doing the same thing as Dreyfuss, but the situation has changed. These people can still influence companies because of their track record as visionaries and the proven demand for the products they design. Most products, however, are defined by less famous designers within a company, and marketing people and managers are highly involved in the process. Marketing has become a much stronger function and very good at ascertaining what the potential customer will buy. But just as marketing has difficulty judging response to an unprecedented product, it has trouble predicting customer reaction to radical aesthetics. Marketing approaches may win in the short term because the customer is likely to be immediately attracted to the product, but they may result in a long-term loss unless they can predict the future sophistication level of their customers and society overall.

Another concern I have is the increasing separation of those involved directly in the design and production of products and those who manage larger companies. The latter typically have backgrounds in finance, and their talents often lie in administration and organizational design and control. This experience may result in company directions that are not consistent with the processes of design and production as far as product quality is concerned. Ford did well when Donald Petersen was president. Petersen's background is in engineering, and he rose through the company in product divisions. He is a self-defined "car guy" who was head of the successful Taurus project before he became president and initiated the successful "Quality is Job 1" campaign.

Petersen's successors did not have as deep a background in product design and production, and Ford products seemed to languish after Petersen left the company. The same situation is true of Hewlett-Packard, a company that seems to do better at product quality and sales when headed by people who have a background in the making of good products. They lagged badly when Carly Fiorina, an impressive woman educated in the liberal arts and business and with a proven record in finance and sales, was president. Compared to most successful HP presidents, she was short in experience in the nuts and bolts of designing and producing good products. Sophistication requires that those who design and build products not only use them but also have a love for them. Boeing concluded an informal study a number of years ago to define the characteristics of their outstanding aircraft designers. It turned out that the key characteristic wasn't education, family background, upbringing, or anything like that. Rather it was love of airplanes.

Sophistication requires hands-on exposure not only to one's own products but also to those of one's competitors and all closely related products. A friend of mine some years ago, on becoming

CEO of a well-known and long-established maker of forklifts, found that all of the small forklifts used in the company were its own. That might seem logical were it not for the fact that the company was being badly beaten up in this niche by its competitors and benchmarking was the rage. To his credit, the new CEO soon had the plant equipped with examples of the competitors' forklifts. He should probably have gone one step more and brought examples of other brands and related machinery into the plant. Forklift makers could probably benefit from taking apart a Volkswagen Beetle and a contemporary industrial robot as well as reverse engineering competing products. But the CEO's attempt to increase the breadth of knowledge and experience of the company designers did not go over well with the board of directors, who were conservative long-timers convinced that the company made by far the best small forklifts in the world. (My friend is no longer with that company, and the company is no longer making small forklifts.)

Finally let me say again that I think, in general, engineering and business schools should do a better job with topics such as aesthetics, sophistication, and elegance. Students indirectly confront elegance and sophistication in Ph.D. research. By dipping their toes into the depths of intellectual specialization, they are given an opportunity to think about the difference between good research and bad. Their advisers have become appreciators of elegance and sophistication, and although they seldom directly discuss such issues, their feedback is often directed toward good methodology and insightful results. However, the poor B.S. and M.S. candidates get almost no opportunities to deal with questions having to do with good and bad. I was originally going to call the Stanford course this book draws from "The Meaning of Good" or "What Does Good Mean?" I chickened out, though, because the title would have been such a poor match for the engineering school mentality.

With some exceptions, engineering schools pay little attention to aesthetics in design, but generally focus on the engineering sciences or basic analytical techniques. As discussed in Chapter 2, students in engineering school tend to be there because of their past performance in science and math courses. Their motivation may be love of technology, but admission neither requires this love nor measures for it. As a result, many of our students are more interested in the process than the results and more interested in optimization than in the actual product.

When I was in college, most of my student colleagues were addicted to some class of product, whether cars, airplanes, audio equipment, explosives, sailboats, submarines, quarry trucks, or whatever. This is no longer necessarily the case. Some students have a product passion (more likely toward computers and bicycles than cars or airplanes). However, many simply like mathematics and science and are looking for a well-paying job leading toward management or a job in a nice place until they go to business school. Where and when are they going to learn about the value of beauty and how to create it or manage the process that creates it?

Chapter 7 *Thought Problem*

Three products this time!

Choose a product that you think is simply beautiful and one that you think is unbelievably repulsive. Choose a third product that you believe to be extremely elegant.

Why do you think one to be simply beautiful, one unbelievably repulsive, and one extremely elegant? Why do you think the repulsive one exists? Could it be improved? What would it take to improve it? Would it cost more? Can you think of a way to aesthetically improve the ugly one that would actually make it less costly to produce?

Problems and Tactics Table: Aesthetics, Elegance, and Sophistication

Problems	Tactics
Inadequate language to discuss and communicate issues having to do with beauty, elegance, and sophistication	Wallow in elegant, sophisticated, beautiful products and spend lots of time with people who make them; take art classes; go to museums and read books about design
Frontier, macho culture values	Realize finite resources and increased population will not allow them to come back—much frontier lore is myth, anyway
Inability to recognize and appreciate beauty, elegance, and sophistication	Practice and try to help others do so; discuss products with other people; analyze why some products please more than others
Possible imagined conflict with maximizing sales and profit	Talk about this issue more within the company, especially top management; aesthetics, elegance, and sophistication should result in increased sales and profit

CHAPTER

Symbolism and Cultural Values

Who Are We?

A symbol is something specific that typically stands for something more abstract. Examples might be the smiley face (happiness), the Hells Angels motorcycle patch (outlaw), the dove (peace), the diagonal bar ("do not"), or the written word. The products of industry are also symbolic. They are specific, and rightly or wrongly, we assume that they convey a message about the owner. Consider what products such as the Chevrolet Corvette, the Birkenstock sandal, the erectile dysfunction pill, the skateboard, the espresso machine, and the assault rifle say to us about their owners. Rightly or wrongly, I assume that people I see in a grocery store who bring their own bags to take their purchases home are politically liberal, sensitive to the environment, and probably neither go deer hunting nor drive a Hummer. I suggest that people who drive Volvo station wagons have a different attitude toward visceral experiences than those who drive Kawasaki Hayabusas. People shopping in REI probably like the out-of-doors and are not eligible for food stamps. Those who have neither inherited nor married money and own a personal jet probably have been quite successful in their field. People wearing highly used clothes and pushing shopping carts full of discarded objects likely do not own large estates.

The symbolism associated with individual products is partly historical, partly a function of the role they play, and partly a function of conscious effort by the producers and distributors. Some products have historically been associated with certain lifestyles. Rolls-Royces, yachts, purebred horses, and dazzling diamond jewelry have always been associated with the wealthy and their activities while scythes, plows, hammers, and, later, lunch boxes, boots, hard hats, and banged-up pickups have typically been associated with members of the working class and their travails. Products such as suits of armor, swords, assault rifles, and tanks symbolize war and violence, and strollers and baby bottles symbolize domesticity.

But aside from symbolism through history and usage, we consciously create symbolism through actions including advertising and brand building. Turn on your television or pick up a magazine and look closely at advertisements. Ads often attempt to portray a specific lifestyle by associating the product with sex appeal (clothing, cosmetics), health (pharmaceuticals), excitement (cars, motorcycles), a happy family (home products), enhanced intelligence (courses, books), entertainment (televisions, travel), or other attractive results one might presumably get from buying and using the product. Companies spend great effort and large amounts of money building a brand that will carry their products to great success. One of BMW's slogans, "The Ultimate Driving Machine," is a good example. It is obviously valuable for BMW to have people associate its products with both luxury and excitement—a combination that is appealing to all of us. BMW's advertising budget for TV alone at the time of this writing is $160 million per year.[1] If you think that is a lot of money, in 2010 U.S. automobile companies and dealer associations spent more than $13 billion on advertising in the United States alone.[2] Much of this spending goes toward building and reinforcing the symbolism of their products.

The symbolism of products is important to us as people. Products proclaim our values and our associations. Armani suits tell the world we are successful and sophisticated, and we may wear them to work in the city with pride. Similarly, Carhartt work clothes show we work out of doors and admire well-made products, and we wear them on the farm or at a construction site with pride. We would not do nearly as well wearing an Armani suit on a construction site, or Carhartt clothes in a Wall Street office.

Producers must stay informed of their products' symbolic nature and ensure that it matches their customers well. This prospect was perhaps easier for the United States 50 or 60 years ago, when "Made in the USA" symbolized the best, import costs were higher, and fewer countries were "developed." But symbolism is changing over time. Because of globalization, more accessible travel, and modern communication, the United States has access to many more products, including ones that were previously symbolic of different cultural values than the ones the country had. Think of imported products that have become endemic to U.S. culture. In the United States there are espresso machines, the Camry, and chopsticks; wine from France, Australia, Chile, and most of the rest of the world is part of U.S. life; and the country has come to depend on "Made in China," although not without a bit of ambivalence. In return, in most of the world you can find jeans, Hollywood movies, and popular U.S. music.

Products, Symbolism, and Cultures

Products are not only symbolic of us as individuals but also of the groups with which we identify. Groups with common customs, attitudes, behaviors, institutions, and achievements are commonly referred to as cultures, and they come in many sizes. We sometimes speak of international culture (all of us) or regional cultures (Southeast Asian, North American, European, and so on). We talk about national (Chinese), state (Oaxacan), and city (Parisian) cultures and an endless number of subcultures. I sometimes refer to *tribes*, because the word connotes commonality of customs, interests, and a feel of belonging. Tribes can be of any size from large (Hutus, Navajos, evangelical Christians) to small (Rotary clubs, inner-city gangs, Stanford undergraduates).

Are there products that are symbolic to all humans? Certainly technology itself seems to qualify. The cell phone is becoming ubiquitous, as is the Internet. Humans are the only known life form that has technology as we define it, and our technology has always been a source of wonder and pride. Imagine the response to the wheel in a society where loads were carried on the back, the plow to people who had historically tilled fields with hand tools, the gun to those accustomed to fighting with swords, and the iron nail to those used to building with wooden pegs. Then, as now, the response was probably not immediate. New technologies are full of glitches and not only unappreciated but also resisted by experts in the old ways. When new technologies are fully born, however, we cannot help but be impressed. Think of the nuclear weapon, the transistor, the xerography process, television, the tomato harvester, GPS, computers, and cell phones. When these inventions were first presented to the public, they showed few indications of the role they would have in our lives. However, we who remember the world before them are now amazed at what they have accomplished, whether for good or evil.

Artists have always selected themes that are symbolic of the human condition, and technology has been well represented. In the cave paintings of 20,000 to 40,000 years ago, there are scenes of people using spears and bows and arrows to hunt animals (or each other). Anyone who has taken an art history course or visited a museum is aware of the products of technology that appear on Grecian or Roman pottery, in ancient friezes on buildings, on tapestries such as the Bayeux Tapestry, and in paintings. In the latter part of the 19th century and the early years of the 20th, technology and the machine were wonders.

The Crystal Palace, built for London's Great Exhibition of 1851, and the Eiffel Tower, finished in 1889, symbolized progress by glorifying technology. Painters often sought technical themes such as railroad stations and engines (for example, Turner's "Rain Steam and Speed," Monet's Gare Saint-Lazare railroad station paintings, Picasso's "Factory in Horta de Ebbo," Delaunay's "Eiffel Tower," and Russolo's "Dynamism of an Automobile"). The Cubists were obviously affected by technological forms in their attempt to reduce their subject matter to a simple geometry. Painters such as Duchamp and Balla attempted to deal with motion in a manner similar to the camera, and Mondrian and Stella were fascinated with industrial and architectural forms. David Smith, Bruce Beasley, Jean Tinguely, and other sculptors have adopted industrial processes and materials for their work. And architects such as Renzo Piano, who designed the Centre Pompidou in Paris, have long utilized industrial products and processes as design elements.

Depictions of technology, however, have not always been a love affair. After the horrors of World War I the Dadaists emerged, who in their destructive and cynical works showed no love of capitalized industrial society and no love of technology. Interestingly, elements of this aesthetic reappeared in the 1960s in the work of such painters as Andy Warhol and Robert Rauschenberg, perhaps in reaction to the post–World War II Cold War mentality and the universally unsatisfying Korean War. But in general, art has reflected the fondness we humans have for technology.

Products and National Cultures

Technology has been particularly important to the United States. Schoolroom history books extol the virtues of McCormick, Edison, and the Wright brothers. The United States was fiercely proud of the industrial capacity that swamped her enemies in World War II. The culture was fascinated by nuclear weapons and energy until many people (certainly not all) began to understand their potential for death and pollution. The country spent a large amount of money and effort to send people to the moon, and its inhabitants were extremely proud when the operation succeeded. There was little of use on the moon, and it was so remote that routine visits were not planned in the near future. Through the moon landing effort, however, technology was advanced, although the advances were bound to be oriented initially toward space travel rather than the commercial sector. The military was undoubtedly interested in the exploration of space and the moon because warriors have always liked high ground, and a quarter of a million miles is pretty high (especially for launching things toward Earth targets). The United States was also motivated to a great extent by technological competition with the Soviet Union and general technological chutzpah. Citizens loved being members of the country that placed the first man on the moon and were thrilled to realize that humans were no longer bound to Earth.

Downsides in efforts toward technological advancement existed as well, with deep disappointment caused by incidents such as the Challenger explosion and the previously mentioned Three Mile Island accident. The Challenger accident was tragic but not unexplainable. The space shuttle was an extremely advanced, complex machine, and its missions were dangerous. We in the United States did not have enough experience sending people into space that we could expect the same reliability as that of commercial air travel, and there are accidents even in that. To me, the wonder was that there had been no accidents before the Challenger. The incident let us down, though, as failures in our technology are conspicuous symbols of failures in our national ability. Three Mile Island elicited a somewhat similar experience and feeling even though no fatalities were involved. Once again, a complicated system was being operated by humans. Unfortunately, in this imperfect world, things break and people screw up. The event was a failure, however, in U.S. technology, and therefore a failure in our competency and in our self-identity.

As far as commercial products are concerned, a good example of national values can be seen in the "American" car. The United States is a large country, with good highways and widely spread snowfall in winter. Many U.S. cities have been built around the automobile. Los Angeles, for instance, although its freeways are often clogged, provides an amount of room for driving and parking that can be compared, say, to the size of Florence, Italy. The United States has also, as a petroleum producer, been committed to low-priced gasoline. As anyone who travels knows, gasoline prices in the United States have historically been approximately half what one finds in most other countries. The country's automobiles therefore evolved into large, heavy machines that could travel extremely rapidly for long distances with a large amount of interior comfort. Crossing the Texas panhandle is best done with air conditioning, compact discs, a cooler full of food and drinks, cruise control, and lots of room to stretch and change position. Our larger cars, however, are not as useful in cramped Japanese cities, on twisty Alpine roads, or in areas where gasoline is seven dollars a gallon.

There is still a market for large, fast, powerful cars loaded with luxuries in the United States and other large, sparsely populated countries such as Canada and Mexico, and they continue to sell as prestige products in countries such as China and even Germany. In the more populated U.S. areas, smaller, nimbler cars are now becoming more attractive. In order to stay in business,

U.S. automobile manufacturers have been forced to produce models that are more efficient, responsive, and economical.

House ownership has become symbolic in the United States as a major part of the "American Dream." Over time this dream has come to include not only a house, but one with a large number of accessories, and perhaps two or more cars. As a result of these values, the United States owns more cars per person than any other country in the world. We also find the anomaly of apartment dwellers in New York City owning cars, although the city is almost completely hostile to the ownership and operation of private automobiles.

Another example of U.S. national values and the role of symbolism can be seen in the case of weapons. The United States has a long tradition of gun ownership, symbolic of "rugged individualism," a frontier with "heroic gunfighters," and perceived success in wars. As a result, the citizens of this country buy, sell, and own a large number of guns. Certainly these weapons are not all made in the United States, but the popularity of guns such as the Colt Single Action Army revolver (known as the Peacemaker), the Winchester lever-action rifle, and the Colt .45-caliber automatic pistol attest to the U.S. love affair with such things, symbolic of a somewhat romanticized past.

Our urge in the United States to replace labor with machinery has led us to home appliances with a high level of automatic function, symbolic of our ability to beat the age-old burden of repetitive work. U.S. kitchens boast small special-purpose devices such as Cuisinarts, bread makers, toaster ovens, mixers, blenders, espresso machines, and rice cookers, in addition to standards such as stoves, refrigerators, and microwave ovens. (A friend of mine from England amuses himself while visiting friends in the United States by counting the control buttons in their houses.)

But the United States is certainly not the only nation in which technology and the technical products of industry are symbolic of national identity and culture. Think of the hallowed historic role of the tank in Russia (which contributed to defeat of the Germans in World War II) and Russia's present achievements in space; also the place of the sailing ship (which helped Britannia rule the seas) and the Battle of Britain fought by the Royal Air Force over England. Countries such as Germany, Switzerland, and Sweden rightfully have great pride in their ability to manufacture fine machinery. In my experience with students from Germany, France, and Japan, they seem to believe that products from their country are superior. Products are objects of national pride and reflect differences in national values in many parts of the world. This national bias also helps preserve diversity in products for all of us.

I recently ran across a paper that had accompanied a presentation on this topic given in one of my classes by a student group consisting of two graduate students from Ireland, one from Turkey, and one from Colorado. The U.S. student, as a minority, was forced to listen as his colleagues expressed disbelief at "bulky cars with fake wood on the inside" and "Californians wearing killer colors that look like they are battery powered" (a reference to clothes). Let me quote a paragraph from a paper the group wrote, since I find that we U.S. academics have been trained not to stereotype as glibly as students from different countries may:

Scandinavians regard design as the most important factor in quality, and so do the Italians. The difference in their ethic is that the Scandinavians must have products that work well both emotionally and technically, while the Italians don't care so much. Germans emphasize functionality and performance of products in a technical hard-engineered sense. Where Germans expect a car window to go up and down a million times between failures, Italians just want the window to work when they want to ogle a *bella donna*. The Dutch, an economically conservative society, like products to be cheap. Our group is divided on

English products. Some members believe they have a certain elegance, but no functionality or simplicity whatsoever, while others find British sports cars to be the epitome of masochistic high quality. The French are careless about environmental issues and their health, but they value products which enhance personal style.

Whether you agree or not, such stereotypes are widely held and probably have some basis on differing national values concerning industrial products.

As another example of national values expressed through technology, think of bathrooms and their fixtures in various countries: the large bathtubs of England, the water rooms of Malaysia with their troughs of water for cleansing and bathing, the bidets of France, the squat toilets and ofuros of Japan. I remember as a graduate student living in a house with four roommates, one of whom was from a country that used squat toilets. He persisted in squatting on the toilet seat with his shoes on because to him, a toilet seat used by countless others is not a pleasant thing for bodily contact. He also considered squat toilets more anatomically correct (he was right).

Products and Subcultures

I broached the topic of subcultures in nations, and cultures that cross national boundaries, when discussing the emotional impact from products that allow one to associate with a particular group of people. Generally speaking, people seem to have a propensity for aligning themselves with social groups, or subcultures, rather than considering themselves to be just one of the 7 billion members of the human race. These groups have the advantage of being more workable in size and of reinforcing one's own personal values. It is common to be a member of several such groups.

One can be an American, a Southern Californian, a mother of young children, an electrician, a member of the Young Republicans, and part of a bowling team. One of the things that distinguish the members of any subculture is preference for certain industrially produced objects over others. This concept is well known to designers and marketing people, and some products are designed specifically for a given group. Skateboards are designed for the young, for example, and reclining chairs for those who seek comfort rather than visual sophistication.

You can see identification with products clearly when you consider products popular with various age groups in the United States. Senior citizens do not often drive four-wheel-drive vehicles with giant tires. However, many of them covet retirement homes that would not appeal to people in their 40s. Teenagers do not want, or care about, new Buicks, matched cooking pots, or gasoline-powered hedge clippers. Most adults don't want "punk" clothing, unless it has been satisfactorily compromised and restated by fashion designers. Can you recall being a teenager and feeling contemptuous of all the boring stuff with which your parents complicated their life?

I still remember while in the air force being proud that all of my worldly possessions fit in the trunk of my Austin Healey. Now all my stuff expands to fill any available space. You may remember being a parent and not understanding why your kids did not seem to place any value in orderliness or why they were careless with things. At the same time, you may have noticed that your parents reached an age where they gave things away more easily and did not become as attached to possessions as you did. If you have now become one of society's elders and have accumulated a large number of things, you might find that other issues are more important. It is quite common for elders to "lighten up" at some point.

It is interesting to watch tastes change in the United States, especially as the baby boomers age. This group consists of some 75 million people who have had a tremendous impact on U.S.

consumption patterns. When they were kids, the country was very aware of toys, supportive of educational bonds, and obsessed with childbearing theory. When they became young adults, we had yuppies, an overflowing of discos and condominiums, and TV commercials and movies featuring people in their early 20s. Now we are seeing older models in clothing ads, older actresses and actors onstage, and greater emphasis on aging, health, and cosmetic surgery. The Cadillac is having a resurgence, and various types of retirement options, activities, and communities are much talked about.

Subcultures also can be defined by income and vocation. I can generalize on the consumption patterns of a number of people I know who have become well off by participating in the growth of Silicon Valley. Many of them are now presidents of companies and members or chairs of boards—so-called executives. As previously mentioned, some of them retain the trappings of the valley—jeans, bicycles, and so on—although their jeans and bicycles are more expensive than they once were. But many now tend toward the conservative taste of successful financial people: dark suits, German cars in muted colors, and perhaps a Porsche or Ferrari on the side. Their houses feature a large amount of white and marble and are meticulously ordered, not showing the ravages of use that mine does. The group tends not to own recreational vehicles, bargain furniture, or lamps made out of old kitchen pumps. They do, however, value and collect art. They tend to listen to music on new and high-quality equipment but not produce it on musical instruments. They eat and drink to moderation and are quite aware of their appearance and their health. There is a concern with apparent taste and decorum. They do not hide their wealth, but they do not flaunt it.

My friends are neither rich nor poor. Their houses are less formal than those mentioned and, in my opinion, more consistent with the business of living. There are books and magazines lying around. There are often signs of kids and grandkids. The TV sets are in plain sight and surrounded by adequate chairs and tables for beer and wine and munchies. Their furniture is more padded and less homogeneous and their housekeeping less meticulous. My wife and I are members of a subculture of people who seem to love offbeat things even though they take up space and "accomplish" very little. Even though we do not consider ourselves collectors, we constantly acquire such things. For example, we have an old dentist's chair in the living room simply because it is fun. Our grandchildren love to give each other rides on the chair, even though some of our older guests cringe at the sight of it. But such an item is a good companion to the antique rifles, jigsaw, hedge trimmer, carpet sweeper, gravel screens, water pump, smudging torches, lead pots, log saw, pathology microscope, Southwest Indian pots, Mexican tree of life, African carvings, orchids, paintings, and sculptures in the room. Since it is our living room, we necessarily have a sofa, music equipment, a secretary desk, and several chairs and tables in it, and around Christmas, my wife adds a couple hundred crèches she has brought home from various travels. We love all the stuff in our living room so much, we carry the theme through the rest of the house.

I suppose we are members of the packrat culture, but so are many of our friends, and it is a big demographic. I recently gave a talk at a small local museum that is interested in mechanical items. The show at the time featured antique tools. At one point, I asked the audience how many of them collected things that their friends did not appreciate. Almost all of them raised their hands. I then asked how many of them had a severe problem because their house was not big enough to contain all the stuff they loved—this time all of them raised their hands. Many successful businesses support this packrat culture. Obviously, eBay is one, while other companies supply original and reproduction parts for almost any product that could be considered old and interesting.

One of my friends quietly collected and restored army tanks and musical organs. Another collected toy trains. Still another one is drawn to steam traction engines and track-laying tractors. A friend from my college days came down with such a train habit that he was led from toys to live steam to narrow gauge to concessionaire of a major tourist railway operation. His life was changed because he had a need to wander from the ordinary. Many in this "antique machine" culture restore old products and make models of them. Two of my friends construct scale 7.5-inch-gauge steam locomotives. I had an opportunity once to meet a man who was a professional ship modeler. He was at one time a physician who originally built ship models as a hobby, but he became so absorbed by it that his health was suffering from lack of sleep. His wife finally convinced him that either his medical practice or his ship modeling had to go. He gave her great credit for posing the problem in such a clear way that it was obvious he should give up medicine. When I met him, he was happily building models of yachts for wealthy owners and models for movies full-time and supporting himself by selling them. I didn't ask if he was still married.

Products also correlate with identity in vocational groups. Construction workers buy fewer notebook computers than do business executives, and machinists and mechanics generally appreciate high-quality tools more than secretaries do. Over time, these preferred products become symbolic of the subculture. If I want to appear more like a successful business executive, I might buy a BlackBerry. When I want to appear more like a farmer, I drive my pickup, though I am of course better accepted by farmers if it is the "right" type of pickup.

As I said earlier, I have owned a pickup for many years, and I often spend time on a farm in California's agricultural valley. In

1976, I bought a small Toyota pickup with a full-size bed and loved it greatly. However, I took quite a bit of abuse from my friends in the valley, who tended toward full-size white Fords. When my Toyota finally wore out, I bought a full-size blue Ford. I did not receive as much flack for the size and make of my pickup, but clearly the blue color confused people. I did not love the pickup as much as I had my Toyota, as it was not as much fun to drive, nor as reliable. But the new truck served me well until it too wore out. I then decided to buy a full-size Toyota pickup, but when my decision came out in a group of my friends I received such veiled disapproval that I bought a white full-size Ford instead. So, I finally had an industrial product consistent with the farmer tribe. Of course, it was not consistent with the professor tribe.

Globalism and Cultures

As I mentioned, one of the big tensions in the world at the time of this writing is due to rapidly increasing globalization. Such technological advances as containerized shipping, satellite and digital communication, and wide-bodied aircraft have simplified the shipping of goods, the travel of people, and the conduction of business across large distances. Products of industry are increasingly assembled from parts made in diverse locations and manufactured long distances from the ultimate consumers. China thinks this concept is wonderful. The United States likes the lower prices of Chinese products, but, as usual, we want the benefits without the costs—cheap products but a balance of payments with the world and full employment at relatively high wages. Many people think that this globalization will continue (I am one of them), although an increasing number are becoming aware of the energy costs of global business and wondering whether it is sustainable in the long run.

This globalization is making it more difficult to correlate products with countries of origin. Many products that proclaim "Made in the USA" contain components from other countries, while others are produced by a plant in another country, or even through a joint venture with a foreign company. One of the effects of globalization is increasing standardization of industrial products. Capital goods, those requiring a large investment and used by businesses in production, are becoming quite standardized. There are tremendous and increasing similarities between the machine tools, trucks, tractors, power plants, and cranes produced in the United States, Germany, Japan, and other industrialized and industrializing countries. The design of such products is heavily influenced by function, and the companies that design and manufacture them are becoming increasingly international in their operations and in their market sensitivity.

We would be surprised if a heavy-duty electrical motor manufactured in Belgium differed significantly from one manufactured in Mexico. Not only are they built for worldwide sales, but we are also becoming used to world standards not only in function and price but also in things such as material, shape, and even color palette. This trend to global standardization is not limited to high-price commercial products by any means. Athletic equipment is another example of international product uniformity. There is not much variation in tennis rackets, golf clubs, boxing gloves, or soccer balls. Some of this uniformity is standardized by rules, some of it simply has evolved into its present form through usage, but some of it is standardized by globalization. Fashion also tends to internationalize products: the present run toward jeans and athletic shoes is a good example.

There is a potential downside, however, to the quality of life in this global standardization. I do not travel overseas for enjoyment as much as I did previously, in part because airports, airlines, ground transportation, and hotels become more standardized over time with an accompanying decrease in the adventure and excitement of visiting a new and different culture. My first overseas trip was to Japan in the 1950s, and coming from the United States it was another world. Now, though strong cultural identity exists, visually the country is much more Western.

There are still countries such as India that have maintained a visual uniqueness, although they too are moving toward the prevalent Western model to cater to increasing international business and tourist travel. There is now a fine new divided toll road between Mumbai and Pune, India, a trip that I have often made. True, the travel time is cut in half and the trip is probably safer, but the new road is devoid of turned-over trucks, oxcarts, three-wheeled tractors, elephants, scooters, Austin cars, pedestrians, cattle, potholes, and other traditional features of Indian roads. To me, as a westerner, the road is less interesting. I fear that the owner-built cab on the truck in India has a limited future as well. Tata will probably soon be selling them in the United States—local purchasing agents and your basic truck-driving cowboy will not be looking for wooden cabs to festoon with totems, fringes, flowers, and other objects found decorating the cabs of the traditional trucks in India. I think there is a good chance, however, that the Indian aesthetic will remain alive—it has survived for thousands of years. A friend of mine who is president of a very successful Indian company loves watches made by Titan, an Indian company that combines traditional Indian design with a modern product. He also is fond of pointing out that successful Indian yuppie businessmen wear kurtas at parties and decorate their homes with traditional Indian crafts.

What will be the eventual price of global standardization as far as cultural diversity is concerned? Are we moving toward a shortage of products that symbolize our differences? Will we become a single global community with a single principal language and industrial products that are common to all? Business seems to be heading that way, but I don't think all *Homo sapiens* will do so. In fact, the more globalization forces tend to standardize products around the world, the more market there may be for products unique to local cultures. Ten billion, six billion, or even just one billion people are still too many to have similar values, beliefs, and tastes, unless we subscribe to mass brainwashing or are lobotomized by invaders from another solar system. China tries hard for a common culture, but looking at the extreme difference between rural and urban life, the huge income gap between the rich and poor, and the lifestyles of the many people of Chinese ancestry living around the world, though a common heritage exists, it is far from homogeneous.

Although industrial products throughout the United States are perhaps not as diverse as those in India and China, they do reflect a collection of subcultures. And subcultures will remain.

As an example, as California's population grows (now at a mere 30 million), one becomes aware of more divisions within the state and more talk of dividing the state into regions of more similar values. For many reasons this is unlikely to happen, but four regions that are quite different are Southern California (growth, entertainment, automobiles, and developers), Central California (the Sacramento and San Joaquin valleys—agriculture and newly influential cities), the San Francisco Bay region (venture capitalists, money, Priuses, and farmers' markets), and the northern portion of the state (timber, marijuana growers, and beautiful scenery—developers not welcome). These regional differences have existed throughout my memory and have allowed Californians the pleasure of not only making rude comments and telling nasty jokes about each other but also making use of different products.

In this increasingly global world, a great deal of product diversity remains among more personal products such as food, furniture, clothing, toothpaste and toothbrushes, razors, deodorant, tampons, and underwear. Subcultures have enough choice to choose products that are consistent with their values. Grocery stores sell both organic vegetables and bacon. Some groups modify off-the-shelf products such as automobiles and computers to better fit their desires. Globalization probably means that divisions based on nations, states, and other political divides will become weaker and other groupings, such as subcultures, stronger.

Some subcultures will be heavily defined by a product: Harley-Davidson motorcycles (the big ones) might be a good example. Originally, the "cruiser" motorcycle was a typically American device. Such motorcycles are comfortable for driving long distances on straight roads. They are not as well designed for twisty roads at high speed or off-road travel through rough terrain. Because of early availability of such motorcycles and the torque and aggressive sound (especially with minimal muffler) made by their large displacement and relatively low-speed engines, they also became the motorcycle of choice for early motorcycle clubs, some of the outlaw variety. Although now most of their sales are to people who are definitely not outlaws, owners of Harley-Davidsons are a tribe. They have an annual powwow in Sturgis, South Dakota, high interest in the Harley-Davidson Company and its products, and similar values in such things as the proper clothing to wear while riding. But interestingly enough, Harley-Davidson is predicting that by 2014, some 40 percent of their sales will be overseas.[3] Apparently the subculture is spreading, and undoubtedly many values of the U.S. tribe will remain intact—a global cult of people who know who Willy G. is and can tell panheads from knuckleheads is good for the company, fun for the tribe members, and fun to joke about for those of us who prefer different types of motorcycles.

The products of industry that we use say who we are. They are symbolic of our place under the sun, and the sun has been very good to us "developed" countries. We have been doing it all —financing, designing, building, selling. We like being technologically dominant in the world. But other countries want, and deserve, their slice of the pie. I think that issues such as immigration, balance of payments, intellectual property, and trade protection will become increasingly talked about in the United States. Many issues associated with industrial production, such as pollution, resource depletion, and energy and water availability, that have formerly been considered local issues, are finally being recognized by the United States as international problems. The issue of political boundaries and international versus national versus religious law will be an issue for some time to come.

In the long run, if *Homo sapiens* are to prosper, there is no choice but to become increasingly international in our thinking. But diversified products that are symbolic of subsets of humanity will endure. I would like to see more diversification. The ease that we have in finding fault with many products is a function of the compromises inherent in our present system of mass production. In the past 20 years, there has been much talk about more customization in products, but not much has happened. It apparently seems cheaper to convince us all to converge than to cater to the diversity in human taste. But I think we will cling to our diversity and the markets will follow.

Chapter 8 *Thought Problem*

Choose a subculture of which you feel a part. Choose the product that is most symbolic of this subculture. Choose the product that is most symbolic of you. Choose a product that is not at all symbolic of you.

What subculture did you choose? What three products did you choose? Why did each of these products fulfill the expressed criteria? To what extent is the product you chose that fits the subculture also symbolic of you?

Problems and Tactics Table: Symbolism and Cultural Values

Problems	Tactics
Belief that symbolism and cultural values are shallow and can be easily changed	Think about when symbolism and culture are a factor in product quality and how more attention to them can improve this quality
Symbolism and culture are difficult to detect and measure for designers and others, especially if they are not used to thinking about them	Become more sensitive to symbolism and values of your own and other cultures; spend more time with people of other cultures
Assumption that everyone's needs, wants, and desires are/ should be the same	Travel and talk to people more; try your products in different cultures, and try products popular in different cultures in your own
Neglect of forces of globalism	Read and talk to people who are directly involved in things such as outsourcing and thinking about tariffs and other sorts of national protection; accept the fact that the past is over

Global Constraints

Does the Product Fit a Finite Earth and Its Inhabitants?

The previous chapters dealt with quality of life now or in the near future—products that fit our bodies and minds, bring us emotional pleasure, keep us healthy and happy, and help us become who we want to be. I have discussed at length the interaction between the product and the individual user, or perhaps small groups of users. This chapter is partly about potential future problems, or possibly catastrophes, that may affect large numbers of people, if not everyone worldwide. Unfortunately the products of industry, through their existence and/or manufacture and usage, can slowly or even suddenly decrease the quality of life on Earth for our species, if not seriously disrupt it. There are, however, opportunities for better products and a better life that may come from efforts to protect, or even improve, our environment and ensure that human life is sustainable on Earth.

Today, topics such as sustainability and the environment are receiving a great deal of attention in much of the world. Students in U.S. business schools are talking about the triple bottom line, a concept originated by John Elkington that tells us businesses must worry about people and the planet as well as profit. Many

U.S. citizens were ashamed of the country's refusal to join in the Kyoto Protocol, an international agreement to reduce greenhouse gas emissions, and believe that the United States should be taking the lead in preserving the environment, rather than dragging its feet. Hybrid and electric automobiles seem to have found a niche in the United States, and people are thinking hard about carbon control, smart grids, solar power generation, sustainable agriculture, and conservation. Universities are blossoming in both research and courses in such areas. Perhaps we in the United States are finally beginning to put some serious thought and effort into the problems of decreasing resources and a suffering ecosystem.

Big Problems

As I write this chapter, I am looking at the May 28–June 3, 2011, edition of *The Economist* magazine. On the cover is a picture of an Earth constructed of riveted steel plates and beams and the leader "Welcome to the Anthropocene," subtitled "Humans have changed the way the world works. Now they have to change the way they think about it, too."[1] Inside the magazine is an article entitled "The Anthropocene: A Man-Made World."[2]

The leader and the article discuss the theory that the earth has moved from the relatively stable geological period called the Holocene, defined by repeated ice ages, into a new one defined by the works of man, christened the Anthropocene by an eminent atmospheric chemist named Paul Crutzen and his colleague Eugene Stoermer. The International Commission on Stratigraphy, responsible for naming various periods, eras, and ages of the Earth, is formally studying this possibility.

Much of the geologic past has been defined by fossils, rock formations, and chemical deposits. Our current era will provide geologists of the future with fossils of cities and widespread domesticated animals and plants. They will find changes in habitat and related extinctions, in the weather and its effects, and in the carbon and nitrogen cycle, and drastically altered sedimentation, all due to the works of humankind. The numbers in the articles are staggering. The industrial fixing of nitrogen has increased the amount of nitrogen on land by 150 percent more than that done by microbes, with results ranging from the encouragement of food plants (good) to the increasing coastal "dead zones" created by runoff water from farming (bad). Rising carbon dioxide levels in the atmosphere due to human activities, although these activities account for only 10 percent of all carbon dioxide produced, are starting to result in worrisome chains of effects.

To add some scale, *The Economist* tells us that the total mass of humans and their livestock not only far outweighs that of other large animals, but the ecosystem in general is being narrowed to those plants and animals that do well in an environment dominated by humans. Another example of the scale of human activity is the Syncrude mine in the Athabasca tar sands in Alberta, Canada. The mining activities there will result in moving 30 billion metric tons of earth—equivalent to twice the amount of sediment that flows down all of the rivers in the world in a year.

One reason the majority of the world population has trouble thinking about terrestrial scale problems is that we are not good at dealing with large quantities. Consider this: If I seriously overloaded my pickup, it could hold a metric ton of earth. This means that this one mine in Canada will result in moving 30 billion pickup loads of earth. That many pickups placed end to end would form a line a bit more than 100 million miles long, which would circle the earth more than 4,000 times. Think of a belt of pickups six and a third miles wide circling the Earth. Alternately, if that amount of earth were spread uniformly over Canada, it would cover the entire nation with a layer about one-quarter of a centimeter thick—clearly visible to future geologists. Fortunately, the dirt being moved is slated to stay in its original location, although its composition will obviously be changed. And though impacts on the environment will be large, they are being closely monitored by the Canadian government. The *Economist*'s coverage of the Anthrocene was especially noteworthy because we are in the midst of a major world recession, and long-term problems having to do with the environment and sustainability of human (and other) life are often given less notice during such times, especially by relatively conservative magazines such as *The Economist*.

Concern with such problems has been slowly increasing during my lifetime, but the magnitude of these problems and the relation of their solution to our economies and values are so large that we generally pay only lip service to solving them. Unfortunately, these problems are complex, involving systems such as electrical power grids and interstate water distribution systems, government regulations and enforcement, and international treaties and cooperation. These issues are controversial, and they have unfortunately become politicized. And people and the media being what they are, we may only be going through a short period of awareness and activity, after which we will sink back to repressing the fact that we are fouling our nest. Strangely, business has traditionally taken a negative position on regulations and expenses to protect the environment, even though there is much money to be made by reorienting the way we approach our ecosphere.

Despite humans' complex hunting and gathering organizations and powerful science and technology, we share a problem with our ancestors. If we run out of resources or destroy our environment, we are in trouble. Our long-ago ancestors, being comparably few in number, could solve such problems by moving to a different location or by taking things away from other tribes. Now we are much more rapidly using up resources that are not easily renewable—critical minerals, animals, plants, open space, arable soils, fresh air, and water. And it is becoming more difficult to find new locations and take things from others, as unexploited locations are becoming rare and tribes have become larger and much better armed.

The Role of Industrially Produced Products

So what do industrially produced products have to do with all of these global issues? Almost everything. The present products that allow us to so efficiently hunt and gather also disturb the environment: take a look at a modern coal mine or deep-sea fishing operation. With our dramatically increased population, increasingly powerful technology, and rising expectations, a desire for more and more industrial products of all sorts has resulted. Unfortunately, the manufacture, maintenance, use, and disposal of these marvelous products depletes the resources required to make and use them. And their use and disposal often, if not always, damage the ecosphere.

One of my sons, Bob, is involved in designing and producing products that will help us move toward a more sustainable lifestyle. As he is fond of saying, industry depends upon "heating, beating, and treating" raw materials. Unfortunately, modern heating, beating, and treating results in a different type of environmental impact, both in quantity and quality, than that of our forebears. Our early ancestors released much fewer pollutants into the air, ground, and water. This material was also more benign, because there was no such thing as a large electronics industry employing toxic chemicals in the manufacture of products that in turn contain heavy metals and other toxic materials that cannot be recycled. Consider nuclear energy, which not only finally convinced us of the danger of nuclear waste but also made us realize the finite nature of uranium ore. Of course, the magnitude of industrial production continues to increase. As an example, modern processes require huge amounts of energy in transforming raw materials into forms that we eventually try to bury or burn, resulting in further problems.

The production of aluminum products is a good example. Although the Earth's crust has always contained a large amount of aluminum in various compounds, it was not until 100 years ago that the necessary processes and sources of electrical energy were available to make metallic aluminum more than an expensive oddity. But the energy cost of creating aluminum is very high. At present, it takes a bit more than six kilowatt-hours of electricity to produce a pound of aluminum. The U.S. aluminum industry directly consumes approximately 55 billion kilowatt-hours of electricity annually to produce aluminum.[3] This amount is equivalent to the electricity consumed by 7 million houses. The United States in total generates approximately 4 trillion kilowatt-hours of electricity per year, so this is 1.4 percent of the total electricity usage in the entire country to produce aluminum. This obviously results in quite a bit more carbon dioxide than that from the entire population of Neanderthals. On the positive side, this energy cost and the physical nature of aluminum have led to successful recycling of products, since it is much cheaper to melt discarded aluminum products than to make new metal from ore. (Hence the nice reward for turning in aluminum cans in certain states.)

Compatibility with the Earth and its ecosphere will unavoidably become increasingly important in product quality. Although attention to problems of the environment and long-term sustainability seems to follow the health of the economy and the interest paid to other problems, we cannot help but increase the attention paid to such things as recycling, alternate sources of energy, the ecosphere, and the design, manufacturing, repairability, and disposal of products: an unprecedented opportunity for industry!

Why These Problems?

Perhaps the most significant cause of our increasing ecosphere and resource problems has been population growth. We have all seen the numbers: the Earth's population was 5 million in 8000 BCE, 250 million in AD 1000, 1.6 billion in 1900, and now is 7 billion—(1 billion increase in the last 12 years) and it is projected to be 9 billion in 2050.[4] The population will not continue to grow exponentially forever, of course, but the alternative to a mass die-off or extermination implies quite a bit of continued growth.

Another cause of these problems is the rising expectations of the population. Wanting more and more new gadgets to increase the quality of life is probably a characteristic of our species. A house, automobile and fuel, refrigerator, TV, washer and dryer, and other such things are considered necessities. Increasingly, so are a computer and a cell phone. Consider the cell-phone camera. A study by the Gartner Group pointed out that 460 million cell phones with cameras were sold in 2006. This product is relatively new, but most people now expect a camera to come with any cell phone, whether they need it or not.

These expectations are enhanced by the increasingly sophisticated ability of manufacturers to influence the desires of potential customers, including governments and companies, through advertising and other promotions. Another factor is the "we can do anything" attitude of modern technologists. Can you send some people to Mars, NASA? Sure. Give us some money, and we will build you what you need. Your great big company has information problems? We'll sell you an IT system that will solve them all. You want a bomb that will kill only bad guys? No problem.

Can the products and processes of industry be designed in a way to be more compatible with global constraints? Sure. But in the past, this has perhaps not been as high a priority as it should have been. Industry produces things in order to sell them to customers, and therefore these products are defined by what customers want (or have been led to believe they want). Organizations and people who design products have their eyes on the market. Except for cost and availability of materials and regulations that constrain them, they typically have not been especially focused upon, or perhaps even aware of, scarcities, environmental damage, and energy consumption associated with the materials they use or the processes of making and using the products. And they haven't been particularly focused on problems having to do with disposing or recycling these products either, unless they faced regulation (for example, if they were exporting to Germany, which has laws regarding these issues) or could make money in doing so (as in the previously mentioned cost benefits of recycling aluminum cans).

Nor have customers been thinking enough about these topics. The hundreds of millions of cell phones that are discarded each year result in hundreds of thousands of tons of waste, some of it highly toxic.[5] Computers and computer displays are now larger and contain even more toxins.[6] The problem has now been recognized, and efforts are being made to solve it, but the problem is outrunning the solutions. An example of the complexity of such situations can be seen in the disposable diaper situation. Each year in the United States 3.5 million tons of waste consists of disposable diapers.[7] These disposables, resplendent with urine, feces, and plastic outer layers, end up in landfills throughout the country. Frighteningly enough, I cannot find documented information on the Internet of the extent of the world problem. I find estimates ranging between 20 million and 40 million tons per year. Perhaps no one even knows.

Fortunately, awareness of this issue led to the availability of so-called eco-friendly disposable diapers, some of which use a wood-based material for an outer layer and a gel for moisture absorbance. Look up Bamboo Diapers on the Internet if you want to see an example of one of these products. The diapers are advertised as being biodegradable and flushable, but on the downside a large amount of energy is needed to manufacture them. There is also a lack of long-term data on the effects of the product on babies. Further, such things do not degrade in a sterile landfill. Even if the flushable diapers will not reach a landfill, will delicate sewer systems, such as the one serving my house, be able to handle them? And flushing toilets takes fresh water. Also, if we can flush waste down the toilet, we will think about it even less. Ironically enough, old-fashioned cloth diapers may still be the gentlest on Mother Earth, but what are the chances of us returning to them?

It is inevitable that products will take better account of constraints placed upon us by the finite nature of Earth. The only question is how soon. Improvements in technology have so far helped ameliorate the difficulties, but at some point in the future, our style of living will not work. This situation will cause major dislocations because economic theories, and capitalism itself, are based on growth and "adding value" to natural resources. The good news is that not only will customers benefit, but manufacturers can also profit from efforts to solve these large and long-term problems before the situation becomes too critical, especially if they take the lead.

Toyota, with support from forward-thinking consumers, got a good grip on a new market from the Prius. General Motors could have had a longer lead on electric vehicles with the EV1, but after making a relatively small number of cars and leasing them, GM recalled and destroyed them. In the process GM disappointed many people, acquired some bad publicity (the movie

Who Killed the Electric Car?), and lost a lot of credibility. There were many reasons for the recall, including organizational timidity, a desire to try to retain the past, and the usual urge to maximize short-term profit. When the EV1 was released in late 1996, there was more money to be made in SUVs. In 2011, Chevrolet released the Volt (a new plug-in hybrid sedan), showing there is now more widespread acceptance of, and interest in, such energy-efficient, environmentally friendly vehicles.

Response to Change

As someone who has been interested for many years in human problem solving, I am fascinated by how slowly we approach solving large and long-term problems such as those dealing with limited resources, the environment, and our unsustainable lifestyle. A good example of this lack of speed in problem solving is the so-called petroleum problem. At this period in history, we seem to almost all agree that the store of petroleum in the Earth's surface is finite, that the majority of it is in an area that the United States has little control over, and that the United States is heavily dependent upon it.

In the introduction to a book entitled *Winning the Oil Endgame* by Amory Lovins (downloadable on the Internet), George Shultz, who served as a senior staff economist on President Eisenhower's Council of Economic Advisers, mentions that one of Eisenhower's chief concerns in the 1950s was dependence on foreign oil. In the 1970s, when OPEC first came into existence and high gasoline prices, shortages, and long lines at service stations occurred, there was much ado and heavy government action. Automobile companies began producing cars with better mileage to respond both to consumers and to new government regulations, money was spent on research in alternate fuels ranging from oil shale to solar energy, and the media blossomed with story after story about decreasing reservoir discoveries, the huge dependence of the United States on foreign oil, and the world's limited petroleum reserves. As soon as gas prices came down, however, the great concern evaporated—not a good approach to a long-term problem. Although the concern has returned due to high gasoline prices and international tensions, U.S. petroleum imports remain more than 300 million barrels per month, and automobile magazines are still enthusiastically reviewing vehicles that continually grow larger and go faster.[8] Every time I see cycles such as this, I realize how quickly we want to forget heavy-impact problems and how unwilling we are to voluntarily control our desires for excess.

In the early years of this century, the situation has worsened, with the United States using more oil than ever before and importing a larger fraction of it. The country is once again talking about the problem, and much more research in alternate energy sources is occurring, but change is quite difficult because of an almost universal love affair with the traditional product on the part of both consumers and producers. In the 1950s, there was no worry about the overall supply of petroleum or of the greenhouse effect of carbon dioxide. In the 1970s, we were well aware of the finite nature of the petroleum supply, but still not worried much about climate change. Now that we are aware of both the limited amount of petroleum on Earth and the greenhouse effect, why do we continue to move so slowly?

Part of the problem is that people underestimate the complexity of the petroleum-based transportation system. More than 100 years have been spent improving not only the automobile but also the myriad highways, filling stations, garages, dealerships, parts stores, manufacturing and assembly plants, and suppliers that comprise the system. Moving toward using more electrical power takes more than simply designing and building an electric car. If we in the United States had known what we now know 100 years ago, we would probably have put more emphasis on mass transportation and transportation planning.

Southern California is a wondrous example of the problems of fully developing an area assuming that the individual automobile would be forever adequate for transportation. Not surprisingly, it is common to encounter fond stories about the old "Red Line" (Pacific Electric Railways), which at one time interconnected the entire region with trolley cars, before it was all dismantled in favor of buses. At the time, there was likely little resistance to this move by most of the local cities. But now that Southern California is completely clogged with smog-producing vehicles barely moving during commuting hours, dismantling the "Red Line" is considered by many to have been a dastardly deed. Although Southern California, like many urban areas, is in the process of strengthening its electric rail system, the task is complex and extremely expensive because the right-of-ways have disappeared. But an increased use of rail is in our future, simply because it is much more efficient and is seemingly more luxurious as other modes of transportation become more expensive and more of a hassle.

Considering our more standardized multiuse vehicles, we are finally beginning to become innovative on decreasing petroleum usage. Honda and Toyota opened people's eyes with the hybrids Insight and Prius. In 2008 there were some 30 company start-ups pursuing electric cars. One of these companies, Tesla Motors, where my son Dan works, is producing an expensive electrically powered sports car with high performance. The vehicle accelerates from zero to 60 in about four seconds and is capable of going 250 miles on one battery charge. The company claims the cars produce only 10 percent of the pollution of equivalent gasoline-fueled sports cars and are six times as efficient (the equivalent of getting 135 miles per gallon and an operating cost of one cent per mile)—it is also beautiful and incredibly fun to drive. To date

Tesla has sold its planned production through the 2011 model, and it is planning to produce a much less expensive sport sedan beginning in 2012. But as a society, we have a long way to go. The buying public must realize that they are being saddled with technology that has remained essentially unchanged for 100 years, and that being part of a large crowd herding two tons of metal propelled by periodic explosions in a machine that heats the atmosphere more than it delivers power to the wheels is somewhat embarrassing.

There is a great deal of opportunity to decrease our need of energy, and it is sometimes surprisingly easy to accomplish. As a specific example of major electrical energy savings through government regulation and more attention paid to efficiency by manufactures, consider home refrigerators. The size of refrigerators has been increasing since the days of the ice box. The energy use per refrigerator increased even more sharply until the early 1970s, a time of great energy concern brought on by gasoline prices (even though little petroleum is used in the generation of electricity). In 1977, California established a set of appliance efficiency regulations, one of these mandating that any refrigerator sold in the state of California must meet a certain reasonable target. Since California represented some 10 percent of the market, and manufacturers had been told that it was coming, the energy use per refrigerator dropped a bit before 1977 and continued to decrease afterward. As energy use dropped, California altered its target toward even greater efficiency. Since all manufacturers wanted to sell in California, all refrigerators sold in the United States met the goal. Therefore, after a bit of time, other states and finally the federal government established similar requirements, and, since then, although refrigerator size has continued to increase, refrigerators use 60 percent less electricity than they did 20 years ago.[9] Interestingly enough, the price of a refrigerator has also dropped. These changes are the result of better approaches to manufacturing and design, but they also demonstrate that improving function does not necessarily lead to higher cost. Also, contrary to early worries, improved function and decreased price did not damage company profits.

Revolutionary Approaches

Happily, today there is a large amount of thinking about more revolutionary approaches to energy systems. There is presently much interest in so-called vehicle-to-grid (V2G) approaches to transportation, in which large numbers of electric cars would be connected to the electrical power grid (plugged into the wall) when not being driven. Owners would pay for having their car charged. Such a system would have several advantages. First, the batteries could be charged when electrical usage is low (at night) and rates are lower. Second, the batteries could act as storage for the electrical grid to help at times of high electrical draw. Such a system also would allow automobiles to act as local power-generating sources in cases of high local demand. Owners would be paid when their car was being discharged. The result would be a dramatically reduced need for central power stations (which are designed to service peak load) and cheaper electrical power for everyone.

Such a scheme would not have been feasible with traditional automobiles because the battery capacity per vehicle is low and lead-acid batteries can undergo only a limited number of charge-discharge cycles. But the battery capacity of an electric car is quite large in terms of the electrical use in most homes. As an example, the battery of the Tesla Motors car (a lithium ion battery) has a capacity of 56 kilowatt-hours, enough to power the average home for two days. Advanced batteries can also withstand more charge-discharge cycles, and they can be discharged more completely without damage to the battery.

Of course, efficiency alone does not necessarily save energy, because historically improvements in efficiency have been more than counterbalanced by increased usage. Neither does the availability of methods of conserving energy guarantee that change will occur, even if this change would be economically beneficial. A good example of this problem can be seen in the case of lighting, another large use of energy and one that we in the United States take to extremes (more than 30 percent of the electricity generated in the United States is used for lighting). When I travel internationally, I am always staggered by the amount of lighting in our cities as I fly over them at, say, 3 A.M. as opposed to that in most non-U.S. cities. I admit that it is impressive—there is no light show that compares to flying into Los Angeles International at night—but we seem to have a nationwide fear of the dark. Buildings stay lit at night even though vacant, and houses are fully lit even though no one is in many rooms.

But people cling to old beliefs about lighting, many of which are false: Reading in dim light does *not* result in poor eyesight. Lighting *does* cost money. Incandescent lightbulbs *do* have shorter lifetimes if they are turned on and off frequently, but lifetime refers to the total amount of time they are lit, and the loss due to cycling (being turned on and off) is usually more than overcome by the time they remain unused—in other words, you probably won't have to change lightbulbs as often if you turn them off when you are not in the room, and you will also use much less energy. Another myth is that fluorescent lights flicker and are not flattering. This belief is based on the behavior of fluorescent lighting in its infancy. Modern fluorescents flicker so rapidly that humans cannot notice. You can even acquire fluorescents tinted to make you look better than you might usually. And, of course, fluorescents are much more efficient than incandescent bulbs. Fluorescent lighting in the home pays for itself many times over the life of the bulb in electrical savings (and the lifetime is much longer than that of incandescents). Unfortunately, the initial cost of fluorescent lightbulbs is higher, and initial cost is a big deal to people. But this, too, will change, and LEDs, or light-emitting diodes (the type found in small white Christmas lights), are growing in size and power and closing fast. Commercial buildings have definitely gotten the message and turned from incandescent lighting to gas discharge lighting. For instance, yellow sodium vapor lamps are heavily used for external lighting. But, overall, most of us in the United States lag.

Beyond refrigerators and lighting, impressive progress is being made at reducing energy cost in the home. Your Internet browser is full of information on everything from ads for new low-energy homes to information on how to cut energy cost in existing homes to descriptions of homes that not only have no energy bills but also sometimes make money by selling energy to the grid. These low-energy homes typically combine solar panels and construction approaches (such as treated windows, proper positioning, thermal inertia, and solar panels) with efficient appliances and lighting. There are many advertisements for homes that require only 50 percent as much energy as "traditional" homes (although they don't specify what "traditional" means). The U.S. Department of Energy has a goal of reducing home energy usage by 70 percent over these "traditional" homes, in addition to reducing the additional cost of building them to near zero, by 2020.[10]

Another example of reducing energy usage is improved control and usage of electric motors. Approximately two-thirds of the electricity used in industry and one-quarter of the energy used in homes goes to powering electric motors. Often, if not usually, electric motors are sized for the largest load they will encounter and little attention is paid to potential energy savings. If, for instance, a motor is powering a pump with a varying load, it will spend some, if not most, of its time loaded at less than its maximum capacity. Although electric motors are extremely efficient at their maximum rated load, they are less so when operating with a lesser load. One solution to this problem is the so-called smart controller. One type of such a device varies the frequency of the electrical input to the motor to change its rotational speed. In the mid-1990s, the 3M Corporation received a lot of attention for using such devices, along with other modifications, in the electric motor systems in one of its buildings. Electrical usage in the building was decreased by 41 percent, saving $77,554 per year.[11] Naturally, the company went on to apply the same thinking to other buildings. The investment required to do this was repaid by savings in energy cost in a little more than one year. Since then there has been much progress in such "smart" controllers and more attention paid to electric motor systems.

There will obviously have to be many alternative solutions to provision of energy in the future, and, at least at the time of this writing, much is happening. As an example, a couple of years ago in an issue of my Caltech alumni magazine I came across an article entitled "Put Some Sunlight in Your Tank."[12] The piece concerned the work of a graduate student named William Chueh and the laboratory of the professor of materials science and chemical engineering, Sossina Haile. The effort had to do with breaking down carbon dioxide using a catalyst and extremely high temperatures (1500 degrees Centigrade). The catalyst Chueh is working with is cerium oxide, used in automobile catalytic converters, and a potential heat source is the sun. Carbon dioxide is ordinarily extremely difficult to break down, because one might have to use as much energy as is gained when carbon forms with oxygen in the first place. But at high temperatures with the proper catalyst, the process goes rapidly, and the sun is a clean source of the needed energy to provide the heat. Once the carbon is separated, it can be reused as a fuel.

A large collector area is necessary for solar energy, and a process like the one Chueh is working on would be associated with a power plant or other such large source, rather than an individual automobile or house. One possibility is continually breaking carbon dioxide down and reusing the carbon in the process of generating electricity. Another would be in a hybrid power plant that during the day would generate electricity through both solar and conventional means, and then use the fuel produced by breaking down the flue gas to produce electricity at night—a method of obtaining large-scale storage. The numbers quoted in the article were quite impressive, and solar-thermochemical research is now widespread.

I mention Chueh's research as an illustration of the type of work that may have major effects on energy production and usage. Independent of research on new approaches to providing and storing energy, many changes will occur with our present sources. Much more use of electricity in transportation will occur since emissions from central power plants that burn hydrocarbons can be more successfully treated than those from movable vehicles, and electrical motors are quite efficient. We will make more use of wind, solar, biomass, and nuclear energy to provide this electrical power, and we will put much more effort into decreasing energy use, cleaning up emissions from electrical generating systems, and developing improved storage devices.

To look at an energy-related example closer to home, let us consider all of those battery-operated toys that overflow stores—some of them are wonderful. We have two of such in our house, one a funky-looking caterpillar that makes various sounds (music, words, letters, and so on) when you push on its feet and one a big soft cube that also plays music, talks, and makes other noises when poked in various places. Not only do they seem to entertain one- and two-year-olds endlessly (priceless for grandparents), but they seem to almost never need batteries and may even be educational. However, counterbalance these with the endless examples of unreliable, breakable pieces of junk that consume endless batteries and are basically lousy toys. How about battery-equipped plastic animals covered with fake fur that wiggle along making animal noises until they break? Or think about battery-driven robots that freeze in midmovement because they are mechanically not up to the task. The end result is expenditure of energy and materials to make the batteries, the production of toxic materials that must be disposed of, and the time and money people use in buying and disposing of them.

Incidentally, this latter example points out a rather elemental method of saving energy: don't use it to do unnecessary things. For instance, an excellent way for people to help decrease the amount of energy used each year in transportation is not to travel so much. One of the advantages of being officially retired is that I can now do my bit to save energy by not taking trips on which I do not want to go. Consider how much unnecessary business travel is involved in this day of electronic communication. We keep talking about teleconferencing and making increasing use of digital communication and the Internet, yet we go through the agony of airports and sitting crammed into ill-fitting seats on unnecessary trips. I believe that one should have an initial chance to spend personal time with colleagues in other locations in order to get to know them, but afterward? Perhaps we need higher-quality communication products.

The Iceberg

But the energy problem is obviously only one of many having to do with using up resources and threatening the environment—the tip of the iceberg, although it is a big tip. Some experts in the field fear that more than half of the species living on Earth may be extinct by the year 2100 due to changes in their habitats, toxins in the biosphere, and intentional killing by us humans.[13] As this depletion of species happens, we may find that a great many of them were important to our well-being. Pharmaceutical companies may find that their raw materials have drastically shrunk as forests are sacrificed. Humans are heading into one of the greatest extinctions in the history of the Earth, and the first one in which we will have had a large role.

Another topic receiving a great deal of worry related to both global constraints and products of industry is the usage of fresh water. Global fresh water use has been climbing more rapidly than the population. In my early days at Stanford, I became interested in the vast quantities of fresh water being used to flush often relatively benign substances down the toilet. At that time, toilets in the United States typically used 3.5 to 7 gallons of water per flush. Consider that amount multiplied by the population, then multiplied by the number of times the average person flushed the toilet per day, and then multiplied by 365—a rather extraordinary amount of fresh water each year that literally went down the toilet. In 1992 new water usage laws limited the flush amount to 1.6 gallons. This change caused some consternation among both plumbers and consumers, but we have accommodated to our new flush levels and are saving part of this vast yearly water expenditure. At some point, however, even 1.6 gallons will seem wasteful, especially in dry climates. Many toilets in Australia (and now being imported into the United States) allow one to select either 1.6 gallons or 0.8, depending on what you have deposited in the bowl. Urine-diverting and waterless composting toilets are on the market to further reduce water loss and are already in some areas. The day will come when the use of fresh water to dispose of human waste will seem anachronistic indeed.

There are vast opportunities for the development of products that use water more efficiently, treat so-called wastewater, and desalinate and purify polluted water cheaply and without large expenditures of energy. There is also a continuing need for more efficient irrigation technology. The major usage of water (70 percent or so) in the world is agriculture, the major proportion of that going to irrigation. In the United States, roughly half of agricultural acreage is irrigated by flooding (surface), more than 40 percent by sprinkling, and only 7 percent by micro-irrigation (such as a drip system). It is possible in many agricultural areas to see miles of sprinkling systems operating in the heat of the day. Evaporation losses are huge, but even my college-educated farmer friends justify this by pointing out that the evaporated water will return to the surface as rain. My answer is yes, but where? Rainfall unfortunately tends to fall in wet areas, where it is not needed, rather than in agricultural areas, which tend to be dry because plants like sun.

More systems will obviously be built to transfer water to areas that desperately need it, with the associated challenge of building such systems in an environmentally sensitive manner. Continued development of irrigation technology and devices is needed, especially for developing countries. There is also an opportunity for digital electronics to control irrigation in a smarter way. There has been a reasonable amount of experimentation with an approach to farming in which acreage is analyzed for various soil and plant characteristics, and then treated accordingly. Treatment is done by using computers and a GPS system to apply fertilizers, pesticides, and water where and when it is needed, rather than uniformly to entire fields. Farming, except for modern machinery, seeds, and chemicals, is done very similarly to the way it has been done for 100 years. One hundred years ago water was plentiful, and to most farmers almost free. Times have changed greatly. So will farming.

And then there is global warming, a large piece of the iceberg and real, even though average temperature fluctuates and the temperature may not be rising where you live. An interesting and alarming talk on this issue entitled "Powering the Planet" was given to a conference held at Caltech in 2007 by Nathan Lewis, a chemistry professor at Caltech whose research focuses on global energy issues.[14] His conclusion is that only solar power can solve our problem. He estimates, incidentally, that the effort needed to accomplish this task is equivalent to that obtainable from 50 Exxon Mobiles. Like many people, he sees the control of the so-called greenhouse effect to be a major business opportunity. But the tone of his paper seems to hint that he doesn't think we will make the target of keeping global warming below 5 degrees Fahrenheit. His paper is well written and interesting, since Caltech has a history of blowing the whistle on large-scale problems such as automobile-produced smog. I recommend you read it and monitor your reactions to it. Do you believe it? Think we'll do much about it? If so, when?

Regulations and Laws

Having talked a bit about improving the fit between industrial products and our Earth, I should say a few words about regulators and the courts, which are major players in the effort. Regulation and judicial actions aimed toward products are a controversial topic as many people in industry consider them unnecessary meddling with the holy free market on the part of government. Some consumers also see them as abridging their individual freedom. After all, automobiles could be cheaper without catalytic converters. With fewer rules, more areas would be accessible to off-road vehicles, we could buy more impressive fireworks for the Fourth of July, we could better enjoy the sound of our modified and unmuffled engines, we would not be hassled in our quest for firearms, we could buy better poison to dispose of pests, we could still get our favorite lead-based paint, and we could buy whatever medicinal material we wanted without having to see doctors or purchase it through foreign websites.

Obviously, one reason for laws and the courts is that one person's freedom is often another person's inconvenience. I am a backpacker. Of course, mountain and dirt bikers want complete freedom to roam the hills, but I don't want to be pushed off of the trail by them. My wife and I (mostly my wife) do our own yard work by hand. Of course, several two-cycle engines running

unmuffled at once allow our neighbors' gardening teams to complete their work more rapidly, but who needs the racket? Sure,
automobile owners have to pay more money to buy and maintain
automobiles with smog equipment, but skies are supposed to at
least occasionally be blue, and air is not supposed to smell bad and
make your eyes hurt. (Having grown up in Southern California
and spent time in places such as Beijing, Delhi, and Mexico City,
I feel strongly about this.)

Another reason for laws and regulations, strangely enough, is
to protect us from ourselves. As an example, the U.S. government, when originally put in place, had no intention of regulating
industrial products. But the process that got them into the activity tells us something. In the early part of the 19th century,
steamboats traveled only a few miles per hour and were powered
by low-pressure, slow-speed engines. They were extremely profit-
able, however, sometimes returning 50 percent of the original
investment in a single year. Competition grew, and what people
desired in the way of performance was greater speed. One secret
to speed is higher pressure, because higher pressure allows lower
engine weight for a given amount of power, and therefore a faster
boat. Although engines and boilers in steamboats continually
improved, the temptation existed to operate engines above safe
pressure levels and scrimp on maintenance to save costs. This led
to an increasing number of fatal boiler explosions, resulting in
the creation of the Joint Regulatory Agency of the federal government in 1852.

Federal regulatory agencies now include the Environmental
Protection Agency, the Federal Aeronautics Administration, the
Food and Drug Administration (FDA), the Federal Communica-
tions Commission (FCC), the Office of Safety and Health
Administration (OSHA), the Interstate Commerce Commission
(ICC), the Nuclear Regulatory Commission (NRC), the Con-
sumer Product Safety Commission (CPSC), and the National
Highway Traffic Safety Administration (NHTSA). There are

also many agencies at the state and local levels regulating products where problems of safety, the environment, or product quality have been detected. Regulation also occurs through technical societies, which often form agencies to provide standardization and quality control. Examples are ASTM (formerly known as the American Society for Testing and Materials) and the American National Standards Institute. Other regulations may be set by purchasing groups. An example is the U.S. military specification system (MilSpecs). Many of these came into being because the private sector did not regulate itself.

The courts and the media also play major roles in environmental quality and safety. Product liability litigation is probably even more controversial than regulation and can cause great damage to companies. The Insurance Information Institute estimates that asbestos litigation will eventually cost insurance companies $65 billion and bankrupt 60 companies. Rather than penalize competitors equally, litigation can focus on a single company (Firestone) or a subset (thalidomide manufacturers). No matter what the case, opinions differ widely. Defendants in product liability cases often feel that they have been adequately cautious in their decisions and that the judge and the jury simply do not understand the risks of doing business. Consumer advocates and those with an antibusiness bent are horrified by the damages and would go for even higher punitive measures.

In the United States, there is no chance that product liability litigation will go away. Companies would not be as eager to recall and modify products without the threat of litigation, and they likely would not put as much thought into safety during the design of their products. Rules may be changed so that more of the settlement goes to the aggrieved parties and less to the attorneys. The constraints on class-action suits also may be changed. More cases may be settled by binding arbitration and negotiation, but there will still be disagreements and rewards to those judged to have been poorly used by products. And the cases that are solved through court action are only the beginning. The majority of product liability claims are settled out of court.

Unfortunately, the threat of litigation is a force for conservatism in product design, and an argument against a litigious climate is its negative impact on innovation. When radical improvement in performance and/or cost is attempted, it is perhaps more liable to produce a product that will be found to have flaws. If sued over those flaws, the company is more likely to lose. One issue that continually comes up in product liability suits is whether the design of the product follows standard practice. A commercial airliner seeking vertical takeoff capability would be much more exposed to liability suits than a slight iteration on presently existing ones. Producers claim, with some justification, that liability litigation therefore causes them to be wary of new directions.

The media does of course have an amplifying effect on court-based disputes, and it is in fact a force in itself. Present-day newspaper, TV, film, and Internet coverage has added greatly to the power of the media. Large accidents or incidents with loss of life, damage to the environment, or harm to property are presented to us continually for days. How can you avoid being angry with BP after viewing all of those oil-soaked beaches and birds and reading out the problems of the fishermen? Aren't we all becoming pretty suspicious about the safety of SUVs? How about those food additives?

The media is extremely powerful at spreading the alarm, but they can be faulted because they do not spread the "all clear" findings nearly as effectively. Stanford University went through a congressional investigation a few years ago having to do with expenditure of overhead moneys on government grants and contracts. The media happily trumpeted the details of all of the accusations and quotes of the accusers for months. In the midst of all this, the rules for apportionment and control of overhead moneys were changed and the media heralded that as a punishment. After a couple of years, when the investigation was complete, the university was exonerated of all of the charges. The media gave this news much less ink.

As an engineer, I can see both sides of the regulation situation. I certainly am aware of the uncertainties in designing and manufacturing new products and the power of the media. After the *Challenger* shuttle explosion, for example, I was interviewed by a reporter for a San Francisco paper on what I thought about it. I gave my opinion, which was that it was a tragedy, but this was a high-risk mission. The shuttle, when designed, was unprecedented and required a high degree of innovation. The *Challenger* vehicle was aging. I held my breath every time a shuttle flew and was not completely surprised when one malfunctioned. If anything, I faulted the judgment of people who would send schoolteachers and senators (except for John Glenn) on missions such as this, but I understood the fragility of complex and lightweight machinery that was called upon to survive launch and reentry to the Earth's atmosphere.

I misjudged the amount of exposure my view would receive. The piece was reprinted in a number of papers, and I received my share of mail attacking me for my cavalier attitude about human life and my "engineeringish" attempt to apologize for an obviously poorly made and negligently operated piece of equipment. I was not surprised, because I had endured quite a bit of this when I worked for JPL in the early 1960s. The employees of JPL were (and are) extremely good at their game and highly motivated. We were working very hard at designing spacecraft, but we had failures that disappointed us, although they did not totally surprise us because no one had built anything like this before. That explanation did not satisfy the public. That was where our congressional investigation came from. The good news was that Congress, or at least the investigating team, learned a lot about what we were doing.

I also, however, see the value of product litigation and media coverage. Businesspeople would like to produce new products, make money, and themselves make the decisions about ethical and social issues concerning their products, but that is a bit much to ask. The public deserves a voice in this process, and that voice is necessarily through legislation, judicial action, and the media. I feel better knowing that the producers of my food, my medicines, my car, my appliances, and other products that might sorely disappoint and/or hurt me are subject to regulations and their makers don't want to be sued. I don't want them so curtailed that they do not continue to develop improved products, and being an engineer, I probably am willing to take more risk than people who are less aware of the process that brings me these products. But life is easier if I don't have to worry about my ladder collapsing, my toaster hooking me directly to my house wiring, or my environment being poisoned. And if my ladder collapses, my toaster electrocutes me, or my environment starts making me sick, I don't mind the media telling the world.

Now What?

To me, when viewed in context of the environment and sustainability, quality is simple to define. The less wasteful and less damaging to the environment a product is, the higher its quality. We can all think of things we do that are not only wasteful but also unrewarding. I can nominate long commutes to work (I grew up in Southern California), waiting for large and/or heavy objects that have been shipped long distances and paying the related charges, building things from increasingly crummy lumber, dealing with plastics that break and discolor, continually telling my computer I don't want upgrades, walking in and out of overheated buildings in the winter and overcooled buildings in the summer, drinking overly chlorinated water, breathing air pollution, driving hours to find a scenic hiking area and finding it full of people, listening to the engine collection of my neighbors' gardeners, airports, long lines in stores, trying to find a parking place, and being buzzed by cars when on my bicycle. Solving some of the outstanding problems having to do with environment and sustainability would, strangely enough, solve some of my gripes.

Many modern packaging techniques are terrible. Plastic packages have traditionally been made from petroleum, and the processes of making and forming them require energy and produce pollutants. Sixty million tons of polyethylene are produced each year, and much of this goes into packing. A large amount of plastic goes into making so-called bubble packages—the kind that surround most products in hardware stores and that one cannot easily break into. My idea of hell for people who design such things is an eternity spent without tools in which all of their food is delivered to them in such packages. Come to think of it, my hate list includes the thin plastic sacks in the produce section that can neither easily be torn from the roll nor be opened, especially if one has one's hands full of produce. But enough already. Protecting the ecosphere and moving ourselves to a sustainable and high-quality level of existence is a huge problem, but the making of the high-quality products needed to do so is a huge opportunity.

Chapter 9 *Thought Problem*

Assume that life on Earth for us will necessarily change in order to protect our resources and environment. Can you think of changes in products that would simultaneously help preserve the environment, help long-term sustainability, and improve your life? How could products change to ameliorate some of your own gripes, and where and how would quality be an important consideration? What should traveling, communicating, housing, and health care be like? How about eating, elimination, exercising, bathing, and entertainment? How could the elements of quality covered in this book be better addressed while simultaneously helping both the economy and the environment and working toward sustainability?

Problems and Tactics Table: Global Constraints

Problems	Tactics
Short-term thinking and economic theory	Think long-term and with concern for the future of the human race
Belief that progress depends on endless growth and consumption of resources	Spend more time in cities, and talk to dedicated and highly educated members of the "green" movement
Technological optimism ("technology will fix it")	Learn more about the problems
Narrow/local thinking	Stay away from fancy "Western" hotels when you travel, and talk to local people about environmental issues

Conclusion

What Have We Learned?
Where Do We Go?

There are many causes for the overall quality of industrially produced products being lower than they might be. As discussed, one is lack of awareness and attention paid to quality. We just don't think about it enough and take those often simple actions that would increase it. When students would finish my course on quality and ask me how to continue to learn about overall product quality, I would advise them to simply keep paying attention to it—if possible to become obsessed with it.

Another cause of low quality is the nature of life in the modern world. We are living in a time of strong materialistic desires and widespread capitalism, even in countries that describe themselves as communist or socialist: Russia, China, Venezuela, and Finland want to make money, as do the United States, England, India, and Germany. It is often possible to make a fast buck by producing an item that is not as good as it might be, especially if it is promoted well and sold cheaply. Eventually, however, high overall quality produces the high value added and profitability that businesses seek. Do we in the United States think we will become the world's leader in making things cheaply? Give me a break. Besides, it is more fun to make the best.

Most of us who buy products are quite occupied with day-to-day activities in life and tend to concentrate on the issues that cry for immediate attention, which may not include the overall quality of the products we purchase. In fact, we typically focus more on quality when a product fails or otherwise disappoints us than we do when we acquire it. Most of us buy a mattress because a friend bought that brand, or because the maker is an old name in mattresses, or because of a good salesperson, or an influential TV ad, or a low price, and maybe because we reclined upon it for a few minutes in a store. But when we really become aware of the bed's quality is after a couple of weeks of sore backs in the morning.

We buy a car with a large number of electrical and electronic features, and love them greatly until after 50,000 miles, when they begin to fail and cost an unexpectedly large amount to have repaired. Only then do we talk to others who have had the same experience and become critical of the car. We buy an expensive formal dress because it is so fashionable, but become unhappy when it becomes unfashionable, well before we have gotten our money's worth out of it, then begin thinking more deeply about the role of fashion in clothing. We are continuously mildly disgruntled owners of many of our possessions.

If we work in a company that manufactures products, many considerations consume our consciousness—schedule, short-term profit, budgets, job reviews, facilities, morale, competition, travel, and how to reduce the amount of e-mail we receive. Specific product goals usually focus on characteristics that are measurable, and these goals are often ambitious enough to squeeze out less tangible considerations. Overall quality again may receive short shrift and not qualify for the level of attention and conscious effort that it deserves.

As I have said many times in the book, quality is a multidimensional and complicated topic. There is no simple way to quantify it, and language leaves us short when discussing it and communicating what we mean. We evaluate the overall quality of a product with a mixture of logical thinking and emotional response.

I began the course that this book is drawn upon because I wanted to cover a number of topics about quality that were hard to discuss logically and treat quantitatively. I underestimated the difficulty of teaching a course of that nature, but fortunately I could put in a large experiential component by having the students rate and attempt to improve existing products and design and make projects of their own. Now here I am writing a book on these topics that are difficult to discuss logically and treat quantitatively. I must like to suffer.

When topics are difficult, it is often easier to think about them by breaking them down into parts—the analytical approach. The topics in Chapters 3 through 9 in the book correspond to useful parts of the whole. I believe that they are basic parts, but I won't argue that they are the only ones. They are ones I have chosen through many years of thinking and teaching about the topic. I have tested these topics on a large number of people in many fields in many countries, and I am convinced that they help people think about the overall quality problem. Hopefully they convey some useful information, stimulate some thought, and make you more aware of the issue.

The Thought Problems at the end of the chapters are paraphrased student assignments. Comparing and consciously criticizing the quality of products demands your attention, increases your awareness, and builds your ability to discriminate between good and bad in a more useful manner. Next time you see something you would love to have, try to figure out why you react to it in that way. Next time you set forth to buy some common product, look at several competing ones and think deeply about why you prefer one over the others. The reason for these exercises was to fill in aspects of quality that are difficult to convey in words. These types of activities and extrinsic knowledge worked well in the classes I taught, and I am immodest enough to think they would also be fun and worthwhile for you. This book contains a large amount of information about product quality and how to improve it, but to change behavior, this information needs to be augmented by experimentation and usage. To really understand product quality, you need to become involved in the issue.

If you would like an easy way to play around with product quality, let me give you a simple matrix based on this book that you can use as an approach to evaluating product quality: Table 10.1, the "Good Product, Bad Product Matrix."

Table 10.1 Good Product, Bad Product Matrix

	Lousy				Super
	1	2	3	4	5
Performance and Cost					
Human Fit					
Craftsmanship					
Emotional Appeal					
Elegance and Sophistication					
Symbolism and Cultural Values					
Global Fit					

Grade some products that you own, would like to own, or are involved in producing, on quality, considering each chapter topic in order. If most of the grades are 4s or 5s, as far as you are concerned, the product is a very good one. If some of the grades are lower, but most are still high, it is still a good product, because not all products can be perfect. It is unusual for a product to reach the top in all categories, but if the scores are mostly 1s, 2s, and 3s, why do you even bother with the product? Aren't we reaching the point where we can no longer afford lousy or even mediocre products? If you are considering buying such a product, don't. If you own it, get rid of it. If your company is considering producing it, stop it while you can. Or improve the product. Can you think of easy ways to improve it based on these grades? If it were improved, would it necessarily cost more, and if so why? This matrix, incidentally, can give insight on comparing competing products. And if you really consider yourself good at using the matrix, try making a version with grades between 1 and 10.

While struggling through writing this book, I sometimes wondered what has brought me from my simpler early days of trying to figure out how things work to trying to figure out how to make things better. Partially it is because I like to think about difficult things like quality. But even more, it is because the time to worry about improving quality in our industrial products has definitely arrived. Our population and expectations have increased to the point where we can no longer afford to make junk and throw it away when it breaks or when we are tired of it. High-quality products, whether they be cheap or expensive, help solve many of our problems, from the individual level to global. Quality, though difficult to quantify, can improve our lives while reducing the damage to the ecosphere on which our lives depend. It can improve value added for corporations producing products ranging from mosquito coil burners costing a few rupees to airliners costing millions of dollars. It can increase pride of ownership as well as the morale of those building the product. A perfect hammer (or nail gun) can ease our day's labor, just as a beautifully designed hybrid can contribute to our feelings of enjoyment and social responsibility as we do our errands. If I were promoting a sound bite, it would be "Better quality is good."

And that's all, folks. Get out there and do some good.

Notes

Introduction

1. *The Oxford Pocket Dictionary of Current English*, Encyclopedia.com, http://www.encyclopedia.com/doc/1O999-quality.html.

Chapter 1

1. Philip Elmer-DeWitt, "iPhone: 4% of Market, 50% of profit," CNN Money, http://tech.fortune.cnn.com/2010/10/30/iphone-4-of-market-50-of-profit.

2. Apple Inc. (APPL) Financial Ratios, Forbes.com, http://finapps.forbes.com/finapps/jsp/finance/compinfo/Ratios.jsp?tkr=AAPL.

3. Charles O'Reilly and Michael Tushman, *Winning Through Innovation: A Practical Guide to Leading Organizational Change and Renewal* (Cambridge, MA: Harvard Business School Press, 1997).

Chapter 2

1. David Garvin, "Competing on the Eight Dimensions of Quality," *Harvard Business Review*, November–December 1987.

Chapter 3

1. Clifford Stoll, *Silicon Snake Oil* (New York: Knopf Doubleday, 1996).

2. "Growing a Nation: The Story of American Agriculture," Utah State University, http://www.agclassroom.org/gan/timeline/farm_tech.htm.

Chapter 4

1. Alexander Kira, *The Bathroom* (New York: The Viking Press, 1976).

2. Peter Lyman and Hal Varian, "How Much Information," University of California, Berkeley, 2003, http://www2.sims.berkeley.edu/research/projects/how-much-info-2003.

3. Paul D. MacLean, *The Triune Brain in Evolution: Role of Paleocerebral Functions* (New York: Springer, 1990).

4. Charles Hampden-Turner, *Maps of the Mind* (New York: Simon and Schuster Adult Publishing Group, 1982).

5. Charles Perrow, *Normal Accidents* (Princeton, NJ: Princeton University Press, 1999).

6. Mitchell Rogovin et al., "Three Mile Island: A Report to the Commissioners and to the Public," vol. 1, http://www.threemileisland.org/downloads/354.pdf.

Chapter 5

1. Matthew Crawford, "Shop Class as Soul Craft," *New Atlantis*, Summer 2006, http://www.thenewatlantis.com/publications/shop-class-as-soulcraft.

2. Thomas J. Stanley and William D. Danko, *The Millionaire Next Door* (New York: Simon and Schuster, 2000).

3. David Pye, *The Nature and Art of Workmanship* (London: A & C Black, 2007).

Chapter 6

1. B. S. Bloom et al., *Taxonomy of Educational Objectives: The Classification of Educational Goals; Handbook I: Cognitive Domain* (New York: Longmans Green, 1956).

2. Antoine Bechara, Hanna Damasio, and Antonio Damasio, "Emotion, Decision Making, and the Orbitofrontal Cortex," *Cerebral Cortex* 10, no. 3: 295–307.

3. Daniel Goleman, *Emotional Intelligence* (New York: Bantam Books, 1995).

4. Robert Plutchik, *Emotion: A Psychoevolutionary Synthesis* (New York: Harper Collins, 1980).

5. "Fatalities on Mount Everest," ExplorersWeb, http://www.adventure stats.com.

6. Michael Cooper, "Happy Motoring: Traffic Deaths at 61-Year Low," *New York Times*, April 1, 2011, http://www.nytimes.com/2011/04/01/us/01driving.html.

7. Paul Bloom, *How Pleasure Works: The New Science of Why We Like What We Like* (New York: W. W. Norton, 2010).

8. Abraham Maslow, "A Theory of Human Motivation," *Psychosomatic Medicine*, 1943, 5.

9. Len Doyal and Ian Gough, *A Theory of Human Need* (New York: Macmillan, 1991).

10. Donald Norman, *Emotional Design: Why We Love (or Hate) Everyday Things* (New York: Basic Books, 2005).

11. James D. Agresti and Reid K. Smith, "Gun Control Facts," *Just Facts*, December 22, 2010, http://justfacts.com/guncontrol.asp.

12. Dev Patnaik, "System Logics: Organizing Your Offerings to Solve People's Big Needs," *Design Management Review* 15, no. 3, Summer 2004.

Chapter 7

1. "Automobiles," History.com, http://www.history.com/topics/auto mobiles.

2. *Webster's New World Dictionary*, 2nd college ed. (New York: Prentice Hall, 1986).

Chapter 8

1. "BMW Plans to Spend $160 Million for Advertising on TV," 4WheelsNews, April 15, 2011, http://www.4wheelsnews.com/bmw -plans-to-spend-160-million-for-advertising-on-tv.

2. "Kantar Media Reports U.S. Advertising Expenditures Increased 6.5 Percent in 2010," Business Wire, March 17, 2011, http://www.busi nesswire.com/news/home/20110317005314/en/Kantar-Media -Reports-U.S.-Advertising-Expenditures-Increased.

3. Annual Report, Harley Davidson Inc., http://www.harley-davidson .com/en_US/Media/downloads/Annual_Reports/2009/10k_2009 .pdf.

Chapter 9

1. "Welcome to the Anthropocene," Economist.com, http://www.econ omist.com/node/18744401.

2. "The Anthropocene: A Man-Made World," Economist.com, http:// www.economist.com/node/18741749.

3. W. T. Choate and J. A. S. Green, "U.S. Energy Requirements for Aluminum Production: Historical Perspective, Theoretical Limits and New Opportunities." Columbia, MD: BCS, Inc., for the U.S. Department of Energy. February 2003.

4. "World Population Estimates," Wikipedia, http://cn.wikipedia.org/ wiki/World_population_estimates.

5. "Frequently Asked Questions," Recycle My Cell Phone, 2011, http:// recyclemycellphone.org/faq.shtml.

6. HiTech Recycling Ltd., 2007, http://www.hitechrecycling.com/ news.html.

7. Megan Gall, "3.5 Tons of Disposable Diapers Fill US Landfills Each Year," Examiner.com, April 19, 2009, http://www.examiner .com/stay-at-home-moms-in-san-diego/3-5-tons0-of-disposable -diapers-fill-us-landfills-each-year.

8. "Petroleum and Other Liquids: Data," U.S. Energy Information Administration, 2011, http://www.eia.gov/dnav/pet/hist/LeafHand ler.ashx?n=PET&s=MTTIMUS1&f=M.

9. "Refrigerators and Freezers," California Energy Commission, Consumer Energy Center, 2011, http://www.consumerenergycenter .org/home/appliances/refrigerators.html.

10. "Building America," U.S. Department of Energy, 2004, http://apps1. eere.energy.gov/buildings/publications/pdfs/building_amer ica/35851.pdf.

11. "3M in the United States," 3M, 2011, http://solutions.3m.com/wps/ portal/3M/en_US/WW2/Country.

12. Douglas Smith, "Put Some Sunlight in Your Tank," *Engineering and Science*, 72, no. 2, Fall 2009.

13. "Warming Puts Species at One in Ten Extinction Risk by 2100," Simple Climate, July 16, 2011, http://simpleclimate.wordpress .com/2011/07/16/warming-puts-species-at-one-in-ten-extinction -risk-by-2100.

14. A PDF version is available at http://www.ccser.caltech.edu/outreach/ powering.pdf.

Further Reading

Ackerman, Diane. *A Natural History of the Senses*. New York: Vintage Books, 1991. A beautifully written book about the senses and the feelings they evoke that can be enjoyed by readers with and without technical backgrounds. One of my longtime favorite books, it is bound to get the reader more interested in the senses.

Adams, James L. *Conceptual Blockbusting: A Guide to Better Ideas*. New York: Basic Books, 2001. My now well-aged collection of common "mental blocks" that, although they ease the brain's burden, inhibit us from creativity and cause us to resist change. Ways to overcome them are included.

Bloom, Paul. *How Pleasure Works: The New Science of Why We Like What We Like*. New York: W. W. Norton, 2010. A refreshing and fun read about the less logical facets of our likes and dislikes. Why would anyone pay three million dollars for a used baseball?

Crawford, Matthew. *Shop Class as Soul Craft*. New York: Penguin, 2009. An impassioned argument for craftsmanship, vocational training and working with the hands, written by a person who both has a Ph.D. in philosophy and works as an antique motorcycle mechanic.

Gladwell, Malcolm. *The Tipping Point*. New York: Little Brown, 2002. A longtime bestselling book about change—in particular about why change sometimes happens so rapidly.

Goleman, Daniel. *Emotional Intelligence*. New York: Bantam Books, 2010. An influential and popular book about the nature and importance of the emotions in problem solving and decision making written by a psychologist and former scientific journalist.

Hawken, Paul, Amory Lovins, and L. Hunter Lovins. *Natural Capitalism*. New York: Little Brown, 1999. A thoughtful, pragmatic, and well-written book about environmental problems and the potential for companies to profit from working toward solving them. The authors feel that a revolution akin to the industrial revolution will occur as capitalism based on exploiting resources evolves into capitalism that respects and conserves them.

Kelley, Tom. *The Art of Innovation*: New York: Currency/Doubleday, 2001. An extremely readable book on creativity and innovation based upon the experiences of and approaches taken by IDEO, a consulting firm renowned for its ability to innovate products and teach other firms how to do the same.

Norman, Donald. *Emotional Design*. New York: Basic Books, 2004. Norman is a cognitive psychologist who has become extremely interested in design and in the products of industry. His book *The Psychology of Everyday Things* was a bestseller, and this one correlates emotions with various aspects of product design.

Patnaik, Dev. *Wired to Care*. Upper Saddle River, NJ: FT Press, 2009. This book argues that empathy is one of the most important ingredients for the success of businesses. The author is cofounder of Jump Associates, a consulting firm that specializes in product strategy and need finding.

Perrow, Charles. *Normal Accidents*. Princeton, NJ: Princeton University Press, 1999. Perrow presents several catastrophic failures in large complicated systems, and he maintains that although we should strive to design systems so that such failures do not occur, contrary to our hopes, they will. He feels that if the cost of such a failure is unacceptable we should not build the system.

Yanagi, Soetsu. *The Unknown Craftsman*. Tokyo: Kodasha International, 1989. A wonderful book about craftsmanship, its nature, and its rewards. The emphasis is on hand craftsmanship, but the book is extremely thought provoking, and it always makes me want to go out and make a samurai sword, or at least throw a pot.

Index

Advertising, 58–59. *See also*
    Marketing
    products and, 11
AEG, 160
Aesthetics. *See also* Industrial
    design
    concerns about today's, 174–78
    elegance and, 164–70
    industrial products and, 155–59
    introduction, 153–55
    problems and tactics table, 179
    product form/function and,
        170–74
    sophistication and, 164–70
    thought problem, 178
Aging populations, addressing
    physical fit and, 74
Airplanes, performance/cost
    ratios, 64
Albers, Josef, 160
Aluminum products, 208
Anthropocene, 204
Anticipation, 126
Apple, 58
    first computer of, 27
    iPhone, 11
Automobile companies, tradition
    and, 29–35

Bamboo Diapers, 211
Bathrooms, human fit and, 69–70

Battery-operated toys, 220–21
Bauhaus, 160–61
Beasley, Bruce, 185
Behrens, Peter, 160
Billington, David, 111
Biotechnology, 67
Bird in Space (Brancusi), 170
Bloom, Benjamin, 121, 135
Bloom, Paul, 135–36
Boeing, 176
Brain, the, 81–84
    Triune Brain theory of, 83–84
Brain function, models of, 84
Brancusi, Constantin, 170
Breuer, Marcel, 160
Business success, product quality
    and, 10

Capital goods, standardization of,
    196–97
Car companies, U.S., tradition
    and, 29–35
Carson, Rachel, 13
Cell-phone cameras, 209
Challenger accident, 186–87, 228
Change
    organizational, creativity and,
        44
    taste and, 10
Chemical sense, 76
China, 19–20

Chueh, William, 219
Cognitive fit, 81–86. *See also* Fit
Cognitive revolution, 81
"Competing on the Eight
  Dimensions of Quality"
  (Garvin), 26
Competition, global, 19–21
Complexity
  human fit and, 87–91
  Three Mile Island nuclear plant
    failure and, 87–89
  trade-off between elegance and,
    173–74
Compromise products, 34
Computers, 47
  human mind compatibility and,
    86
  problem-solving and, 85–86
*Conceptual Blockbusting: A Guide to
  Better Ideas* (Adams), 44
Conjoint analysis, 27
Consumer safety, 92–93
Cortex, 133–34
Cost. *See also* Price
  balancing act between
    performance and, 59–63
  complexity of, 56–59
  introduction, 51–52
  problems and tactics table, 66
  thought problem, 65–66
  "true," debate about, 57
Cost/performance ratios
  of airplanes, 64
  of products, 64
Craftsmanship
  industry/culture problem of,
    104–9
  introduction, 97
  nature of, 109–14
  pleasure and pride of, 100–104

problems and tactics table, 120
reasons for importance of,
  98–100
suggestions for improving,
  114–19
thought problem, 119
workmanship and, 109–14
Crawford, Matthew, 108
Creativity
  design and, 44
  organizational change and, 44
  organizational characteristics
    for, 44–46
Cross-functional interdisciplinary
  team approach, 28
Crutzen, Paul, 204
Crystal Palace, 185
Cultural values, problems and
  tactics table, 201
Cultures
  globalism and, 195–200
  products and, 186–90

Dadaists, 185
Danko, William, 108
Day-to-day annoyances, reasons
  for accepting, 8
Death, fascination with, 128–31
Deming, W. Edwards, 17
Design
  changing nature of, 37–44
  creativity and, 44
  defined, 37
  global constraints and, 210
  increased sophistication of, 39
  industrial, 159–64
  process, for physical fit, 73
  of products, 28
  safety and, 93–94
  threat of litigation and, 227

Design for manufacturing, 16
Design groups, attributes of, 38
Designers
   complexity of systems and,
      89–90
   duality of consciousness/
      unconsciousness and,
      84–85
   human fit and, 68–69
Diapers, disposable, 210–11
Doyal, Len, 138–39
Dreyfuss, Henry, 152, 161
Drug Importation Act (1848), 92
Duchamp, Marcel, 185

Economic theory, flaws in, 35–37
Ecosphere problems, 204–7
   causes of, 209–12
   response to, 212–16
   revolutionary approaches to,
      216–21
   role of industrial products,
      207–9
Eiffel Tower, 185
Electric motors, 218–19
Elegance, 164–70, 172
   problems and tactics table, 179
   trade-off between complexity
      and, 173–74
Elkington, John, 203–4
Emotional Design (Norman), 140
Emotional Intelligence (Goleman),
   125–26
Emotions
   complexity of, 125–31
   diversity in responses to, 131–33
   introduction, 121–22
   labels for, 125–26
   mechanisms of, 133–36
   needs and, 140–44

problems and tactics table, 152
   role of, 122–25
   thought problem, 152
Employees, retaining and
   motivating high-quality, 10
Empowerment, worker, 16
   recognition/rewards for, 113–14
Energy systems, revolutionary
   approaches to, 216–19
Entrepreneurship, 18
Environmental problems. *See*
   Ecosphere problems
Environmentalism, 13
Ergonomics, 67
Essentialism, 135
Esteem needs, 145–46
EV1, 212
Expectations, population, 209

Farm equipment
   effect of, on farming, 63
   performance, cost, and price of,
      61–62
Farming, effect of farm equipment
   on, 63
Faste, Rolf, 149
Fayol, Henry, 71
Feature creep, 54–55
Federal regulatory agencies,
   225–26
Fiorina, Carly, 176
Fit
   cognitive, 81–86
   human, 67–70
   physical, 70–75
   sensory, 75–81
Fluorescent lighting, 217–18
Food and Drug Act (1906), 92
Forbes, Fahrad, 102
Forbes, Naushad, 102–3

Forbes Marshall, 102–3
Ford Motor Company, 115, 176
Free workmanship, 109, 110, 113, 114
Fresh water, global use of, 222
Freud, Sigmund, 127–28
Future creep, 54–55

Garvin, David, 26
Gates, Bill, 10
Gehry, Frank, 175
General Motors, 40
German Modernism, 160
Global competition, 19–21
Global constraints
design and, 210
problems and tactics table, 231
Global Positioning System (GPS), 41–42
Global warming, 223–24
Globalism, cultures and, 195–200
Goleman, Daniel, 125–26, 132
Good Product, Bad Product Matrix, 236
Gough, Ian, 138–39
Gropius, Walter, 160
Gulick, Luther, 71

Haile, Sossina, 219
Hampden-Turner, Charles, 84
Harley-Davidson motorcycles, 131, 199
Hasso Plattner Institute of Design, 48
Head, Howard, 147
Hearing sense, 76, 78–79
Hewlett, Bill, 60, 147
Hewlett-Packard, 115, 176
Hierarchy of needs (Maslow), 137
Holocene, 204

Home energy costs, reducing, 218
Home ownership, in U.S., 188
Honesty, 59
Human emotions. *See* Emotions
Human factors engineering, 67
Human fit
bathrooms and, 69–70
complexity and, 87–91
designers and, 68–69
problems and tactics table, 95
problems with, 67–68
safety and, 91–94
thought problem, 95
Human interface, 67
Human needs. *See* Needs, human
Hunter Engineering, 39, 40, 42

India, 20, 197
Industrial design, background, 159–64. *See also* Design
Industrial products, 9. *See also* Products
aesthetics and, 155–59
design of, 37–38
future trends in, 9–11
role of, 207–9
Industrial safety, 92
Information revolution, 81–82
Innovation, 18
Insight, Honda, 214
Intel Corp, 63
Intellectual needs, 148–49
International Commission on Stratigraphy, 204
International Data Corporation (IDC), 11
International style, 160
Introduction to design, 39–41
iPhone, 11
Irrigation, 222–23

Jet Propulsion Laboratory
   (JPL), 11–17, 40, 42–43
Jobs, Steve, 60, 147
Joint Regulatory Agency,
   225
Joy, 126
Jump Associates, 149
Juran, Joseph M., 17, 18

Kandinsky, Wassily, 160
Kelley, David, 48
Kennedy, John F., 60
Klee, Paul, 160
Kyoto Protocol, 204

Lauren, Ralph, 175
Laws, 224–29
LEDs (light-emitting diodes),
   218
Levi Strauss, 34
Lewis, Nathan, 223
Lifestyle changes, physical fit and,
   74–75
Lighting, 217–18
Living National Treasures
   program (Japan), 113–14
Loewy, Raymond, 161, 175
Lovins, Amory, 212
Lutz, Bob, 175
Luxury products, 146
Lyman, Peter, 81

MacLean, Paul, 83–84
Magazines, 35
Maslow, Abraham, 137–38, 150–51
Manufacturing quality
   beyond, 17–19
   changes in organizational
      structures and procedures
      for improving, 16

focus on, 15–16
improvement in, 28
responsibility for, 16
Maps of the Mind (Hampden-
   Turner), 84
Marketing. See also Advertising
   intent of, 28
   product design and, 175
   product quality and,
      26–28
   unprecedented products and,
      27
   values of people in business
      and, 27
McCartney, Stella, 175
McKim, Bob, 149
Mechatronics, 46
Microsoft Word, 172–73
Midbrain, 84
Mies van der Rohe, Ludwig,
   160
Millionaire Next Door,
   The (Stanely and Danko),
   108
Mind, the, 82–84
Mockups, 73
Moholy-Nagy, László, 160
Mondrian, Piet, 185
Moore, Gordon, 63
Moore curve, 63
Movement sense, 76
Myerson, Bess, 93

Nader, Ralph, 93
Nature and Art of Workmanship
   (Pye), 109
Needs, human, 136–40
   emotions and, 140
   esteem, 145–46
   finding, 149–52

hierarchy of, 137–38
intellectual, 148–49
safety, 143–44
social, 144–47
survival, 140–44
thought problem, 152
"New feature" solution, 150
New Science of Why We Like What We Like, The (Bloom), 135–36
Nikon camera, 173–74
Normal Accidents (Perrow), 87
Norman, Donald, 140

Occupational Safety and Health Act (1970), 92
O'Reilly, Charles, 13–14
Organic sense, 76
Organizational change, creativity and, 44

Pacific Electric Railways "Red Line," 214
Packard, David, 147
Panasonic, 34
Parkinson, Brad, 41–42
Patnaik, Dev, 149–51
Perfect products, 7
Performance
balancing act between cost and, 59–63
introduction, 51–52
problems and tactics table, 66
quantifying, 52–56
thought problem, 65–66
Performance/cost ratios
of airplanes, 64
of products, 64
Perrow, Charles, 87
Petersen, Donald, 15, 115, 176

Petroleum-based transportation system, 213–14
Physical fit, 70–75. *See also* Fit
addressing aging population and, 74
data for, 73
design process for better, 73
lifestyle changes and, 74–75
mockups for, 73
prototyping and, 74
testing time for, 74
World War II and understanding, 72–73
Piano, Renzo, 185
Pickup trucks, as example of quality problem, 31–34
Pininfarina, Battista, 175
Plattner, Hasso, 48
Plutchik, Robert, 126, 132, 135
Price. *See also* Cost
complexity of, 56–59
introduction, 51–52
problems and tactics table, 66
Prius, Toyota, 211, 214
Problem solving
computers and, 85–86
quality and, 24–29
Problems
quality, example of, 31–34
reasons for, 63–65
Problems and tactics tables
for aesthetics, 179
for cost, performance, and price, 66
for craftsmanship, 120
for cultural values, 201
for elegance, 179
for emotions, 152
for global constraints, 231

for human fit, 95
for sophistication, 179
for symbolism, 201
Product design. *See* Design
Product form/function, aesthetics
    and, 170–74
Product liability litigation, 226–27
Product quality. *See also* Quality
    business success and, 10
    design group attributes for, 38
    marketing and, 26–28
    thought problem, 22
Product simplification, 162
Product standardization, 162
Product uniformity, international,
    196–97
Products. *See also* Industrial
    products
    advertising and, 11
    aluminum, 208
    compromise, 34
    cultures and, 186–90
    design and, 28
    effects of improved quality of,
        11
    emotions and, 121–22
    improvement and, 8
    luxury, 146
    perfect, 7
    performance/cost ratios of, 64
    subcultures and, 190–95
Prototyping, 74
Pye, David, 109–13

Quality, 1. *See also* Product quality
    as abstract concept, 2
    aspects of, 26
    criteria for, 2–3
    marketing and, 26–28

problem solving and, 24–29
product, business success and,
    10
thinking and, 24–29
thought problem, 22
Quality improvement, example of,
    11–17
Quality problems, example of,
    31–34
Quantity, tradition of producing,
    31

Rauschenberg, Robert, 185
Recognition, for worker
    empowerment, 113–14
"Red Line" (Pacific Electric
    Railways), 214
Refrigerators, 215–16
Regulated workmanship, 109, 110
Regulations, 224–29
Rewards, for worker
    empowerment, 113–14
Rick, John, 99
Rogovin, Mitchell, 87
Rough workmanship, 109–10,
    112–13
Rutan, Burtan, 175

Safety
    consumer, 92–93
    designing products for, 93–94
    human fit and, 91–94
    industrial, 92
Safety needs, 143–44
Schiaparelli, Elsa, 175
Schimandle, Bill, 60
Scientific management, 71–72
Senses, 75–76
Sensory fit, 75–81. *See also* Fit

Shell Oil Company, 40
"Shop Class as Soul Craft"
    (Crawford), 108
Silent Spring (Carson), 13
Silicon Snake Oil (Stoll), 55–56
Skin sense, 76
Smith, David, 185
Social needs, 144–47
Solar energy, 219–20
Sophistication, 164–70, 176–77
    problems and tactics table,
    179
Sputnik, 12
Standardization, global, 196–97
Stanley, Thomas, 108
Starck, Philippe, 175
Stella, Frank, 185
Stoermer, Eugene, 204
Stoll, Clifford, 55–56
Subcultures, 198–99
    products and, 190–95
    thought problem about, 200
Success, business, product quality
    and, 10
Survival needs, 140–44
SUVs, 35, 75, 212, 227
Symbolism
    introduction, 182–83
    problems and tactics table,
    201
    products and, 183–85
Symbols, defined, 181
Systemic solutions, 151

Taste, change and, 10
Tata Group, 21, 197
Taylor, Frederick W., 71
Teague, Walter Dorwin, 161
Technical balance, 42

Technology
    depictions of, 185
    importance of, 188–90
    United States and, 186
Tesla Motors, 214–15, 216
Theory of Human Need, A (Doyal
    and Gough), 138–39
Thinking, quality and, 24–29
Thought problems
    about aesthetics, 178
    about craftsmanship, 119–20
    about emotions and needs,
    152
    about environment problems,
    230–31
    about human fit, 95
    about narrow-mindedness or
    tradition, 48–49
    about performance and cost,
    65–66
    about product quality, 22
    about subcultures, 200
Three Mile Island nuclear plant
    failure, 60, 186
    complexity of, 87–89
Thresholds, 77–78
Time sense, 76
Tinguely, Jean, 185
Toilets, 222
Total Quality Management
    (TQM), 16
Toxic waste, 210
Tradition
    car companies and, 29–35
    of producing quantity vs.
    quality, 31
Triple bottom line, 203–4
Triune Brain theory, 83–84
"True" cost, debate about, 57

Trust, 126
Tushman, Michael, 13–14

United States
    cars in, 187–88
    focus on manufacturing quality
        in, 15
    house ownership in, 188
    importance of technology to,
        186
    kitchen appliances in, 188
    tradition of producing quantity
        vs. quality in, 31
    weapons and, 188
    worry about product quality in,
        13–15
Urwick, Lyndall, 71
U.S. Pharmacopeia, 92

Varian, Hal, 81
Vision sense, 76
Volt, Chevrolet, 212

War, 128
Warhol, Andy, 185
Warner and Swasey Company,
    105–6

Water, global use of, 222
Weapons, in U.S., 188
Werkbund, 160
Winning the Oil Endgame
    (Lovins), 212
*Winning Through Innovation:
    A Practical Guide to Leading
    Organizational Change and
    Renewal* (O'Reilly and
    Tushman), 13
Worker empowerment, 16
    recognition/rewards needed
        for, 113–14
Workmanship. *See also*
    Craftsmanship
    of certainty, 110
    free, 109, 110, 113, 114
    regulated, 109, 110
    of risk, 110
    rough, 109–10, 112–13
World War II, understanding
    physical fit and, 72–73
Wozniak, Steve, 147
Wright, Frank Lloyd,
    175

Young, John, 15, 115

About the Author

James L. (Jim) Adams is an emeritus professor in the Department of Mechanical Engineering, the Department of Management Science and Engineering, and the Program in Science, Technology, and Society at Stanford University. He received his B.S. degree from the California Institute of Technology and his graduate degrees in engineering from Stanford University. He also spent a period of time as an art student at U.C.L.A., served a tour in the air force, and held several jobs in design and development in industry before receiving his Ph.D.

Before returning to Stanford as a faculty member, Adams was employed by the Jet Propulsion Laboratory in Pasadena, California, where he was involved in the design of the first spacecraft to explore the Moon, Venus, and Mars. His teaching at Stanford has ranged from mechanical and product design through creativity and innovation, product quality, and the nature of technology. He has held many administrative jobs at Stanford and won a number of awards for outstanding teaching and service to both students and alumni.

In addition to his Stanford work, he has been retained to consult and/or lecture or conduct workshops by more than 100 commercial clients, ranging from large to small and technical to financial; served as a consultant and/or lecturer to a large number of government, educational, and professional groups; and been a faculty member in many executive programs.

Adams is the author of *Conceptual Blockbusting*, a popular book on creative thinking, *The Care and Feeding of Ideas*, a book directed toward the management of creativity and change, and *Flying Buttresses, Entropy, and O-Rings*, a book on the nature of engineering. He and his wife, Marian, have four children and eight grandchildren and live on the Stanford Campus, where he spends his spare time restoring old machinery, reading and writing, eating and drinking, and working for Marian. He maintains a blog at http://www.jamesladams.typepad.com.